Globalisation, Global Justice and Social Work

Globalisation has become a seemingly unstoppable force over recent decades and, in its wake, global notions of social justice have developed in response to its negative aspects. Neo-liberal economic policies have been a key element in the wider processes of globalisation, and these policies have had a profound impact on welfare provision and the shape of social work practice. Arising dissatisfaction among users of welfare and social work services is fuelling the search for a new, more radical social work that is firmly rooted in principles of social justice.

This book explores the effects of neo-liberal policies on welfare services in different countries, with contributions from social work academics, practitioners and welfare activists around the world. The first section of the book presents case studies exploring the impact of neo-liberalism on welfare systems, social service provision and the practice of social work. In the second section the chapters explore the relationship between social work practice and the struggle for social justice. Authors discuss the personal and political dilemmas they have had to address in seeking to link a personal commitment to social justice with their daily practice as workers and educators in social work. The final section assesses the prospects for social work practice based on notions of social justice, by looking at what can be learned from the experience of previous radical movements as well as from emergent global and local movements.

Iain Ferguson is a Senior Lecturer in Social Work at the University of Stirling. Before moving into social work teaching, he practised as a social worker and community worker for many years in the west of Scotland. His main research interests are in the areas of mental health, asylum-seekers and critical social theory, and he has published widely in all of these areas.

Michael Lavalette is a Senior Lecturer in Social Policy at the University of Liverpool. He teaches, researches and writes in three interrelated areas: aspects of child labour, studies of collective action and collective responses to oppression, and various aspects of Marxist welfare theory and Marxist approaches to engaged social work practice.

Elizabeth Whitmore is Professor at the School of Social Work, Carleton University in Ottawa, Canada. Her main areas of interest are in participatory approaches to research and evaluation, and international social development.

social work/political sociology/social policy

D0082191

Globalisation, Global Justice and Social Work

Edited by

Iain Ferguson, Michael Lavalette and Elizabeth Whitmore

To Roslini,
You are my teacher,
mentor & friend.
Thank you
for all
[illegible]

Bessa

Routledge
Taylor & Francis Group

LONDON AND NEW YORK

© 2005 Taylor & Francis, an imprint of the Taylor & Francis Group

First published in the United Kingdom in 2005
by Routledge, an imprint of the Taylor & Francis Group, 2 Park Square,
Milton Park, Abingdon, Oxfordshire, OX14 4RN

Tel.:   +44 (0) 20 7017 6000
Fax.:   +44 (0) 20 7017 6699
Website: http://www.routledge.com

Simultaneously published in the USA and Canada by Routledge, an
imprint of the Taylor & Francis Group, 270 Madison Avenue, New York,
NY 10016, USA.

A CIP record for this book is available from the British Library.

Library of Congress Cataloging-in-Publication Data

Data available on application

ISBN 0–415–32537–4 (hbk)
ISBN 0–415–32538–2 (pbk)

Composition by J&L Composition, Filey, North Yorkshire, UK
Printed and bound in Great Britain by TJ International Ltd, Padstow,
Cornwall

Contents

Contributors

Norberto Alayón is a Professor of Social Work at the University of Buenos Aires, Argentina.

Manuel Boucher is a researcher in the Laboratory of Studies and Social Researches (LERS), Institut du Développement Social, IDS.

Linda Briskman is an Associate Professor of Social Work at RMIT University, Melbourne, Australia.

Ingrid Burkett teaches social work at the School of Social Work and Social Policy, University of Queensland, Brisbane, Australia.

Suzanne Dudziak teaches social work at the Social Work Department, St Thomas University, Fredericton NB, Canada.

Iain Ferguson is a Senior Lecturer in Social Work at the University of Stirling, Scotland.

Heather Fraser is a Senior Lecturer in Social Work at RMIT University, Melbourne, Australia.

Estela Grassi works in the Social Work Department at the University of Buenos Aires, Argentina.

John Harris is a Professor in the School of Health and Social Studies, University of Warwick, England.

Chris Jones is Professor of Social Work at the University of Liverpool, England.

Susan Kuruvilla completed her Masters degree in Social Work from the Tata Institute of Social Sciences, Mumbai, India. She was a social worker in an NGO working with fishing communities for a short while, and then a trainer in a project for Women Panchayat members. Since then, she has pursued her interests in development studies.

Michael Lavalette is a Senior Lecturer in Social Policy at the University of Liverpool, England.

Catherine McDonald teaches social work at the School of Social Work and Social Policy, University of Queensland, Brisbane, Australia.

Ed Mynott is based in Manchester. He has been involved in campaigns against deportation and in defence of asylum seekers for the past decade. Formerly an academic researcher specialising in the field of immigration and asylum, he currently works as an assistant caseworker at the Greater Manchester Immigration Aid Unit. He has also worked as a volunteer with the National Coalition of Anti Deportation Campaigns and the Citizens Advice Bureau in Manchester.

Maria del Carmen Mendoza Rangel is a Professor of Community Development, Social Work Theory and Practice at the National Autonomous University of Mexico (ENTS-UNAM).

Michael Reisch is a Professor of Social Work at the School of Social Work, University of Michigan, Ann Arbor, MI, USA.

Fatou Sarr was the first African woman in the West to receive her doctorate in social services from the University of Laval. She works at l'Institut Fondamental d'Afrique Noire (IFAN) de l'Université Cheikh Anta.

Abye Tasse was born in Ethiopia and has lived in France since 1979. At present he is Dean of the Graduate School in Social Work at Addis Ababa University, Ethiopia. He is also President of the International Association of Schools of Social Work.

Elizabeth Whitmore is a Professor at the School of Social Work, Carleton University (Ottawa, Canada).

Maureen Wilson is a Professor in the Faculty of Social Work, University of Calgary, Alberta, Canada.

Acknowledgements

We would like to thank a number of people who have helped us put together this book. First a big thank you to Mike Gonzalez and Andy Stafford for their help in translating chapters 1, 2, 4 and 5. The speed with which they did this was amazing—and their grasp of the political issues being discussed invaluable. Second, each of the contributors has met the deadlines we set—and our thanks are due to them for this and their patience and understanding at dealing with our frantic e-mails. Finally, we would like to thank the team at Routledge for their advice and help in putting the book together.

Iain Ferguson
Michael Lavalette
Elizabeth Whitmore

Introduction

Iain Ferguson, Michael Lavalette and Elizabeth Whitmore

> The passing-off of market fundamentalism as the new common sense has helped to drive home the critical lesson which underpins the 'reform' of the welfare state: the role of the state 'nowadays' is not to support the less fortunate or powerful but to help individuals themselves to provide for all their social needs. Those who can must. The rest must be targeted, means-tested and kept to a minimum of provision lest the burden threaten 'wealth creation'.
>
> (Hall 2003)

Over the past two decades the world has been dramatically reshaped by the development of neo-liberal globalisation. Neo-liberal advocates argue that economic and social liberalism will benefit everyone; wealth will trickle down from the wealthiest nations and individuals to the very poorest across the globe. The solution to debt and poverty, so they would have us believe, is structural adjustment: lowering trade barriers and opening economies up to multinational companies, encouraging direct foreign investments, welfare retrenchment and privatisation of state-owned enterprises, abolition of subsidies and price controls, and the withdrawal of controls on capital movements. By following these simple measures economic growth and expansion is sure to follow and the lives of the poor vastly improved.

This prescription—the 'Washington Consensus'—dominates the thinking of the major international financial institutions: the IMF, the World Bank and the World Trade Organization (WTO). It dominates the strategic economic planning of the US state and the Federal Bank. And it directly shapes the activities of governments across the globe.

But it is a perspective that rings hollow. As Joseph Stiglitz, chief economist at the World Bank from 1997 to 2000 and Nobel prize winner for economics in 2001, has written:

> Liberalization has . . . too often, not been followed by the promised growth but by increased misery. And even those who have not lost their jobs have been hit by a heightened sense of insecurity.
>
> (Stiglitz 2002, p. 17)

The extent of that increased misery is vividly reflected in the Human Development Reports, produced each year by the United Nations. The 2003 report showed that in 54 countries average income actually declined in the 1990s and that in 21 countries, mainly in Africa, society went backwards on measures such as income and life expectancy.

But immiserisation is not only an African phenomenon. In Latin America, countries such as Ecuador, Venezuela and Paraguay have seen living standards fall over the last 10 years, while Argentina, once the IMF's 'star student', now lurches from crisis to crisis. Similar falls have also taken place in the Ukraine, Kazakhstan, Tajikistan and Russia. In addition, the global gulf between rich and poor has also grown over the past decade, with the richest 1% now having as much income as the poorest 57%. In human terms, this means that every day throughout the world, 30 000 children die of preventable diseases (UNDP 2003). As Bertinotti argues: 'Capitalist globalisation contains deeply regressive elements that are leading to a real crisis of civilisation' (Bertinotti 2003).

Faced with this crisis governments have not changed tack but simply repeat another mantra—that 'there is no alternative'. This is a slogan that has also been taken up by a number of social democratic-inclined academics such as Anthony Giddens (1984) who wrapped 'neo-liberalism' in the cloak of 'Third Way' politics. As Stuart Hall, taking New Labour in Britain, the global brand leaders of Third Wayism, as his case-study, argues:

> New Labour has a long-term strategy, a 'project': the transformation of social democracy into a particular variant of free market neo-liberalism. Thus New Labour has worked—both domestically and globally—to set the corporate economy free. It has renounced attempts to graft wider social goals on to the corporate world. It has deregulated labour and other markets, maintained restrictive trade union legislation, and established weak and compliant regulatory regimes. It has 'cosied up to business', favouring its interests in multiple ways. It has pursued a splendidly variable range of privatisations— sustaining the sell-off of critical public assets and stealthily opening doors for the corporate penetration of the public sector.
>
> (Hall, 2003)

This process, of course, directly affects many of those involved in social work and social care, both as workers and as service users. In Britain, for example, the implications of this unquestioning acceptance of capitalist rationality for social work have been profound. It has led to the growth of what John Harris has described as 'the social work business' (Harris 2003) which is dominated not by notions of social justice and equality but rather of 'value for money', led by managers whose primary remit is often to manage budgets rather than to meet the needs of clients, and too often staffed by demoralised practitioners who feel increasingly alienated from their organisations and from what now passes as social work (Jones 2000).

Yet while the claim that 'there is no alternative' may have held near total sway in the 1990s it is increasingly questioned both by 'insiders' such as Stiglitz and, more importantly, by the emergence since Seattle 1999 of a global social movement with the vision that a different world *is* possible.

This movement has many names. Some, especially in the media, portray it as the 'anti-globalisation movement'. This though is the least accurate descriptor. As Susan George, a writer who is readily associated with the movement, said at the first World Social Forum in Porto Alegre in January 2001: 'We are "pro-globalisation" for we are in favour of sharing friendship, culture, cooking, solidarity, wealth and resources' (in Callinicos 2003a, pp 13–14).

Others, including leading activists in North America, for example, prefer the 'movement for social justice'. The Council of Canadians suggests this name allows us to take control of our movement and give it a positive focus. We are for a more equitable, more just and more harmonious future. By formulating it in this way we immediately halt those rather silly claims that suggest that, while this is a movement that knows what it is against, it does not know what it is for.

In contrast, in Britain, the dominant descriptor is the 'anti-capitalist movement' (Callinicos 2003a). For proponents of this perspective, it is not that everyone involved in the movement thinks that it is either possible or desirable to get rid of capitalism but, rather, that the movement has moved beyond its roots in a variety of 'single-issue' movements to point to the interconnection between a variety of grievances. And as part of this process, there is an 'anti-systemic' kernel or logic within the movement.

These differences reflect real debates within the movement, and in this collection different authors use a variety of labels to describe the movement of which we are apart. We feel this is not something to get overly concerned about. We are marching together in a common direction and with a common goal and while we march together we debate and discuss important issues.

In both world and regional social forums, the movement has started to debate the viability of alternatives to neo-liberal globalisation: to assert that 'another world is possible'. It is the growth and expansion of this movement over the last few years that has revived social criticism and posted notice that, in fact, there *are* real alternatives. As Stiglitz notes:

> until the protestors came along there was little hope for change and no out-lets for complaint. *Some* of the protestors went to excesses; *some* of the protestors were arguing for higher protectionist barriers against developing countries, which would have made their plight even worse. But despite these problems, it is the trade unionists, students, environmentalists—ordinary citizens—marching in the streets of Prague, Seattle, Washington and Genoa who have put the need for reform on the agenda of the developed world.
>
> (Stiglitz 2002, p. 9).

This book situates itself within this movement. It's a book about social work and, for all of us in the collection, that means assessing what is happening to the world of social work practitioners, social service users and, more generally, the poor and dispossessed amongst whom we work. The book has a number of

purposes therefore. First, we want to explore the social costs of neo-liberal globalisation, to emphasise that, for the people we work most closely with, another
world is necessary. Second, we want to look at the growth of the anti-
capitalist/social justice movement and look at what resources of hope it offers for
the social work academic and practitioner—and for those we work beside in the
user movements and both urban and rural communities. We want to assess the
seeds of hope that make *another world possible*. Third, we want to focus on examples of 'engaged practice' where individuals and projects have grappled with
social and political restrictions to work in ways that reflect the goals of the new
movement and enhance the lives of those they work with. And finally, we want to
consider what implications this has for the future of social work—what can we
learn from the movement. Too often academics assume their role is to pronounce
new ideas and developments from on high. We feel strongly that often the reverse
is more viable and more valuable—we have much to learn from studying and
working with those who are involved in the struggle for a better world.

Book outline

In the first part of the book, social work academics and practitioners from
Mexico, Argentina, Senegal, India, Britain and France assess the impact of neo-
liberal globalisation on the welfare regimes and social work services in their
respective countries, beginning with Maria del Carmen Mendoza Rangel's
account of the experience in Mexico over the past few decades. It is fitting that
this collection should open with a chapter from a Mexican contributor. Not only
has that country experienced the full force of neo-liberal globalisation, in part
through the geographical accident of its location in Uncle Sam's backyard, but it
was also the site of the first real rebellion against neo-liberalism in the shape of
the rising of the indigenous peoples of the Chiapas region against the Mexican
government, under the leadership of the Zapatista National Liberation Front.
Maria's chapter analyses the interaction of global social forces, the rise of these
new popular movements and the struggle of social workers in Mexico to relate to
these struggles and become part of the struggle for social justice.

For much of the 1990s, Argentina was held up as the 'miracle economy' of
Latin America, a shining example of what the economic strategy dictated by the
'Washington Consensus' could achieve. 'It's springtime in Buenos Aires. The government is selling everything in sight' the *Wall Street Journal* gushed when the government's privatisation programme was launched in 1991. Less than a decade
later, these policies had produced poverty on a scale which was unprecedented in
the history of Argentina, resulting in massive spontaneous street protests, the
downfall of president after president and creating a near-revolutionary situation.
It is this experience and the implications of the 'cycle of neo-liberalism' for welfare services and social work practice that Estela Grassi and Norberto Alayón
explore in their chapter.

Within the international social work literature, social development models are
growing in influence and popularity, as a more appropriate model for practice for

social workers in the South than the traditional remedial models of British and American social work. Yet as Susan Kuruvilla argues in her discussion of social work in India, the concept of 'development' can mean very different things to different people and needs to be used carefully. Reviewing the experience of both the state-led economic development which followed Indian independence in 1947 and the neo-liberal development policies in place since the early 1990s, she shows, through a discussion of the experience of fishery workers in Kerala, that the first form of development was often harmful both to the environment and to the interests of local communities, while the latter has also resulted in 'a very doubtful kind of progress'. On a positive note, however, her discussion of the role of social workers in working with these fishing communities to protect their rights and in the establishment of a campaigning organisation, the National Association of Peoples' Movements (NAPM), gives a glimpse of a type of social work which has all but disappeared in the West and which seems a million miles away from the care management approaches which currently dominate in Britain and the US.

As Fatou Sarr reminds us in her chapter on Senegal, in a divided society social policy is never simply about 'meeting needs'. From its inception, the development of forms of welfare in Senegal, as in many other African countries, was inextricably linked to the requirements of the dominant colonial power (in this case, France), leaving the majority of the population excluded from any type of state support. Far from improving the situation of the mass of people, the implementation of neo-liberal policies in the form of structural adjustment polices in the 1990s has left a desperately poor country even poorer and less able to deal with a series of 'natural' catastrophes, including the sinking of the *Joola* in 2002 (with the loss of almost 2000 lives) and massive influxes of refugees fleeing wars and conflicts in surrounding countries. In this context, the inappropriateness of the 'Western' model of social work has become glaringly obvious and Sarr argues convincingly for the superiority of traditional models of social solidarity and mutual aid in meeting the needs of the mass of the people.

A central element of the radical critique of traditional social work in the 1970s concerned the professionalisation of social work, which was seen by many radicals as a means of distancing social workers from the clients with whom they worked (Bailey and Brake 1975). In their discussion of social work in France, Abye Tasse and Manuel Boucher discuss the ways in which the market has undermined social work professionalism from a very different direction, through the replacement of a 'logic of qualification' by a 'logic of competence' and through the development of new forms of welfare (similar to Supporting People in the UK), based on employing untrained and unskilled workers who exercise limited care and control functions on behalf of the state or private agencies. The development of new forms of professionalism that can resist the pressures of the market and can connect with the aspiration on the part of many of these new social agents to develop more empowering forms of practice is the central focus of this chapter.

Care management approaches came to prominence in Britain as an integral feature of the neo-liberal reshaping of social work organisation and practice which took place under the third Thatcher administration in the late 1980s and early 1990s. In the final chapter of the first section, John Harris traces the process by which British social work moved from being a universalist, generic service, firmly located within a welfare state, to the much more fragmented service it is today. In this 'modern' social work, notions of 'value for money' have become the overriding consideration of the managers who have dominated every aspect of social work organisation, practice and education for more than a decade. As Harris makes clear, the election of a New Labour government in 1997 (and its re-election in 2001) has seen a continuation, and even intensification, of this market-driven and managerial approach (albeit with some minor 'Third Way' differences), underpinned by an unwavering acceptance of the dogma that 'there is no alternative' to the market. The picture he paints is a fairly bleak one and, given that British social work might be seen as being 'ahead' of social work in most other countries in the extent of its penetration by market forces and ideology, might be read as a warning of what is to come elsewhere unless alternative models of social work can be developed.

In the second part of the book, the perspective narrows to allow for a more detailed exploration of the ways in which the market has impacted on three particular areas of social work. First, the practitioner experience. Drawing on his research into the experience of front-line workers in local authorities in the UK, Chris Jones paints a vivid, if depressing, picture of a demoralised and alienated workforce, weighed down by lack of resources, growing bureaucracy and managerialism. This is the reality of life in 'the social work business' with Jones' chapter providing an essential qualitative underpinning to the analysis contained in Harris' chapter in the first section.

The next two chapters explore the role of social work in relation to a group of people whose needs are massive but who can hardly be described as service users since they are excluded by law from most of the welfare entitlements available to full citizens—namely, asylum seekers. Writing from the perspective of both practitioner and political activist in this field, Ed Mynott outlines the increasingly punitive and racist direction which British asylum seeker policy has taken, first under Conservative governments and since 1997 under New Labour, and challenges social workers to think through the implications of the different strategies they employ in relation to work with this group of people, strategies which he describes as compromise, collaboration or collective resistance. As the world discovered when the Australian government in 2003 refused to allow a boatload of destitute asylum seekers to dock in Australian waters, preferring to leave them drifting in the ocean, that government's policy is no less punitive or racist than that of New Labour in Britain. Heather Fraser and Linda Briskman trace the development of Australian asylum seeker policy and its links to government policy towards its 'own' aboriginal people since the end of the Second World War. While social workers have been active in defending the rights of both groups, there is clearly scope for greater involvement and through a friendly critique of radical social work theory, they outline what they see as the basis for a new, engaged practice.

The last chapter in this section is concerned with social work education. This too is an area which, in the UK especially, has been dominated for the past decade by employer interests and managerialist perspectives, through the imposition of competence-based approaches, for example, and the dilution of anti-oppressive perspectives (Jones 1996). In her inspiring chapter, however, Suzanne Dudziak shows how social work education can become an arena for the development of a new theory and practice of resistance, of the sort which the previous three chapters have called for. Her account of a social work class field trip to the protests at the Summit of the Americas in Quebec City shows how notions of social justice and collective action can be made real to new generations of social workers and prefigures the arguments of several of the contributors to the final section of the book on the need to make links with this new and growing movement.

The four chapters in the final section seek to map new ways forward for social work and to locate the sources from which a new, engaged practice might emerge. The section opens with an overview by Michael Reisch of the history of radical social work in the USA, from the late nineteenth century to the present day. This chapter is particularly important for two reasons. First, radical social work in the US, like so much of the rich history of struggle against oppression in America (including recent opposition to the Iraq war), is often 'hidden from history', air-brushed out in favour of a crude media caricature of Americans as God-fearing, Dubya-loving patriots. As far as the development of social work in the US is concerned, Reisch's chapter shows how false that view is. The chapter is also important, however, in providing a context for current debates about the future of a critical social work practice. 'Back to the 1970s' is not an adequate basis for building a critical social work movement and practice in an era of neo-liberal globalisation but it would be equally foolish not to draw on, and learn from, the rich heritage that Reisch's work has uncovered and documented.

Reference was made earlier to the potential shortfalls of the concept of 'development' as a basis for a more radical social work practice. While acknowledging these shortfalls, Ingrid Burkett and Catherine McDonald draw on the Australian experience to argue that a critical understanding of social development, if underpinned by notions of diversity and difference and informed by post-colonial theory, does offer new spaces for thinking about different forms of practice. Many of the dilemmas now faced by critical social workers (in relation to the ambiguities of 'participation' for example) are already familiar within social development theory and practice and lessons can be learned from that experience.

One of the 'contributions' of managerialism to social work in the 1990s has been a 'dumbing-down' of social work education and practice, with theory often seen in an instrumental way ('sociology for social workers', etc) and/or as simply one element (often subordinate to 'skills') of employer-driven competencies. In contrast to that approach, Elizabeth Whitmore and Maureen Wilson's chapter seeks to critically engage with some major (if contentious) current sociological concepts, including notions of 'social capital' and theories of 'new social movements', and to explore their relevance for practice. One challenge facing anyone seeking to develop new forms of practice is how to relate to service users as individuals, groups and organisations in non-oppressive ways and Whitmore and Wilson's notion of *acompaniemento*, drawn from their reading of Gramsci and Friere, offers one potentially very fruitful way of achieving that goal.

Finally, the past few years have seen the development of a critical, international body of social work theory which is particularly strong on identifying the ways in which managerial and market-based approaches have undermined the social justice agenda within social work but is less strong at identifying ways forward. The last chapter in the collection by Iain Ferguson and Michael Lavalette seeks to address this perceived weakness by posing the question of where the impetus for a new, engaged practice will come from. Recognising that some of the major paradigm shifts that have taken place in social work in the past have been the result, not of internal developments, but of social work academics and practitioners engaging with wider social movements, they explore the scope for links between the 'anti-capitalist' or 'social justice' movement that has arisen in recent years and a new, critical practice. They identify several potential areas of convergence between the two projects and in the spirit of Dudziak's chapter, argue for social workers to involve themselves more fully in the forums of these new movements than they have done to date.

Unsurprisingly within a relatively new critical social work current, there is considerable diversity amongst the contributors to this collection in respect both of their theoretical perspectives and their practical proposals. While most, for example, are critical of the relativism of post-modernist perspectives, several contributors nevertheless see them as having some contribution to make to a new critical social work, while others see post-modernism's pessimism about the possibilities for structural change and its rejection of 'grand narratives' as a block to making sense of a global neo-liberal project and developing appropriate strategies of resistance. What unites the contributors, however, is a shared rejection of the marketisation of social work, a commitment to a social work practice based on a model of social justice that respects diversity and difference, and a desire to explore and encourage new critical currents within and without social work. In all these respects, the collection mirrors the wider social justice/anti-capitalist movement itself. This, then, is not 'back to the 1970s'. Rather, it is forward to a new, engaged social work practice.

Part 1

Social work, social welfare and the impact of neo-liberal globalisation

1 Social work in Mexico: towards a different practice

Maria del Carmen Mendoza Rangel
(Trans: Mike Gonzalez, University of Glasgow)

Introduction

The Association of Mexican Social Workers (ATSMAC) was founded on 20 March 1982 by a group of practitioners with the aim of opening a space for reflection on our professional activity where we could develop new methodologies for our interventions as well as contribute to the growth of the popular movement. It was the 1980s, and we were emerging from two decades in a methodological desert. Most countries in Latin America were experiencing confrontations that forced the social sciences to reconceptualise their theoretical frameworks and their models of intervention.

The Cuban revolution, the failure of developmentalism, the lost decade, the emergence of armed movements from Patagonia in the south to the Mexican border with the United States in the north, and the wars that were unfolding across the continent provoked a deep crisis in the social sciences. The ideological debate shook Latin America's social workers to the core and opened the way to a theoretical, philosophical and political exploration of the issues involved in the transition to a new society; hence the significance of the practice of community organisation.

That is the perspective that informs the work of our association and provides the starting point of our efforts to develop a different professional practice informed by historical understanding.

A different practice in Mexican social work

The history of our profession is certainly marked by a whole series of initiatives undertaken to enable us to intervene in a specific situation with a more professional orientation. Much of the literature emerging out of social work represents

For Maria Luisa Herrasti Aguirre, 'La China' to us, sister, comrade, colleague, friend, a lodestar for me and many others. She flew through life and opened a path for many of us. And on social work in Mexico left a mark that will endure forever.

an attempt to systematise a professional experience born out of a proposal to intervene.

In Mexico, it is assumed that social work arose out of a community perspective. In its early phase we find a number of experiences which, while they were described in terms of 'assistance', took on forms which owed much to community interventions. This was true during the period of Spanish colonisation, for example, of the religious position adopted by Vasco de Quiroga. His work began as a form of charitable assistance but little by little took on forms of organisation and mobilisation through the craft cooperatives he established. For Mexico, this is a seminal founding example of social work as community organisation. Centuries later, the Education Ministry under José Vasconcelos created, in 1921, the so-called 'cultural missions' whose purpose was to improve and promote the community both economically and socially.

Although it had antecedents in the colonial period, it was not until 1933 that the first degree course in social work was approved under the aegis of the School of Domestic Economy of the Education Ministry. The school was located in the Tepito district in the centre of Mexico City, an area noted for its high concentration of market traders; the result was that many of its students provided services for and worked with the traders and their families. The story goes that when the first group of students graduated, General Lázaro Cárdenas, then President of Mexico, supported their right to be recognised as professionals. Although their role within the political system remained unclear, Cárdenas' patronage determined that social work would take on the 'popular, socialist and revolutionary' character of his Presidency.

Four years later, a new degree course was initiated in the Law School of Mexico's National University (the UNAM) under the direction of the Children's Courts; this was the predecessor of the degree in technical social work whose framework was basically paralegal. From the outset, its courses were taught by professionals from other fields and very little was done to give it an orientation more appropriate to the needs of a world on the threshold of war.

By then the United States had become hegemonic in terms of professional education, so that social work was shaped by the US and assumed the anodyne methodology usually denoted by the term 'agent of change', a role then reinforced by developmentalist policies which emphasised the technical and neutral nature of social work.

The victory of the Cuban revolution in 1959, creating Latin America's first socialist state, struck a note of warning to US hegemony; in response the Alliance for Progress (A for P) was set up with the aim of designing development strategies and policies based on a series of indicators which literally measured underdevelopment and the elaboration of policies for, or 'roads to' development. From the 1960s onwards, Latin America entered a period of crisis which produced a number of movements in opposition to military dictatorship including armed guerrilla groups in Argentina, Brazil, Peru, Chile and Uruguay, and later in Colombia, Guatemala, El Salvador and Nicaragua. All of them were evidence of the failure of developmentalism and exposed the dependency at the heart of our economic backwardness. In Central America, in areas like Guatemala, El Salvador and Nicaragua, the struggle to overthrow dictatorships was carried to its ultimate conclusion, unleashing internal wars which brought in their wake massive human devastation, because of the difference in the military resources available to each side.

The reconceptualisation process set in motion in Latin America in the 1960s began by questioning the theoretical and methodological foundations of social work as well as the role that the profession had played in society. The result was a qualitative leap, as the profession began to define not only new frameworks and purposes but also positioned social workers side by side with the masses, whether they were called the 'exploited', the 'marginalised' or the 'excluded'. In the framework of a transition to a new society, the demand was for community practices and models which encouraged the integration of theory and practice, with particular emphasis on ideology.

By 1968, social work had become a full degree course at UNAM, and a new course of professional training was established, though it was not as yet defined by the expectations embedded in the Movement for the Reconceptualization of Latin America. In 1975 the Mexican Congress of Community Development brought together social work professionals. Their conclusions proved to be a turning point for professional training, for they argued the need to overcome a developmentalist vision and seek to work in the community with a new emancipatory perspective at the core of which was dependency theory rather than developmentalism.

The Mexican Association of Schools of Social Work was set up in the same year. It organised a series of national seminars at which students and teachers reflected together on the new perspective emerging from the Latin American Centre for Social Work (CELATS). CELATS was the organiser of the Latin American congresses where new frames of reference were already being elaborated on the basis of historical and dialectical materialism and political economy.

In 1973, the social work qualification became separated from the School of Law at UNAM and the National School of Social Work was founded. It was a time of deep crisis within the university when forms of self-management were proposed as the basis for reform; these proposals had a determining influence on both the organisation of and the course content at the School of Social Work. However, it was not until the1980s that the School was directed by social work-qualified staff, and paradoxically it was that leadership which led to the first student protests against authoritarianism and the imposition of academic criteria.

The 1980s saw us involved in conceptual, ideological and methodological debates, yet at the same time we were also able to produce a more finished and appropriate proposal for social work in which we defined both conceptually and operationally the area of our intervention in the context of social policy. This produced professional and intellectual efforts designed to define and understand these issues, and the result was an important body of work on the theory of the profession.

In 1982, the Mexican Association of Social Workers was formed and the professional colleges set up. It was the period when social policy became defined as the ambit of professional activity and a decade in which the urban masses became a stronger collective subject as social movements grew across the continent. Paulo Freire's psychopedagogy and his proposal for education and learning within the perspective of conscientisation become the reference point in that period for new theoretical and conceptual discussions (Freire 1970a&b).

On 19 September 1985, an earthquake destroyed a large part of the capital. On the level of organisation, it had important repercussions; the popular response to the earthquake brought a qualitative change among the social movements in the struggle for democracy. Its impact was such that 1988 saw the beginning of the decline of the one-party system with the defeat of the Institutional Revolutionary Party (PRI), which had held power for 70 years as the official party of the state. At that time, liberation theology, Christianity committed to popular struggles through the Christian Base Communities, infused community social work with a new impulse to become committed to the popular movements.

The development of social and civic organisation produced a growth in non-governmental organisations, which became the privileged space for a social work that developed a gendered perspective and focused on the construction of identity, mass action, civic involvement and democracy. The alternatives available with regard to public policy, the defence of the environment and sustainable development, the struggle against Aids and respect for choice in sexual preference were increasing.

By 1992, the 500th anniversary of the Spanish Conquest, a new articulation among indigenous peoples began to emerge in Latin America, and later at a global level. The Latin American Council for Indigenous and Black Mass Resistance was formed and later a Mexican Council, which gave unity and direction to the struggles of indigenous peoples and raised their profile within the processes of transition to democracy. These movements were the immediate predecessors to the Zapatista indigenous rising of 1 January 1994. They raised the banners of human rights, peace and development and developed the resistance in defence of indigenous rights and culture, while at the same time taking the first steps towards the construction of autonomous, or self-governing indigenous communities.

Social work in Mexico suffered from the same methodological shortcomings as the rest of the world, shortcomings that became very apparent when, in the 1960s, a series of conflicts throughout Latin America forced the social sciences to revise their theoretical frameworks and their methods of intervention. The uncertainty that followed this questioning of the ideas that had guided our actions until then forced social work to seek out solutions and methods that could give their intervention a more solid and scientific foundation.

In an attempt to combine orientations, intentions, procedures, instruments and techniques in a way that would allow us to act in a given context, from the 1980s onwards we approached the design of mechanisms and procedures in a more rigorous and scientific way. This enabled us not only to address issues of consciousness but also to analyse reality and design strategies to solve social needs. At this point we again turned back to proposals on social intervention and fundamental training in the certainty that neither ideology, nor the individual, nor techniques and processes could be prioritised or sacrificed to the benefit or disadvantage of the others.

For social work this represented a major leap forward, for we took on a notion of professional intervention and emphasised process in order to overcome the partial and unilateral perspective we had tended to adopt until then. We took professional responsibility for a methodology which went from understanding to planning actions and interventions which we ourselves designed, executed and evaluated. This gave us an integrated framework which allowed reflection and collective construction.

This enabled us to participate as social workers in a continuum that took us from knowledge through analysis to intervention, defined in three stages or methodological moments in the construction and application of rigorous scientific procedures for investigating, ordering, classifying, interpreting, analysing and systematising our information. We could then plan actions and propose initiatives that would resonate in the leadership of social processes. This also enabled us to win a place among social science professionals where we could debate our political position in the reality of our country and argue our decision, based on our experience, to place ourselves side by side with popular movements explicitly devoted to bringing about social change.

In the 1990s, the recomposition of the world power blocks and the fall of the Berlin Wall, which repositioned the subjects of change, opened a range of new possibilities arising out of new social movements and political processes. We took this as the ambit of our professional intervention and this in turn allowed us to develop an array of new practices and expectations which we reflected upon and conceptualised continuously.

Neo-liberalism and globalisation: generators of a society of exclusion and confrontation

Neo-liberalism, capitalism's new political strategy, drove forward a globalisation that produced an increase in extreme poverty. The creation of new complex economic functions also produced new centres of power and new economic blocks, removing the process of production, circulation and consumption from the national context and relocating them within a transnational ambit. The result was a world of fragmented and dependent economies in permanent crisis, stigmatised by corruption and political and institutional decline.

Structural adjustment, the volatility of capital, economic and fiscal rationalisation meant shrinking resources for social spending, which in turn brought increasing poverty, marginality and exclusion, widening the economic gap and intensifying the struggle for survival, a struggle which, in modern society, assumed the character of political conflict. However, unlike previous epochs, there is no need today to declare war before eliminating human beings. Today those of us who do not belong to any power group are easily excluded, eliminated, conceptualised as disposable. The most appalling thing, however, is that humanity seems to have lost the capacity to be shocked by this.

We are no longer frightened by violence; it has become an everyday thing since the media have introduced it into our homes. One no longer has to go out into the street to experience terror, mass murder or to see the spilling of blood. This logic of war sustains the model of death and exclusion that globalisation has prepared for our future. The dirty war is an accomplice of modernity, inhibiting criticism and silencing the voices that are raised against repeated crises, war, nuclear proliferation, global warning and the danger of annihilation. We live in the interstices between conflict and confrontation; we provide the dead of history, we are subsumed in uncertainty, we are imprisoned by the market as our sense of identity fades, we are destined to be the disappeared after conflict or the disasters that await us or to be the victims of the slow environmental collapse, the GM foods, the epidemics.

Globalisation is a perspective which constructs subjectivities on a model of violence. It infiltrates our imaginary and our daily life, our public and private actions. It creates a society of risk and changes the values which have shaped human behaviour until now, replacing them with institutionalised violence.

As a system of government and a model of living, neo-liberalism rests on a policy of excluding the poor and the marginalised, denoting them 'disposable', 'marginal' and enemies of those who enjoy freedom of thought and collective consciousness or who labour collectively and organise in communities. The system has no difficulty in eliminating street kids, indigenous peoples, peasants—as it did, for example, in the case of the Mexican communities of Acteal and Aguas Blancas. Theirs is a 'project of death and destruction of all that is human, in the widest sense'.

For social subjects this has profound implications: the destructuring of collective identities; the violent dismantling of social networks through the new mechanisms of social control; and domination and repression accentuating social contradictions and deepening conflict. Experts have suggested that Mexico could very soon find itself facing an explosive situation with the disappearance of the middle sectors, as the number of jobs declines due to the disappearance of small and medium-sized industry. Even now the picture in the Mexican countryside is desolate. Peasants have been expelled from their land because of a lack of credit and resources to cultivate their land, leaving behind communities of women and children waiting for their men to find the means by hiring themselves out as labour on Mexican farms or as immigrant labour in the US, where they work with no security and often at great risk.

There is a deep discontent among all social and political sectors, and in the population in general. There was an assumption that the removal from power of the PRI would bring changes. In fact, the new government of the Partido de Acción Nacional (PAN: National Action Party) has not been able to resolve the crisis, nor improve the national economy. Its loss of credibility is creating a general dissatisfaction which takes a number of forms, some peaceful, others violent, but all expressing the insecurity and uncertainty that infuses daily life at every level and in every area of social reproduction.

Another consequence of neo-liberalism and globalisation is the re-emergence of repression and measures violating individual and human rights as elements of social control in the hands of ruling groups. In the 1990s, we assumed that the Central American experience had produced a general acceptance that 'there should be no more deaths'. Yet that recognition now lies in ruins as governments have proved incapable of responding to popular demands and because an economic model has been implemented that pays scant attention to popular needs but protects only the market and the interests of a small number of capitalists. Governments are returning to the use of force to silence the voices that are raised to denounce their living conditions, combining the use of institutional security agencies with other paramilitary forms in defence of public order, the guarantee of the law and governability.

Yet poverty continues to increase and becomes ever more extreme; the country is facing a crisis in its principal industries, such as electricity and oil production. Unemployment is growing by leaps and bounds. The assembly plants (*maquiladoras*), which had always been considered capable of absorbing the reserve army of labour, are now closing. According to the National Institute of Statistics, 450 have closed in recent years, leaving 219 500 people without jobs. The privatisation of basic services such as water, electricity, education and health imposed by neo-liberalism leaves the mass of people defenceless and unable to satisfy their most basic needs.

On the other hand, our closeness to the United States makes us vulnerable to the policies that that country has adopted in recent years in relation to free trade, and which are designed to conquer markets and hegemonise patterns of consumption. The so-called Free Tree Agreement for the Americas (FTAA), for example, has generated the Puebla–Panama Plan and the Plan Colombia as measures that could establish an oil–energy bloc (Argentina, Brazil, Peru, Venezuela and Mexico) that would function like a multinational company.

The consequence will be that the indigenous peoples will be robbed of their inheritance, the land assigned to them by the Spanish Crown after the Conquest. They will be expelled from their ancestral lands and alienated from the sources of their culture and their identity. The slogans raised by indigenous movements in recent years have suggested a people reaching the end of their tolerance—'Ya Basta' (Enough), 'El campo no aguanta más' (The land will take no more), 'Sin maíz no hoy país' (Without maize there is no homeland), 'Nunca más un México sin nosotros' (Never again a Mexico without us).

Identity and social subjectivity: key factors in the popular resistance in Mexico

As we have suggested, the process of resistance has produced expressions of rejection and forms of mobilisation over the last decade which have given the lie to the new dogmas issued by the dominant powers in the world as if they were original truths: 'the paradigms have fallen', 'we have reached the end of history' or 'the subject is dead'. Yet these processes of resistance have unfolded in the context of predominant financial, economic, technological, communication and politico-military structures, which have forced them to seek new forms of struggle as well as a recomposition of social and political forces. This desperate search has produced many different expressions and states of mind.

In the 1980s, two major events had a particular impact on civic consciousness: the 1985 earthquake; and the electoral fraud of 1988. The earthquake, at 8.7 on the Richter scale, destroyed much of Mexico City's historic centre and was a tragedy that moved a whole city. Having woken up to the horror of death, the city was transformed into a recuperation of life; out of the loss of shelter and the camps came new forms of organisation. Civil society took a qualitative step forward, producing forms of self-organisation and direct management of the resources mobilised by international aid.

The second key event, in the context of a Presidential election campaign, was the use of fraud to deny victory to Cuauhtemoc Cárdenas, candidate of the left and challenger to the power of the PRI. Thousands of voters took to the streets, spontaneously at first and then in an organised way to defend the will of the people. The demonstrations went far beyond the traditional protest movements and produced a number of new social movements which then took to the streets in defence of their own local or sectional interests, and demanded the satisfaction of their needs, the recognition of their right to dignity and equality of access to education, work, culture, representation and the exercise of government. As examples we might cite the following.

- The struggle of the students to raise the quality of education and to defend the right to a free education: their huge mobilisations created new forms of struggle and generated a new kind of direct, public negotiation with the authorities.
- The struggle of the Indian peoples: excluded from all services, deeply impoverished, deprived of natural resources that were their rightful inheritance, they launched a movement against the celebration of the quincentennial of Spanish intervention. In 1992, they created the Councils of Black, Indian and Popular Resistance at local, regional, national and continental levels. These struggles in fact became the central feature of the time, and as their creativity developed they began to play a central role as protagonists of a new history. They introduced a new way of acting politically, which embraced the diversity of identities and the pluriculturalism that are involved in all social and political processes.
- The struggles of small farmers who gathered in a movement against bankruptcy called 'El Barzón'. They took on the national banks and the financial sectors, creating new links and new expressions of a section of the middle class and professionals who supported them.
- The struggle against violations of human rights and individual rights: initiated by a committee of Mothers of the Disappeared and led by Rosario

Ibarra de Piedra, later set up the first human rights organisations and which was later incorporated into the 'Todos los Derechos por Todos' (All rights for everyone) Network.

- The struggle of women for the recognition of their gender identity and the defence of their rights in the context of a battle for equal rights, equal access to work, representation and government. They began with sectional groups of women, linked to the urban mass movement, and later forged broader organisations like the Benita Galeana Women's Coordinating Committee. More recently they have linked up with international organisations and movements like Towards Peking and the Feminist Millennium.

The Zapatista proposal: an historic opportunity

On 1 January 1994, the indigenous communities of Chiapas, under the banner of the Zapatista National Liberation Front, revealed to the world the grave situation of inequality and repression to which they were subject. They called on civil society to listen to the voice of those who had for so long been silent and forgotten. Through the Zapatistas, the indigenous communities of Chiapas broke their own silence and our indifference, and called on the whole nation to stand up and participate in the search for democracy, peace, justice and a dignified life. By doing this, they were making a real contribution to history.

Their declaration of war against the then Mexican president, Carlos Salinas, had been preceded by a long period of consultation, discussion and communal decision-making. Their communiqués and statements to the nation reflected the indigenous cosmology rather than the politico-military discourse of the guerrillas. They did not seek war; they had risen up to speak out and communicate their understanding, and to say 'Enough' (Ya Basta!) after centuries of exclusion, misery and the slow death they have lived through for 500 years.

Their calls for the building of 'peace belts' to protect the first dialogues between the federal government and the Zapatistas, the 'Declaration of Autonomy' issued by 19 indigenous communities in October 1994 together with a proposal for the resolution of ancestral problems and for development, and the 'National Democratic Convention' which took place in August that year in Chiapas to which the nation was invited to discuss the question of the transition to democracy in Mexico, mobilised both the organisations of civil society and the population in general.

In 1996, the 'Dialogue on Indigenous Culture and Indian Rights', created a precedent in our history by demonstrating the possibility of jointly building democratic procedures for dialogue. In the same way the International Meetings organised in 1997 mobilised our dreams and created in our imaginations the possibility of the creation of a new nation and a different world. In March 1999, a call was issued for a National Consultation: 5000 Zapatistas left their communities and visited schools, universities, factories, legislative chambers and sought out their brothers and sisters in the communities in the mountains and other indigenous peoples to explain the purposes of their struggles. The National

Consultation was a symbolic occupation of the nation; by peaceful means, the Zapatistas took over the national terrain and embarked on a dialogue with Mexican men and women throughout the country; they shared other identities and visions, they were received by organisations, by citizens, by local governments, and they exchanged feelings and proposals on indigenous culture and the rights of Indian peoples. In this way, the Zapatistas have established important precedents; they returned to us the instruments of Utopia so that we could continue the necessary construction of our democracy towards a society based on peace, justice and dignity.

The attempt by the government of Ernest Zedillo (1996–2002) to begin the persecution of the Zapatista leadership and its issue of twelve detention orders on 9 February 1995, was overturned for the good of the nation by a new law, approved on 9 March 1995 by the National Congress, entitled the 'Law of Dialogue, Conciliation and for a Just Peace in Chiapas'. A Commission of Concord and Pacification (COCOPA) was established in conformity with the new law, including members of the different parliamentary organisations, which joined the process of dialogue and mediation already set in motion by the National Conciliation Commission (CONAI) headed by Bishop Samuel Ruiz of Chiapas.

Within this legal framework the main actors designed and agreed principles, criteria and procedures for a series of 'Dialogues on Indigenous Rights and Culture and the Transition to Democracy'. Representatives of federal government sat with representatives of the Zapatistas and other civic organisations, personalities, experts, academics and government institutions in a discussion which produced the documents known today as the 'San Andrés Accords'. To facilitate their implementation COSEVER (Commission for Verification and Completion of the Accords) was established to design and put into operation mechanisms to carry through the agreements. Unfortunately, there has been no progress and the dialogue is frozen.

As time passed, and despite the gains that were made, the increasing militarisation of the region has put the lives of the communities at risk. The men, women and children of the communities are trapped in a situation of permanent tension and insecurity that has prevented them from working their lands and travelling freely across their territory. As mute witnesses to these assaults on their life, more than 15 000 indigenous people emigrated to the refugee camps. These camps became the scene of one of the most tragic massacres of our history, the Acteal massacre, which took place on 22 December 1997. The events there set off a chain of events which gave every appearance of being a strategy for the elimination of the Zapatistas.

In the first 6 months of 1998, one military operation followed another in the autonomous communities of Taniperla, Tierra y Libertad, Nicolás Ruiz, San Juan de la Libertad and finally El Bosque, where a strategy of state terror towards the communities was initiated with the public display of the mangled corpses of nine Indian men murdered while they were being taken to recover from wounds they had received during the confrontation.

Yet the struggle of the indigenous peoples has a horizon far more distant than the simple provision of immediate services or the satisfaction of needs in a near future. Their struggle was undertaken to ensure the life of future generations. What they propose is rooted in the indigenous 'cosmovision': a new relationship with nature and mother earth; a new definition of territory, local, regional and national; a new model of education for their children; a new relationship between society and government and of both with the indigenous communities; that is to say, a new ethics and the possibility of moving forward towards a new civilization.

If we did not have a struggle today, we would have no Utopian vision to inform our construction of democracy. Without those struggles, we would not be governing the world's largest city today and we could not continue our efforts to build a future founded on peace, justice and dignity.

The challenges to our profession

We must initiate a new debate on our professional identity and its specificity, inviting other social science professionals to join us in seeking new mechanisms to aspire to new levels of action, and to build a broader strategy as a contribution to the development of nations and peoples. We must counterpose inclusion and exclusion, participation and imposition, listening and indifference and contribute to the building of new relationships in our daily life: academic, professional, and political, through new forms of dialogue and horizontal linkages. We must contribute to the elaboration of public policies and provide more integrated and powerful answers that improve the level of attention given to the most vulnerable and traditionally excluded sectors, developing a new culture of collaboration and co-responsibility.

It is a strategic necessity today to contribute to the formation of subjects who individually and collectively can undertake the struggle against the new paradigm of the market and the project of death and exclusion that is being imposed on us in ever more numerous areas of life. This requires that we take our professional responsibility seriously, linking education with the exercise of our profession and social practices, linking culture and economy, language and languages, identity and communication, memory and calculation, poetry and science, emotion and reason.

It is our responsibility to contribute to the construction of a new paradigm with a humanist conception at its heart, and from that perspective contest those traditional political practices at whose heart are lies, corruption and simulation. We must adopt new attitudes and new styles of work in every area of cultural, political and daily work and contribute to the rebuilding of the nation.

Pedagogy can only overcome technique if it sets out to create a 'didactic of creation over action'. We must look for ways to overcome the risks of innovation and participate in the 'being as becoming' that will transform us into social subjects and ensure a new confidence. In this shared work we will create the confidence of a community elaborating new ways of living.

The new educational programmes should resolve the social and environmental emergency, creating allegorical territories where cultural diversity can find expression and intercultural being be realised so that life itself may flourish. Education should create a being for our time who does not sell his or her labour nor be anyone's employer; in that way it can contribute to ending human exploitation and speculation, assimilate technological advance and give it a human purpose and direction.

Whether we are a science or not, a social movement, a body of ideas or a social force, our only alternative as social workers is to build autonomous beings. The challenge for us is to recover an education whose values can contribute to the search for the enduringly human.

2 Neo-liberalism in Argentina: social policy, welfare and the conditions for the development of social work

Estela Grassi and Norberto Alayón
(Trans: Mike Gonzalez, University of Glasgow)

Introduction

For Argentina, the last decade of the twentieth century was a period of profound social, political and cultural transformation. It revealed a society that was growing poorer, and more fundamentally, more unequal, and a state (its political expression) becoming more subordinate to external powers and more determined in its defence of the interests of one class. To this end, the state used its capacity to instrumentalise and legalise the systematic expropriation of workers rights, to which the development of social rights in Argentina had always been directly connected.

The period of the last military dictatorship (1976–1983) initiated a cycle of regression by paralysing the levels of social participation and creating the conditions for an external debt which grew unceasingly from then on, and opening the door, at the same time, to growing intervention by international organisms in the country's internal affairs. Yet it was the democratically elected government, which ran the state between 1989 and 1999 which was responsible for implanting and consolidating, consciously and deliberately, the neo-liberal political project which was to produce an extraordinary social catastrophe. A food-producing country with significant energy reserves and high levels of employment was transformed into a country in which half of the population lived in poverty (and a significant proportion of them had no means of fulfilling their basic food needs) and where unemployment reached 20% of the economically active population. Even more significant were the conditions in which people worked: of those in work, the vast majority were in temporary and unstable jobs with incomes that did not lift them above poverty level and with no social protections which might compensate for their lost labour rights.

Social policy is not a simple reflection of economics, but rather the expression of the general character of a political project and of its social values. The systematic ideological critique and the disarticulation (whether formal or because of the state's failure to act) of the norms and institutions which protected the rights of workers led to their gradual replacement by a politics of welfare limited to emergency responses. It was expressed through specific and temporary programmes which substituted for the basic rights associated with the modern state (equality of access to the resources necessary to satisfy the needs created by new levels of human development) and miserable allocations which destroyed the dignity of socially necessary labour by demanding that workers carry out tasks that were sometimes simply useless and at other times served only the ends of political patronage.

In this chapter we will offer a brief survey of the cycle of neo-liberal hegemony in Argentina, the context of which explains both the terms in which the social question is addressed in this country, and the reasons why the indicators of social inequality have evolved in the way that they have over the last 25 years. We go on to offer a synthetic description of the main social welfare policies for the poor which developed over the same period, because those policies reveal the general direction of a social policy in which they came to occupy a larger and larger relative space (there was no precedent for this in the history of Argentina, just as there was no precedent for the levels of poverty and the widening gulf between rich and poor). Yet if the policy of social welfare provides the evidence, the explanation needs to be sought in labour policy which, given the constraints of the chapter, we can only refer to briefly (but see Grassi 2003). Finally we analyse this development of social policy as social welfare and its role in the construction of a neo-liberal society. We will discuss the replacement of social rights by more or less temporary forms of social welfare, counterposing it to the *right to welfare* (see Alayón, 1980, 2000) which implies the collective and organic assumption of responsibility for ensuring the reproduction of the members of the national political community as a whole. We should clarify that the policy orientation we are analysing corresponds to a political cycle beginning in 2001 whose socio-economic and cultural consequences we will describe. The political process that followed led to a reorientation of state policy which opened the way to alternative policies. Those conditions, and the new context, provide the background against which a critical social work capable of proposing and carrying through integrated social policy programmes would have to develop.

The cycle of neo-liberal hegemony in Argentina

The neo-liberal cycle began with the military dictatorship which assumed power in March 1976 with a traditionalist and authoritarian ideology supported by sections of the church and the armed forces, reinforced by military repression and shaped by the free-market ideology of those political groups which most closely reflected the interests of local oligarchies. The international ideological context, which focused on neo-liberal policies and a critique of the welfare state, served to reinforce the fact that the second half of the 1970s were lost years, indeed years of regression, for the country. State terrorism obstructed political life and prevented debate and reflection on society. At the same time the nation slipped deeper into debt and its state institutions lost their autonomy as the international organisms were given free rein, in particular the International Monetary Fund (IMF), which from then on imposed its own definition of the problems and the solutions that should guide the decisions of the state.

From that moment onwards the main socio-economic indicators, which had shown that Argentina was a relatively homogeneous country, began to move into reverse. The first sign was the growth of the informal sector, which exposed in its turn the limitations of the protection available to workers. Although the authoritarian discourse denied it, it became clear that poverty was increasing, marking the demise of the myth of an egalitarian Argentina where no-one was hungry or unemployed.

The democratic cycle was re-established in 1983. The first democratically elected president, Raúl Alfonsín,[1] believed that the crisis he was facing was temporary: the result of bad government under military rule. However, then came the Latin American debt crisis; the values of a society of full employment and a universal welfare state which Alfonsin had promised had already been significantly eroded by neo-liberal critiques originating in the metropolitan countries, particularly Britain and the US. Because of these external conditions, and because of the role of the business corporations whose power had been reinforced under the military dictatorship (Azpiazu 1997), the persistence of authoritarian groups in positions of influence and the systematic opposition to government of the trade union organisations linked to Peronism, the 1980s too proved to be a lost decade. By its end, the country had a negative GDP and almost 40% of the population were living below the poverty line, the victims of an uncontrollable inflationary spiral which reached levels close to 50,000%. There was a dramatic decline in the number of people covered by social security, and a consequent loss of legitimacy of all the state institutions. The situation was becoming explosive; and while the ruling sectors precipitated economic collapse with what were described as 'price cushions',[2] the poor launched a wave of lootings of supermarkets in response to increasingly desperate food shortages.[3]

The hyperinflation of 1988–1990 left society defenceless in the face of the neo-liberal discourse concerning the crisis, a discourse enthusiastically embraced by the president elected in 1989, Carlos Menem, who represented the Partido

1   Alfonsín represented the UCR (Radical Civic Union), one of the traditional mass parties. He expressed a humanistic and social democratic current within the party, but it also included liberal and conservative wings.

2   The big economic conglomerates, organised in powerful business organisations (like the Union Industrial), were identified as the 'price fixers' because they established price levels which would ensure their profit levels throughout the hyperinflationary crisis (or thanks to it). This was described as 'establishing price cushions'—and it contributed in its turn to inflation.

3   It is worth noting that a similar social crisis, which included looting of supermarkets, also marked the end of the 1990s, brought down the De la Rúa government and marked the end of neo-liberal hegemony, of the unrestricted opening of the economy and of the convertibility model originally established in 1991.

Justicialista.[4] His Peronist ideology, among other things, materialised in a political project and state policies whose discourse began from the assertion that the state was inefficient and that stagnation and crisis were the result of state intervention, particularly in its measures to protect the working class which represented a disincentive to capital investment and undermined the will to work of the workers themselves. Furthermore, the growth of the state's economic functions through the development of state enterprises in service and energy sectors had served to undermine the market and led directly to an unprecedented increase in bureaucratic regulatory mechanisms. For their part, social security, collective consumption and policies of universal social benefits (including health and education) had entailed a rise in public spending which only tax increases or inflation could continue to finance.

Driven by these socio-political and economic perspectives, the primary policy objective (albeit an unattainable one) was the reduction of public spending; the resulting public spending cuts and reallocations became the core of a state policy which effected the most extraordinary regressive redistribution of wealth. The income gap grew by 30% (from the already wide imbalance that was the legacy of the military government),[5] as did the indices of poverty and unemployment as we shall see below. In the name of the rationalisation of state spending, investment in fundamental public services such as health, social security and infrastructure, education and scientific research was severely cut back. Government policy towards state employees led to the misuse of contracts for the location of services which served to undermine stability of employment, reinforce the deprofessionalisation of civil service jobs and encourage clientilism in state institutions. Public services were privatised in their entirety—and the same thing happened to social services. The benefit system was privatised[6] with the specific purpose of opening up a new financial market whose beneficiaries would be the organs administering the retirement and pension funds. The rhetoric of the campaign for reform stressed the need to lower the level of state contributions to pension funds in order to improve the situation of those already in retirement. Yet privatisation led to a great imbalance in state finances by depriving the state of most of the tax income which was now redirected into the pension funds run by the new private companies.

The common sense in the country was that the 'crisis' was something that happened irrespective of political decisions or intentions; this left very little room for

---

4   The party was the expression of the socio-political movement founded by Juan Domingo Perón in the 1940s, which largely shaped the identity of the Argentine working class, gave birth to the Argentine welfare state and established the constitution which included the provision of labour and social rights.

5   In 1982 the earnings of the richest were 14.3 times greater than those of the poor; in 1988, the figure was 18.2, in 1991 it fell to 15, but in 1995 it rose again to 22, staying at that level until 2002.

6   The initial reforms were intended to bring about the total privatisation of the economy; in the end, however, a partial voluntary welfare system did persist to provide a Basic Universal Payment (PBU) which was the minimum given to all the beneficiaries of the welfare system, whether those in the state scheme or those who were clients of the AFJP.

understanding the power games which determined how problems were posed, what political priorities prevailed and how decisions were made about policy directions. Over and above anything else, these decisions were designed to ensure maximum profits on capital investment and continuing payment on the foreign debt.[7] And this in turn demanded the disciplining of labour, as much for political as for economic reasons.

The principal means for achieving these objectives were a series of key laws approved by the National Congress at the beginning of the Menem government: the Economic Emergency Law, which permitted the virtually uncontrolled privatisation of state enterprises; the Law of Deregulation of the Economy; and finally the Monetary Convertibility Law, which was the foundation of the economic model which existed until 2002.[8] As far as labour was concerned, the policy followed the demands of creditor organisations who among other things demanded law reforms to maximise the flexibility of labour and the lowering of labour costs. This continued to be a priority throughout the 1990s. The first new National Employment Law was passed in 1991 and the last Stable Employment Law (number 25.250) in 2001; a series of other reforms were enacted in the intervening years.[9] Beyond the letter of these laws, which did not always emerge as their sponsors would have wished, the policy on labour was aimed at adapting the labour force to a supposed demand for skilled workers, making the use of the labour force more flexible and reducing labour costs, under the general slogan of 'modernising industrial relations'. Each of these measures was supposed to make local industry more competitive and provide incentives for the creation of new jobs, thus reducing unemployment. In reality, however, the result was a fall in wage levels, the de facto lengthening of the working day, an increase in temporary contracts and the growth in unregistered and unprotected jobs, together with a continuous rise in unemployment, underemployment and subcontracting (Gonzalez and Bonofoglio 2002; Grassi 2003b; Lindenboim 2002).

---

7   The state budget is a good indicator of policy priorities; even when the purpose was to reduce public spending, the element set aside for external payments rose continuously. That is where the income from the sale of public enterprises and other state goods was directed, as were the IMF loans for overdue service payments—all of which, naturally enough, increased the level of public debt during this period (see Grassi 2003b, Lozaño 1999).

8   It is worth noting another coincidence; the Economic Emergency Law ended convertibility in 2002. The result was the devaluation of the Argentine peso, after the confiscation of dollar bank accounts. This measure marked both the beginning and the end of the politico-economic model imposed on the country by neo-liberalism; in 1991, savers were given share certificates, just as they were in 2002.

9   The new Employment Promotion Law was passed in 1995, establishing long-term and promoted contracts; it was repealed in 1998. In this period there were some 300 laws modifying labour contracts. A different government (the coalition headed by Fernando De la Rúa) presented the 2000 Law whose rapid passage through the Senate was later explained when it emerged that the Executive had paid bribes to some of its own senators, as well as others in the opposition. The Vice-President, who had exposed the corruption, later resigned. The issue is in the public arena again in 2004 and the Law has been withdrawn.

Growing insecurity and the fall in household incomes obviously created a larger pool of labour, which in turn brought pressure to bear on the labour market; at the same time, the possibility of more intensive exploitation and longer working hours led to the reduction of the number of available jobs rather than the reverse. Flexibility proved to be an ambiguous notion since in reality it meant an increasing dependence on work for survival and correspondingly rigid new rules imposed by the labour market which placed severe limits on workers' demands—hence, for example, falling wage levels.

If free-market ideology did not explicitly justify it, the radicalism of those in charge of the policy in Argentina and the incompetence of those in charge of public affairs under Menem's government (1989–1999) reinforced the socially and economically regressive decisions it took.[10]

The terms of the social question in Argentina and the indicators of the crisis of social reproduction[11]

The most important socio-economic indicators in recent decades have been those relating to poverty and unemployment. They provide a clear image of a society which was never envisaged by Argentines nor anticipated in any of the national plans or projects set out in the course of the twentieth century and which gave direction to state policies, and to the common sense on social issues until the political crisis of the 1970s.

The Economic Ministry's Convertibility Plan, initiated in 1991, did bring inflation under control, stabilise prices and permit the recovery of GDP, which grew steadily and significantly until 1997. During the same period, employment levels remained stable at first and then began a slide which continues today. In the most critical years (1994–1995),[12] not only were the wages of new workers entering the labour market held down but also existing jobs were lost, in particular stable, permanent and pensioned posts. Unemployment levels reached double figures: 13% in October 1994 and up to 17.3% the following year.

Up to that point, the 'social problem' that moved the state's and the new philanthropists' social policies concentrated on 'poverty', defined in terms which recognised no link between the living conditions of the population and the state of the economy, the labour market or the level of employment. In the terms that

---

10 In the final crisis of the political cycle (2001–2002) this aspect of the Argentine crisis became increasingly visible: the lack of control over the privatisation of state enterprises in strategic sectors like communications, energy production and the airlines, and the extent to which the protection of workers rights and the most elementary social needs had simply been ignored. By the end, half the population were feeding on the leftovers of the consumption of the other half, while foreign banks and enterprises were pressing to be able to remove every last cent from the dollar reserves and were demanding from the provisional government (January 2002–May 2003) 'compensation' for the losses suffered as a result of the asymmetrical devaluation of the peso in 2002.

11 All the data used hereafter refer to Greater Buenos Aires which express the processes with which this article is concerned.

12 The situation was repeated in 2002.

were hegemonic in political discourse at the time, the economy (which was grow-ing) demonstrated the success of the model; the labour market was showing signs of automatic adjustments just like any other market; and the guarantees of living standards were proving problematic in terms of competitiveness because they raised the costs of labour. So in these terms industrial relations needed to be 'modernised' and labour must adapt to the new market conditions governing the flexibility and conditions of labour contracts. Poverty embraced the traditional poor and the 'new poor', who were defined by local politicians in terms of 'over-flow theory' as 'the victims of market adjustments' that were a necessary accom-paniment of economic growth and whose benefits would 'later' be more widely distributed. In this ideological discourse, *poverty* was a dehistoricised phenomenon which could be described in terms of a 'needy' or 'poor' subject requiring state welfare. These criteria allowed the poor to be described and classified and poli-cies to be graded according to levels of need, vulnerability and so on: lack of goods, services and resources for survival, of education, of cultural capital, of aspirations, of power, of work and ultimately of norms. The common sense was now turning back to Durkheim's concept of anomie, to complete the picture of the heterogeneous poverty of the 1990s (Giddens 1972).

Consequently, despite the very low wage levels of the growing number of tem-porary and unregistered workers, despite the lack of health cover and the loss of welfare rights (like pensions and health and safety at work), quite apart from the levels of unemployment themselves, the situation only became a 'social problem' at the point when the employment statistics were presented in the press in cata-strophic terms. Only then was a relationship between poverty and work acknowl-edged, but not in terms of the working conditions that these figures pointed to, but simply as another privation suffered by the poor, namely the 'lack' of work. And that lack was linked to other lacks (of education, cultural capital, of the flex-ibility necessary to enable them to adapt to technological and social change) which together rendered them 'unemployable'. So labour was placed now at the centre of the social question and not just at the heart of the economy. Work now became the subject of abstract and ahistorical analyses, disengaged from produc-tion, for example, it was constructed as the need of the subject and the reified conception of work as a condition of humanisation in itself was resurrected, with no consideration of the social relations which frame the way in which the human capacity for producing and distributing wealth is realised or of the purposes to which production is dedicated.

The consequence was that 'having a job' became the principal requirement for overcoming the subject's various 'lacks' and 'providing work' the unilateral act of goodwill on the part of employers. All this despite the large number of studies which showed that 'the poor' included not only the unemployed but also people in employment, temporary workers and even people receiving social security, as was the case for example of the majority of pensioners whose income generally fell below the poverty line.

If these were the more or less explicit terms in which the social question was posed under neo-liberal hegemony in Argentina, the indicators which registered and quantified the social situation showed that the number of households whose income was insufficient to guarantee their reproduction at reasonable levels of consumption and access to services had reached a point where statistically, albeit with some variations over time, Argentina could now be characterised as an increasingly unequal society.

As several studies of the issue showed (Murmis and Feldman 1992) after the peak of 1989, when almost half the population was poor, the situation improved up to 1994 as hyperinflation was brought under control and affected both consumption and the rising availability of credit. The impact of the Mexican crisis at the end of that year was to increase the levels of poverty again until almost half the population was affected. In May 1995, 22.2% of the population was living below the poverty level (while 5.7% were technically indigent, i.e. without the resources necessary to cover their basic food needs); by May 1997 26.3% were poor (and 5.7% indigent). By May 2001 the figures had risen to 32.7% in poverty and 10.7% indigent. At the height of the crisis, in October 2002, the National Household Survey identified 42.3% of households in Greater Buenos Aires as below the poverty level—that represented some 667 200 people or 54.3% of the total population of the area. One-third of these were indigent, the figure that revealed the depths of the crisis of survival (insofar as figures can ever reflect the reality); in some regions, like the north-east of the country, 26.8% of the population did not have sufficient income to feed themselves. We can only guess at the survival strategies that people employ when they reach the very edge of disaster; in the urban context they include the collection of rubbish, begging and other activities both illegal and dangerous that the education and social service professionals can only imagine. There is a complex relationship between these factors, social welfare programmes and the local activities of political parties. In rural or less urbanised areas, hunting, fishing, picking fruit and vegetables and peasant subsistence production are some of the alternatives to which the population there can turn.

From a social point of view, the results of the period of economic recovery were even more negative than during the 'lost decade' of the 1980s. While the production of wealth increased significantly until 1998, the appropriation of that wealth was extremely unequal. So the problem was not simply economic—it was political and social. And it was the institutions of the neo-liberal state that were responsible for creating and maintaining the vulnerability of the working class.

In terms of unemployment,1995 was a terrible year. The May figures showed that 20% of the population were workless, more than double the number unemployed at the beginning of the decade. In the same period, productivity per worker per hour had risen, while the value of wages fell and the average working day lengthened. In subsequent years the levels of unemployment remained at a 'normal' level of 15%; in fact 80% of new jobs were fixed term and 11% of the labour force was officially 'working a trial period' in the terms set out in the Employment Law of 1995. The December crisis of 2001 pushed the figures back up to 22% the following year in Greater Buenos Aires, and the situation was equally serious in the rest of the country though there were significant variations between provinces and regions.

At the same time as levels of unemployment were rising, so too was the tendency towards the super-exploitation of workers. In October 2001, the proportion of the labour force working more than 45 hours was more or less the same as the underemployed and the unemployed combined (that is, above 31%) as well as the numbers working a normal working day. Concretely this meant 3 080 150 super-exploited workers as opposed to 3 409 272 with insufficient work or no work at all and 3 058 552 working normal hours. Out of the total number of super-exploited workers, 2 024 049 worked between 46 and 61 hours a week and 1 045 821 worked an even longer working week. The following year, in the midst of the crisis, super-exploitation diminished, yet it still remained above the levels of underemployment, which rose in their turn by 65%, and unemployment, which increased by 41%. The vast majority of these people were wage-earners; since multiple employment affects a relatively small number (a little over 330 000) it follows that super-exploitation is common among workers with only one job.

In relation to global activity and the number of years spent in work, two phenomena marked this period: a global increase in the rate of economic activity among the population, from 39% in 1985 to around 45% in 1997 and thereafter; and an increase in the proportion of the group at the top of the age profile still economically active; in 1985 the economically active proportion of the 50–64 age group was 49.4%; by 1995 it was 59.5%, by 1997 63%, 65.2% in 1997 and by 2001 the figure reached 67.2%. A year later, in October 2002, it stood at 67.5%.

From this we can conclude that by the end of the wave of liberalisation there were growing numbers of people working more hours and longer days in order to earn sufficient to feed and clothe themselves and their families. One part of the group was permanently in work, the other permanently available. A shrinking number earned enough and enjoyed protection, although their jobs were increasingly insecure; the other group had an income insufficient for their needs, and in many cases it could not even assure a basic basket of food. The crisis at the end of the cycle destroyed more jobs, and brought rising levels of unemployment as the value of wages declined and prices rose, particularly of the basic items of popular consumption. According to the calculations of one specialised institute (Lozano 2002), by May 2002 wages lost 20.6% of their value, which meant 30% for the indigent population because the biggest increases came on the most basic food products.[13]

13 The analysis of the impact of a possible wage increase in the private sector by the CGT (General Labour Confederation) and the main Chambers of Commerce, in June 2002, started from the 'need to re-establish the ability of the wage to feed the worker'. This recognition says all that needs to be said about the perceived relationship between labour policy, poverty and indigence. The agreement on the point of departure for the studies was a tacit recognition of that relationship, but also assumed that the needs with regard to health, clothing, education, housing and recreation could remain outside the equation. Thus wages need only be enough to buy food.

Social policy and social welfare: principal plans and programmes

The process of pauperisation, the removal of protections for workers and the growing number of temporary and unstable jobs began under the military dictatorship; yet it was only after their departure from power that it was recognised that a large number of households were unable to guarantee sufficient nourishment to ensure their reproduction, even though Argentina is a food producer and a food exporter (Hintze 1989). There had been food policies previously (control of the prices of basic products, provision of additional nourishment in schools, like milk, free distribution of milk to pregnant women and small children through health centres, for example) but they were linked to politically oriented universal interventions aimed at improving the general level of incomes. The social situation in the early 1980s, however, led to the implementation of the first global food welfare plan (PAN, Plan Alimentario Nacional) which provided a basket of food for households with problems of nutrition. The beneficiaries of the plan did have to fulfil certain conditions; it was a focused plan, though it applied widely, carried out in a context of political optimism. The democratic government that came to power in 1983 assumed that the plan would only be needed transitionally, until the 'normal' conditions of democratic life were restored.[14] Its political analysis located the causes of poverty in the previous authoritarian government, and resolved to break with its practices, which saw poverty as a failing of the poor and created 'poverty certificates' which would have to be obtained at the Department of Social Security before medical attention could be given in public hospitals. Despite the democratic will, neither of these aims was achieved as far as the PAN was concerned: food welfare had to continue throughout the period of the so-called 'democratic transition' and beyond; and despite the wide eligibility for food baskets, they were ultimately used as elements of patronage by a series of political mediators.

The accession of Carlos Menem to the presidency in 1989, in contrast to the previous government and against the expectations of many of his early supporters, was marked by the clear decision to follow a political project in full accord with the politico-ideological tendencies prevailing in the hegemonic countries. In this framework the role of social welfare programmes was clearer; although it too was intended to be transitional (on the basis of the expectations generated by the 'disarmament theory' elaborated by the experts of the international organisms), it was clear that those who needed government or charitable support were to be the victims of structural adjustment policies. Aid to the poor (old or new, but always the losers) was subject to that general strategy and had two explicit purposes: to contain social conflict (when it was directed to those in extreme poverty

---

14 President Alfonsín had affirmed, with conviction: 'In a democracy there is food, there is education, there is health'.

who had nothing left to lose by their actions[15]); and to compensate the new poor, the immediate victims of the model.

Nevertheless, in the Argentine case it is important to distinguish between different modes and moments of social policy at different phases of the Menem government; their differences derived among other things from the fact that the neo-liberal project was being carried through by a government whose origins lay in a populist movement which had, in the mid-twentieth century, actively pursued protectionist and redistributionist policies. Social welfare was a key component of its political practice and demanded a certain kind of political conduct of its active agents.

Two issues came together here: one concerned the way in which the problems were defined as worthy of aid or welfare; as we have seen this involved moving from an abstract concept of poverty to that of *lack of work* as the main question; the other matter concerned the role of social welfare within political practices, especially Peronist practices, which were unfolding in a context of a new orientation driven by the international agencies who were financing social policy.

In this framework, the most significant political programmes and decisions as far as their capacity to institute new social relations was concerned (rather than the impact on the problems they claimed to be concerned to solve, which was irrelevant) were those we set out below, which in their turn illustrate the different conceptions of social welfare in play during this period.

The Emergency Solidarity Certificate

The Emergency Solidarity Certificate was the first project designed to replace the PAN and address the social crisis of 1989–1990. It was inspired by the representatives of the principal corporations linked to government and organised under the ephemeral but influential banner of a Private Enterprise Action Foundation. The Solidarity initiative of which the certificate formed part was intended to address the emergency in a short-term way by issuing scrip that could be exchanged for a list of foods. In the first place it was to be financed with funds provided by the Foundation; in return they required a labour quota and an identification of their beneficiaries by having them dress in 'labour overalls'. In the end the initiative was financed from public funds through an ad hoc tax which was bitterly resisted by employers representatives in Congress and its distribution proved to be fairly haphazard; the beneficiaries were not given identifying work clothes, but they did have to form pathetic queues on the public highway to receive what amounted to five dollars.

The Solidarity Certificate had a short shelf life but it did make manifest the role of social welfare in traditional political practice, for its whole existence was marked by arguments over its distribution among civil servants and the various

---

15 'The distribution of food is a preventive measure, like the state of emergency' was how one political functionary put it at a high point of conflict in 1990.

provincial deputies. What they were fighting over was the private accumulation of political capital and local loyalties.

At that classic point where social support, politics and philanthropy meet, the Solidarity Certificate was followed by other plans like Emergency Solidarity Aid for families, which was given in exchange for the labour of some of its members; an ephemeral attempt to create productive mini-enterprises by some NGOs; and then, in 1993, by the First Social Plan.

The creation of the Social Development Secretariat

The launch of the Plan got no further than an announcement, but it was the beginning of a transition to the establishment of a different type of social welfare inspired by the ideologies of state management. A year after the announcement (in January 1994) the most important institutional structure of social promotion and welfare created by the neo-liberal state was set up—the Social Development Secretariat under the direct control of the Department of the Presidency. The government's social policy was now associated with the new Secretariat which undertook to coordinate the Social Plan, which brought under a single umbrella a range of social programmes in every area of government and added its own programmes. The following year, the Secretary launched the Second Social Plan and announced his intention to end the clientilistic and voluntaristic social policies of his predecessors, with all their defects, to bring greater efficiency into government actions in the field. The new policy would be founded on the following principles: focusing on specific client groups, ensuring the integrity and sustainability of the plans, controlling social investment and strengthening communities, including local government and the organisations of civil society. In reality, the Secretariat's policy was to pass social intervention to third parties, creating a register of NGOs like the National Centre of Community Organisations (CENOC). This organ, like the Social Programmes Information Monitoring and Evaluation System (SIEMPRO), the General Social Account and the Centralised Social Tribunals Programme, were instruments for achieving *a higher level of rationalisation*. The Secretariat brought together a number of different programmes—emergency programmes directed at minors; food programmes; community gardens, productive mini-enterprises, indigenous community development schemes, individual social welfare programmes and so on. In addition to programmes co-ordinated by the Secretariat, others were developed which were focused on other ministries— Health, Education, Agriculture, Interior, Cabinet Office, the Economy, Labour and Social Security.

Job promotion plans

Under the aegis of the Labour Ministry so-called job promotion plans were developed which were in fact modes of social welfare to the unemployed, since the policy specifically undertook not to interfere with the labour market. The Employment Law of 1991 (number 24013) instituted unemployment insurance under the title of the Integrated System for Payment to the Unemployed, that is those legal workers who had been made redundant and had contributed to the National Labour Fund, created to finance promotion and training programmes. The demand for a legal contract of employment was a major restriction, given the nature of the local job market and the numbers of people employed outside the legal framework. The so-called 'active job promotion and training policies' covered fixed contracts exempted from employers' social security contributions, and other programmes which included some type of work in exchange for welfare.

Several plans along similar lines were set in motion; the PIT (Intensive Work Programmes) of 1992 were among the first and most important in political and cultural terms because like its successors in 1995 (Plan Trabajar) and 2001 (Plan Jefes y Jefas de Hogar) they were initially condemned by both employed and unemployed workers' organisations and later contested and resisted by them. The PIT employed unskilled workers in labour intensive activities; its beneficiaries were known as 'the pits' and were identifiable when excessive numbers of workers were employed on undemanding tasks. The Plan Trabajar offered 'non-remunerative economic aid' to unemployed people to work on infrastructural projects and was important in local areas affected by the privatisation of state-owned extractive industries where the protests which gave birth to the *piquetero* movement.[16] The Plan Jefes y Jefas de Hogar Desocupados (Unemployed Heads of Household) was launched by the provisional government in 2001 in response to the profound social crisis produced by the devaluation of the local currency. It also envisaged a work for benefits system, but on a much larger scale; today it involves over 2 million people receiving payments of 150 pesos (around 50 dollars) per month.

These are the best known schemes, but they are far from being the only ones developed during this period; all of them had in common short-term jobs (of 3–6 months) in exchange for 'economic welfare' (offering low-paid jobs that would be a disincentive to staying on the scheme). Others supported productive micro-enterprises (almost always subsistence activities, given the lack of any specific policy for the provision of protection, training or credit), training for work, professional retraining programmes, etc.

These programmes were highly focused and developed in conjunction with a labour policy which in the name of labour flexibility restricted the institutional resources and protective measures available to workers (related to wages and conditions); on the other hand the individual nature of state welfare made it less efficient in the framework of state policies which were producing unemployment, insecurity and unfulfilled needs and the so-called job creation plans proved to be little different from earlier poverty plans aside from their central use of often

---

16 The term refers to those unemployed workers' movements whose name derives from their form of protest—blockading highways. The 'piquetes' or pickets link arms to block the road and prevent the passage of vehicles as a way of drawing attention to their demands. These would last for varying lengths of time—sometimes hours, sometimes days.

discredited work plans in exchange for 'non-remunerative economic aid'. In the end the plans were applied according to the criteria set out by the agencies responsible for their implementation rather than those that figured in the plans themselves. This contributed to their ineffectiveness in solving the problems they were ostensibly created to address, although they were 'efficient' from the point of view of the accumulation of political capital by their respective mediators. Throughout this period there were complaints that the lists of beneficiaries were not available and that the conditions for eligibility were not held to; whether these complaints were right or not, they were the direct consequence of state policies based on not very scientific criteria of 'deserving cases' which were combined with traditional uses and conceptions of social welfare as something given at the discretion of individuals irrespective of the legal equality of all citizens.

The transformation of social policy into social welfare, and its significance in the constitution of society

Social policy is a sign of the politicisation of the social question, or to put it differently, of the perspective that the social question is a matter for the state from the moment at which the tensions arising out of 'dependence of wages on free labour' can no longer be resolved by philanthropy or Christian charity. With this as its point of departure, the social state represents the meeting of politics and economics in the form of a new democratic consensus which extends equality into the social field; but it also establishes conditions that arise out of accumulation itself—a guarantee of social peace, a growth in mass consumption, creation of a disposable healthy and educated workforce, to name only some elements of a complex question. So the social state and its policies express not only the tendency to secure the reproduction of the labour force (and taking into account unemployment, retirement and industrial accidents) but also of capital, to the extent required by the technical and organisational needs of production.

If this fits the general movement of history, the concrete forms assumed by national states arose out of local conditions and the mode of insertion (hegemonic or subordinate) into the global system. In the Argentine case, the political commitment to social rights in the mid-twentieth century was a chapter in the development of labour rights.[17] The particular character of the Argentine labour market, with high levels of employment and relatively homogeneous living conditions, gave a universal appearance to systems that depended on formal wage relations and/or on the contribution of both blue- and white-collar workers.

As these systems of social protection developed, social welfare was restricted to particular vulnerable groups. The Argentine social state took shape in the 1940s, under the specific conditions of the government headed by Perón, who at the

17 With the exception of public education which was secular, compulsory and free. In the case of health, the institution of social security as a social responsibility of the trade union movement divided the system into three sections: public, private and welfare. For an analysis and discussion of this see Danani (2003).

same time was advocating a wide-ranging intervention in welfare issues by an organisation parallel to, but not part of the state (the Eva Perón Foundation). This produced the classic discussion about the ideology of welfare, despite the discourse of the founder of the Foundation who affirmed the *right of the poor to welfare*.

As we suggested earlier, the more recent historical cycle moved in the reverse direction. The conditions of the labour market stripped away the systems of protection while the notion of the right to that protection was gradually eroded. Far from creating alternatives capable of superseding those limits and disengaging rights to protection from the condition of the labour market, welfare itself came to be discussed in terms of 'privileges' and the tendency was towards the formation of private insurance enterprises (although it was compulsory to belong to them) which depended on the savings of each individual. Thus protection and security became associated with the individual's success in accumulating more of these new commodities. The market for these services (whose agents were the AFJP and the pre-paid medical enterprises) became legitimate. The unemployed and those working in the informal sector whose income was not sufficient to cover such regular payments were left outside the new system to become the present and future clients of state welfare.

Thus a welfare system emerged out of the general direction of politics and the concrete solutions to the crisis whose origins lay in the 1970s, and global social policy became 'welfare-ised'. Social intervention was now focused on the *weak* in counterpoint to the rules of the market (rules followed by those who have been able to adapt to it successfully) and initiated by the state to regulate social life as a whole and then reproduced in political discourse and other social interventions. The maximum marketisation of the labour force and the destructuring of the institutions regulating the use and the protection of workers coincided with and determined the nature of welfare whose subject was now the unprotected, actually or potentially poor, worker. As far as the state was concerned, the result was a system in which the regulations made the use of the labour force more flexible and at the same time restricted the disposition and capacity of workers to challenge their working conditions. The labour policy which both produced and flowed from this new order shaped the character of a state intervention in welfare globally designed to address the crisis of reproduction faced by those who had been left 'free' on the labour market. This new orientation then combined with the old practices which interpreted the payment as the moral response of a specific individual (a person, a government, a leader or political group, or a civil servant), undermining its institutional character as an expression of collective will.

The right to welfare and the meaning of social policy

Welfare policies arose from measures necessary to address social emergencies and unpredictable situations, to ensure the protection and care of people with chronic or congenital disabilities, to compensate for family loss (for children or the elderly), to defend and protect the victims of socio-family violence (children or women victims of domestic violence or rape, for example) among other issues which do not necessarily derive from poverty, yet which produce specific needs and which are not embraced by the social security system. It also embraced those actions necessary to ensure the defence, protection and social and cultural promotion of those groups most affected by drug addiction, truancy or the general devaluing of their own and other people's life; together they represented a new social problematic born out of the conditions and the culture imposed by neo-liberal solutions to socio-economic crisis. These problems, together with the loss of protection occasioned by these same policies, required specific responses to deal with the loss of autonomy of these subjects, a loss which could not be resolved by the kind of immediate actions focused on the subject's 'lacks' (in the sense defined earlier).

In principle, there would be nothing negative about welfare policies set within a general framework of rights and guarantees which took on board the historical and structural reality that social reproduction might occasionally be at risk for circumstantial reasons or because of the conditions prevailing in the labour market. These would express the normative agreement across the whole of society to assume collective responsibility for the security of all its members. This does not emerge automatically from such a framework, however, but depends on the social and cultural processes shaping social policy. So what such welfare policies require is the development of strategies devoted to maintaining the potential of the subject and his or her recognition as an active member of society; and this in turn requires a political and professional practice among the agencies involved directed at the construction of a new hegemony.

We must take account of the needs of social reproduction, but within a framework of rights and guarantees. One attitude might be that its definition cannot be limited to issues of day to day survival or mere subsistence which simply reduces the person, the subject, to a collection of biological needs. Those needs, therefore, must be those that arise from the conditions of reproduction of all members of society, all of which could be satisfied by the development of human capacities (productive or cultural forces) which do not place at risk the life or resources of the planet, which communities or other social groups (as social subjects) regard as desirable or positive for their own development and welfare and to which individuals can aspire legitimately and equally. In this context, the subject may then freely choose to live the life of an ascete or a hermit.

These assumptions are the point of departure and the conceptual framework for discussions about policy. In the immediate future, effective, efficient and wide-ranging policies are required to address issues of survival, giving immediate guarantees of adequate food, shelter, health and housing and with an eye to preventing the deterioration that causes suffering and produces other social problems which are difficult to cure, like the abandonment of their home by responsible adults and children whose lives then spin out of control and into begging, addiction, crime, etc.

In the medium term, we should review the systems of protection linked to individual wages and savings, because they underline the vulnerability that comes with unemployment or a loss of income.

As far as employment is concerned, the labour policies established by neo-liberalism should be revised, establishing norms for the use of labour, among other things by fixing limits to the length of the working day and the degree of exploitation and establishing minimum wage levels corresponding to the costs of the reproduction of labour.

As far as labour in general is concerned, as a condition of participation in social production, we must abandon the strategy of creating short-term unskilled jobs which carry a social stigma, like the promotion of mini-enterprises which are no more than subsistence activities. Policy in this area has to go beyond subsidies; it demands training, credits, rules governing competition and commercialisation, etc.—that is, economic policies designed to develop and extend these markets.

Finally, in regard to social work, the political conditions we have described also severely restricted the exercise of the profession whose agents were always severely constrained by the social institutions.

Yet we can identify a practice of resistance, both at the level of discourse and of day-to-day practice, fundamentally opposing the moral principles of neo-liberalism; this leaves the profession well-placed to rebuild the links of communication and understanding, particularly at the level of the daily life of social groups and communities. It remains to be seen, however, what role social work can play in defining the alternative integrative social policies (i.e. those capable of rearticulating the many sectors into which state intervention has divided us) which will tend to produce horizontal social relations based on solidarity among subjects capable of building their lives with greater autonomy and participating reflectively in political life.

In the present circumstances, in which poverty grows deeper and the expressions of social problems grow in number, the perspectives of social work should be articulated in two intimately linked contexts: the structural situation of the country and the wide range of social problems requiring urgent attention which that situation has produced.

3 Social work and social development in India

Susan Kuruvilla

Introduction

This chapter attempts to articulate social work in India as an integral part of the post-World War II development discourse that emerged with respect to Third World countries in the context of modernisation. As social workers in the 'developed' and 'developing' countries converge on 'social development' as the common banner under which to join hands, the problematic biography of 'development' as a practised concept and the modernist background of social work are apparently out of the discussion. A global interactive discourse on the practical and realistic function of social work in the world today is necessary, but this needs to be achieved by acknowledging the realities of people's experiences in the context of post-colonialism, development, industrialisation and globalisation. Social workers are in direct interaction with people's lives, and are able to situate individuals and groups within the larger context of global systems. This opens up avenues for critical reflection on the current state of affairs so that social workers may articulate today's problems to make efforts towards global social justice effective.

Here, I attempt to illustrate the need for reflexivity regarding social work and social development through the example of some aspects of Indian experience in the past few decades. Therefore, the first section seeks to acquaint the readers with social work in India, followed by a brief presentation of India's fisheries development efforts. The concluding part deals with some musings that can perhaps aid critical reflection.

Situating Indian social work

Social work in India has been influenced by several aspects of Indian socio-cultural ethos and political history. Some of these are: presence of voluntary social work since ancient times, caste-based social hierarchy, rich diversity in cultural and linguistic groups; experience of colonisation, independence movement and birth of a new nation about six decades ago. When professional social work was 'imported' to India from the West, it had been squeezed into the social fabric and forced to deal with all the factors mentioned above. Thus the experience of professional social workers is somewhat complex and requires a constant dance between different social systems and cultural ideologies. Some of the influencing factors are elaborated in the ensuing paragraphs.

Voluntary/professional social work

Social work in India generally seems to comprise two co-existing spheres of work styles, corresponding to the social systems of modern and pre-modern. These are: one that recognises social work as a charitable response by individuals or groups to the perceived problems of society, and a second that situates it in the context of modernisation and industrialisation. Correlating with these work styles are the two groups of social workers: voluntary social workers and professional social workers. Throughout India it is rare to find professional social workers in voluntary organisations, though this situation seems to be changing with the increased presence of NGOs (non-governmental organisations). Cities like Mumbai have NGOs employing professional social workers and accommodating student social workers for placement (student placement in actual work settings being part of the academic requirements). A study of voluntary organisations in Solapur district in Maharashtra shows that only about 23% applied any kind of professional social work approach, or employed trained social workers (Lawani 1999).

Caste-based hierarchy

The history of caste in India is complex and there are many viewpoints about it. The experience of it used to be that in most parts of India, individuals belonged to one caste or the other, which determined their social relation to others in society. The ancient general hierarchy had the Brahmins or the religious scholars at the top and the 'untouchables' virtually below the hierarchy and outside it. However, scholars disagree on the geographical and temporal homogeneity of the caste system. Currently, experiences vary throughout India with respect to caste. In some regions caste hierarchies, now mixed with class differences, have an overwhelming influence on people's lives, whereas in some other areas, class, rather than caste distinctions, governs social relations. Though caste hierarchies are more often associated with the traditional Hindu religion, it still plays out in other religious communities on the basis of the caste origins of individuals, before conversion to, for example, Christianity. Tribal communities, though they have no caste/class differences among themselves, also fall in the lower rungs of the hierarchy in the eyes of the larger society. Caste features prominently in almost all avenues of social work. It crops up in personal issues such as marriage and even in larger systemic issues like access to drinking water and other basic needs. Fitting into the overall 'development' direction, the Indian government has been trying to 'uplift' the marginalised castes and tribal groups by institutionalising concessions for them in education and employment opportunities. The overall effects of these measures have been controversial.

Colonial past and independence

The Indian sub-continent has been in trade relationships with other parts of the globe for centuries, and this is evident in the socio-cultural life of the people and artefacts that they use. However, it is only since the seventeenth century that trade relations grew into colonial relationships with erstwhile trading partners. The French, Dutch, Portuguese and British have been colonisers in different regions of India. This had a tremendous social, economic and political impact on the lived experiences of people in India. The entire geographical region became geared to ultimately serving the interests of a population far displaced from the lives of local people. India also became the scene of altruistic missions to 'civilise' barbarians while being the fascinating theme for orientalists. Ironically, to a large extent, independence became possible through the institutions that the colonialists had established. The new nation, 'India', that was born through the process of fighting for independence, did not have the economic and social infrastructure to be a logically productive unit in itself. The widespread implications of this continue to play out in all spheres of life. Social workers may notice the lack of coherence between the lives of people and the possibilities offered through the formal institutions. For example, there is a wide gap between educational courses offered and the employment structure. Many university degrees do not link up to job opportunities.

Cultural and linguistic diversity

India has 18 officially recognised languages and several dialects stemming from these, and a related variety of culturally distinctive communities, each with its own norms and mores. The social worker's language and cultural background have a great influence on practice and, depending on the context, they can be limitations or advantages in work. For example, while both may confine a social worker's communication capacity to a linguistic or cultural boundary, at times, being skilled in the language and culture of the dominant group may assist advocacy of the marginalised.

Areas of work

There are many sites of social work (professional and voluntary) activity going on in India, in extremely diverse conditions. Professional social workers find employment with government welfare agencies, NGOs (including those that receive international financial assistance) and semi-governmental organisations. Urban areas attract social workers interested in adoption, school counselling, medical, correctional and correctional settings, as well as those desiring to work with urban community groups with different goals—street children, slum dwellers and women. Rural development programmes, like agriculture-related projects and women's empowerment groups, employ social workers in rural areas. There are several scenes of social activism as well, for example various social movements like the ongoing struggle of the fish-workers along the Indian coast and the protest movements of the tribal villages displaced by the Narmada Valley Project. A list of past recruiters on the website of the Tata Institute of Social Sciences shows a variety of organisations from rural community-based NGOs to industries and social movements (**http://www.tiss.edu/**).

India and development

Since social work is intricately linked to the development endeavour in India, a brief foray into India's industrialisation and development experience will enlighten the ensuing section about the fisheries sector development. With this in mind, the following section touches on some relevant aspects of India's past.

India was pulled into the train of development discourse from its birth in the global situation of World War II and its aftermath. This was in an atmosphere of the Cold War, the threat of communist popularity and the proclamation of the development mission for Third World countries. India, the young nation state formed through the process of overcoming colonisation, became one of the countries to be 'developed' with foreign assistance. In the short stretch of time since India's independence in 1947, its policies have run concurrent with the global development discourse to a large extent. Thus, India's development experience provides an ongoing critique of development economics in India and the various turns it has taken (Chakravarty 1987).

The first few years after independence saw an emphasis on becoming self-sufficient, so as not to repeat the experience of dependency on foreign powers. Two prominent political figures in the time leading up to independence, Jawaharlal Nehru and M.K. Gandhi (Mahatma Gandhi) symbolised two alternative strategies in post-independence planning. Jawaharlal Nehru emphasised modernisation and industrialisation, while Gandhi advocated village-based growth and ecological balance.

Both Gandhi and Nehru had their own insights into the problems and potentials of India. While Nehru's view conformed more to that of development economists and the Left, in terms of the stress on industrialisation, the Gandhian approach was more the ideology expressed in E.F. Schumacher's work *Small is Beautiful: A Study of Economics as if People Mattered* (1973). It focused attention on small-scale and cottage industries, while at the same time calling for fundamental changes in the hierarchical caste system. However, the Gandhian approach was eclipsed by the Nehruvian perspective, though some institutional structures do survive to the present that owe their existence to the Gandhian viewpoint, like the handloom industry.

India has taken a definite turn into neo-liberal economics since the early 1990s, with the New Economic Policy. The nation has been challenged by the invasion of raw materials from markets abroad and foreign-produced goods. Liberalised fiscal policies and a focus on export promotion have changed parts of India dramatically. The hi-tech boom has also been a cause for explosive changes, again, for some Indians. Reinstating the Panchayat system (institutions of local self-governance), to make it a more effective executive body, has been another nation-wide influence in social change. However, cultural variations across India and weak political access for the marginalised majority question the supposed prosperity of the invisible hand. Reduced onus by the government to support those who are not able to 'move with the times' for whatever reason, has resulted in a very doubtful kind of progress. Thus the rapid pace of life, the alteration of time–space linkages and the erosion of social relationships are all parts of the urban experience in India now, while some rural areas remain without electricity and convenient water supply.

Indian social work and modernisation

As mentioned earlier, professional social work and voluntary social work conform to two types of societal structures. Currently, professional social work forms part of the modernisation endeavour and its transmittance to the 'Third World' coincides with the idea of 'progress' and 'development'. This is evident from the fact that the history of voluntary social work has been tied to religious and cultural values in India since ancient times, whereas the first school for professional social work was started only in 1936 under the directorship of an American, Dr Clifford Manshardt (Desai 2002). The curriculum was built closely along the lines of British and American schools of social work, and the bibliography was prepared by the University of Chicago library. This shows the direct link between professional social work in India and the 'export' of ideology and philosophy from the 'West'.

Schools of social work later made conscious attempts to indigenise professional social work, and to distinguish it from the American version of it (Desai 2002). Indian social work was influenced by contextual factors like India's social scenario and distinctive demography. Interactive discourse with the Gandhian approach brought in the notion of social action and social change, which did not feature strongly in the remedial social work practice of the West at that time. Absence of basic necessities among the majority of the Indian population related to the hierarchical caste and class structure in India, and the issues arising from a comparatively later, accelerated industrialisation brought a different colour to Indian social work.

Despite measures and attempts to indigenise 'professional' social work in India, it forms part of the modernisation endeavour, its general orientation being to integrate the marginalised into the mainstream, and to succour those who have fallen through the cracks of the 'prosperity' following industrialisation. Professional social work also fills the gaps of traditional social work, and in this sense enables the transition from social systems based on some of the crippling traditional values/beliefs to the 'modern' society and notions of human rights and individual liberty.

India's history of social work could imply that international social work, in order to be relevant and functional, needs to undertake a reflexive critique of social work as experienced and undertaken by the participating countries. The Western countries had a biography of a particular kind: the era of Enlightenment, the Treaty of Westphalia and formation of nation states, industrialisation and increasing institutionalisation of various aspects of life. Most other countries around the globe, on the other hand, had entirely different experiences as plural societies. Thus, a critique of the situatedness of social work, in terms of its functions and relevance in societies across continents, would enhance thoughts on the orientation of international social work under the conditions of globalisation.

Responses to globalisation

Groups of academics, literary figures, economists and local activists have been vociferously criticising the neo-liberal policies of the Indian government. Interestingly, in one of the struggles against environmental pollution by a textile corporation in Mavoor, Kerala, it was a group of prominent writers who actively lobbied and brought the issue to the limelight. The global communications network helped to carry this issue to other countries and communities that faced similar problems.

The Indian government's adoption of neo-liberal practices has meant a reduction in government support in social service sectors, and it appears to have sent out the message that NGOs should hunt for financial support elsewhere—their own communities, local corporations, national and international funding agencies (**http://socialjustice.nic.in/grants/welcome.htm**). This has invited global players into the lives of villagers and urbanites. Strategies of 'development' as envisaged by the donor organisations can now be realised in the 'field' through NGOs which are dependent on them for sustenance.

One of the major responses to globalisation by social workers generally (including both professional and voluntary social workers) has been the formation of the National Association of Peoples' Movements (NAPM) in 1992. Gabriele Dietrich, an active participant in NAPM, describes it as a second freedom struggle (the first being the national independence movement) for social justice and ecology (**http://www.aidindia.org/hq/publications/proceedings/india_1999/speaker12.htm**). Narmada Bacchao Andolan (NBA) is one of the movements that form the NAPM. It was created as a response to the dam project along various points of the River Narmada in North-west India, sponsored by the World Bank. The active lobbying by the activists, including processions and hunger fasts, caused a rare re-examination of the project by the World Bank and the eventual cancellation of some parts of the project. NBA speaks for and with the tribals/villagers along the Narmada who are displaced by the project. Another well-known movement that had its beginnings in the Indo-Norwegian Fisheries project is the Fish-workers' movement.

The Indo-Norwegian Project

When India gained freedom from the British colonialists in 1947 and declared itself a sovereign, secular, socialist republic in 1950, the basic economic policy was import substitution, as opposed to export promotion. The idea was, as mentioned before, to be independent of foreign powers and to be self-reliant. To further this purpose, India opted for industrialisation, with foreign collaboration where necessary. One such enterprise was with Norway, to develop the fisheries sector.

Origins

Fisheries development started off with a tripartite agreement (between the United Nations, Norway and India) by which Norway agreed to assist India on development programmes. In 1953 a supplementary agreement gave rise to the Indo-Norwegian Project to develop the fisheries sector and the fishing communities. Though the project started off on an experimental basis in Kerala (**http://ifp kochi.nic.in/history.htm**), the 1960s saw the project spreading to other coastal regions in India. Technological increments such as fleets of trawlers and research vessels were acquired, and infrastructural supports provided for. In 1972, the Indian government assumed full charge of the project, and it was renamed the 'Integrated' Fisheries Project, since the goals of the project included improvement of technical skills and infrastructure, as well as the consequent social and economic development of coastal communities. Non-project aid continued to flow from Norway as the project was made a permanent organisation.

Thus, for about two decades, populations along the Kerala coast experienced active intervention for technical, social and economic development by professionals and volunteers. Fishing communities along the coast were shocked into immobility, their life-world being so impetuously invaded. For a time, the larger society apparently did not register the drastic changes, or ignored the issue, probably because the fishermen were in the lowest rungs of caste/class in society, though they provided a significant service. The motivation for the fishing communities to 'develop' did not come from the communities themselves. It is perhaps not unlikely that the underlying desire of the decision-makers might have been the industrialisation of the fishing industry so as to enable increased productivity and to capture a part of the world market. However, it is also possible that resonating with the idea of uplifting all sections of society to be productive capital in the economy, fishing communities were seen as a group to be 'developed'.

Klausen, a Norwegian researcher, who undertook a socio-anthropological study of the Norwegian project, gives a detailed sketch of the first few years of the project and the limitations already observed (Klausen 1968). Kurien portrays the impact of globalisation on small-scale fisheries as well, and maps out some strategies for the future (Kurien 1998). The limitations of the project were, I suppose, very similar to any of the non-participatory, top-down, industrialising activities that have taken place anywhere else in the world. The project to maximise exploitation of marine resources has upset the delicate balance of the coastal ecosystem as a whole, including the livelihood of the fisher-folk. Some of the problems associated with the project are as follows.

Effects

- The industrial-scale harvesting of marine resources was not selective in terms of which fish to catch and when, with a view to allowing regeneration and continuation of the species. Thus, not only was the method of fishing defective but also its large-scale use made matters worse.
- Fishing technology in terms of the types of fishing methods was more suited to temperate waters where the variety of fish is less and the quantity of each species more. In tropical waters, there is a greater variety of fish, so that a single harvest may bring in a great many species, some of which are not in demand on the market. Consequently, the less popular fish are thrown back into the sea, sometimes mutilated and dying.
- Bottom-trawling, used off the Indian coast, greatly disturbs life-systems on the ocean floor, interfering with spawning and upsetting ecological balance.
- The Indian government's decision to grant licenses to foreign fishing vessels to fish beyond the EEZ (exclusive economic zone) enabled fishing vessels from other countries to fish without supervision, sometimes entering into the EEZ. Some Indian companies were also allowed to lease foreign vessels, and later, to buy them by paying in installments. Processing of the fish harvested by these vessels was done on-board, so that Indian citizens had no idea which variety of fish and in what number were harvested and transported by these factory ships. (Recent lobbying on the part of the NFF has forced the review committee to recommend that the government ban the system of granting licenses to foreign fishing vessels.)
- The technological innovations introduced to the traditional fisher-folk without their consultation has not improved their livelihood in the long term. Often, they have been found to be capital intensive (again, unsuitable for a well-populated country like India), and have led to the growth and influence of money lenders.
- Traditional fishing communities, who had been the sole suppliers of fish (other than those who fished for individual needs) to the larger society for centuries, found themselves excluded from their profession, and marginalised by the 'developed' society.
- The crumbling life-world of the fishing communities dragged down their meaning systems in such a way that they do not find it easy to 'integrate' into the mainstream.
- Most local people began to find fish an expensive source of nutrition contrary to the earlier state of affairs.

As the limitations of the project slowly became visible, another set of interventions was triggered off for the fish-workers' communities. The coastal areas became the scene, once more, of professional, voluntary, local, national and international involvement. Some of the activities of voluntary and professional social workers in NGOs have been as follows.

- Acting as mediators and interpreters between the fish-workers and those from outside the community.
- Supporting struggles against the changes in the lives of the community and the forces that are causing it, like the state and national fisheries departments and international trawlers.
- Presenting alternative occupations for those reliant on traditional fishing methods, and networking with other agencies to provide training for those occupations.
- Assisting government efforts to start thrift societies, particularly among women.
- Forming groups in the community so that a common platform is found for addressing concerns and finding solutions.
- Enabling children to come through the national formal education system so that they 'integrate' with the mainstream society.
- Conducting sessions on various aspects of health, environment, politics and any other issue that might be useful and relevant to the community.
- Enabling community members to take leadership in their 'development', gaining confidence to address members outside their community, and to take their future into their own hands.
- Social movements like the NFF lobbies with the state for laws protecting the livelihood of the fish-workers as well as nurturing marine ecology. Some NGOs along the coast assist the local arm of the NFF, in different ways.

Thus, NGOs and charitable organisations are engaged in mitigating the circumstances of these fisher-folk by certain types of activities: activities that will probably help the fishing communities to undergo the transition from a more or less traditional lifestyle to a modern lifestyle; activities oriented towards protecting the rights of the traditional fish-workers and thus limiting the power and influence of the new industrial fisheries lobby that has mushroomed; and activities aimed towards protecting the coastal ecology.

International presence plays some significant roles in this situation: the compulsion for an export orientation and liberalised industrial relations came from the IFIs (international financial institutions); and NGOs working among fishermen receive economic assistance and ideological/conceptual/strategic guidelines from foreign donors. Both these roles are intimately connected to the idea of 'development', though from different perspectives.

The preceding paragraphs briefly illustrate an attempt for socio-economic development within a liberalised, export-oriented framework, and it shows how such a process has not been a life-enhancing experience for the people involved. This should serve as an amber light for those of us ready to embark on social development without sufficient critique. Are social workers who have directly witnessed these situations able to form a coherent argument against this kind of development and social engineering? It does not seem so at present. Social development interventions with the erstwhile fishing communities paint an eerie picture. Present programmes appear to be taking place in the same headlong rush that triggered off the chain of varieties of 'development' programmes in the 1960s. A large section of NGO activity is centred on integrating the marginalised fishing communities with mainstream society and the Ministry of Social Justice and Empowerment (Government of India) also takes a similar stand (**http://socialjustice.nic.in/grants/welcome.htm**).

To the professional or voluntary social worker, integrating marginalised people to the mainstream is perhaps the most obvious and commonsensical solution to the problem of dealing with the devastating effects of popular development. But is the modernising endeavour undertaken with a fairly comprehensive idea of its problems? For example, inexpensive and renewable fishing technology perfected over the centuries is being lost with the advent of 'modern' capital-intensive and polluting technology. Knowledge handed down through generations has been cut off and replaced with a set of experiments and hypothetical notions of future prosperity. This is not to suggest a return to the past, since the fishing community would seem to have had a much less than ideal life, as we look now through the lenses of human rights and cultural plurality. Though they served an important function and had their own ethos, they were not recognised as such or accepted by the higher castes/classes as being 'equal but different'. What is needed now in the globalised context, is a conscious attempt to craft a strategy that will support livelihoods without loss of dignity, allow self-reliance at the community level and nourish the delicate threads of socio-cultural life that makes an economy possible. How can social workers contribute to this end?

Perspectives for social work

Some perspectives regarding the history of social work and the cultural milieu in which social work practice takes place may prove useful for social workers attempting international dialogue and interaction. A primary orientation would be as follows: that an awareness of 'development' as the linear movement forward along the path of industrialisation and liberalisation, with the West being somehow further ahead the rest of the world, is not the only future worth working towards. In order to appreciate such a perspective, social work as a profession needs to undertake a critique of itself, and its situatedness within industrialisation and modernisation. It also needs to have a balanced and in-depth understanding of as many different notions of society and societal relations as possible. This would enhance comprehension of social systems in different cultural contexts.

Some authors give an inkling of how fundamentally different assumptions/interpretations of life processes can affect notions of social life. Sahlins, for example, holds up his study on the 'hunter-gatherer' society to show that a perception of limited wants (as opposed to unlimited wants) can change the picture of life as a whole, not just the economics of it (Sahlins 1997). Whereas modern economics is based on the idea of unlimited wants and insufficient resources, limited wants could coincide with a perception of sufficient/abundant resources. Psychology is a field that social workers often draw upon to interpret behaviour. However, Norberg-Hodge relates how basic human behaviour in certain cultures can question the universal notions of modern psychology, which draws out the patterns of human relations according to a limited understanding of cultures and behaviours (Norberg-Hodge 1997). These ideas provide tempting glimpses outside the dominant perspective.

In the Indian context, Mahatma Gandhi's idea of development provides interesting alternatives. A difference in his viewpoint, which stands out from prominent streams of development ideas, is that he gives a spiritual basis for pursuing development. He does not prescribe any particular religion, but finds the value of a human being as a spiritual entity. In India, where 'secular' in the nation state refers to inclusiveness of all religions rather than the divorce of the state from religion, Gandhi's ideas fit the context. He was not a supporter of large-scale industrialisation, rather, he suggested village-based growth and development, and equality among different social sub-groups, whether class or caste-based. Gandhian notions of economics, which assumes limited wants of human beings, also reveal an alternative for economic and social transactions that may seem drastic in comparison with the consumerism advocated by international financial institutions today.

With regard to social work as social development activity in the 'Third World', Van Ufford's study on the intricacies of 'report writing' merits respectful attention (Van Ufford and Quarles 1993). It refers to the process by which funding beneficiaries, expected to follow the donor's policy and objective guidelines, write project reports that will satisfy the donor and thereby ensure future flow of funds. When social workers are reliant on external funding, as is usually the case since social work is rarely directly an economically productive work, then a peculiar set of dynamics comes into play. The donor agency that is external to the community follows a kind of policy-based funding: i.e. money has to be spent in ways and for goals that fit into the funding agency's meaning framework or paradigm. In this way, policies/strategies that are linked to concepts alien to the actual site of practice are filtered down. However, social workers in the field may find it impractical to implement the objectives directly, while also being unwilling to displease the donor. Therefore, report writing would be in such a way as to tailor the account of actual activities in the field to fit into the requirements of the donor, and so the actual practice can be very different from the eventual project report. Reports of activities can, in this way, mask the actual issues and methodology in social work practice, and thus dissuade social workers from bringing the reality in the field to a venue open to creative and reflexive thought and action. National and international interactions between social workers would enhance the profession, if they would acknowledge this situation and act. A point to note in terms of external funding is the way in which policies and strategies formed external to the community can change social, economic, political and cultural structures within it, in unexpected and sometimes calamitous ways (as the experience of traditional fishermen attest).

Another interesting site of mutual sharing could be the social systems of different contexts and what they contribute to global knowledge. This is with particular reference to the breakdown of informal social relationship networks in highly modernised society, where a process of 'de-individualisation', or a feeling of individual divisiveness among the institutions that control people's lives, is experienced. Less industrialised societies may provide an opportunity to comprehend alternative human relationship possibilities and the tremendously supportive role of the life world. On the other hand, less industrialised societies can search for solutions to the problems that high industrialisation can bring, if they are exposed to it through discussions and studies. In this way, societies can 'inform' one another. Midgley (2002) writes about such a sharing in terms of industrialised welfare states in the North learning from the social development orientation of the South states, so as to counter the effects of neo-liberalisation. In this context, he perceives social development under the umbrella of economic development. It would be more of a realistic representation if both economic and social aspects of life were viewed as equally significant and contributing to each other.

A healthier way of approaching economic development would be, as Kurien (1998) suggests, to pose the ethical question 'how should one live?' concurrent to the engineering aspects of economics. The neo-liberal free-market strategy that allows sections of community to suffer for a time (supposedly only temporarily, though there is no guarantee) for potential gains in the future, based on hypothetical assumptions, does not answer well to the question of how a community should live. The tendency to divorce economic and social aspects of life is strange, under critical reflection, and runs parallel to the modernist tendency to compartmentalise and segment life with increased institutionalisation.

Approaching an arena of work in the international sphere is a delicate process for social workers. Yet, as Giddens expresses it, our bounds of knowledgeability intersect at different points, and as protest movements in different parts of the world acknowledge, mutual sharing of knowledge and experiences has a power of its own. The notion of accompaniment (Whitmore and Wilson 2000), along with the recognition that communities, groups and individuals have different spheres of knowledgeability, point to the need for social work to be non-hierarchical across the globe.

Midgley (2000), Pieterse (2001) and Drucker (2003) all call for a vision of social development in the practice of international social work. This seems appropriate and reasonable if undertaken with reflexivity and, among other things, an understanding of the political economy of aid and 'development' in the field. As Pieterse clearly presents, there are many interpretations of 'development' (Pieterse 2001), depending on who is articulating it, the current dominant one being economic neo-liberalism. Social workers, as professionals who are in direct and dynamic contact with people often in trying situations, need to be aware of long-term consequences of ideologies and concepts in practice, so that they can be reasonably confident of not being swept away in the current without sufficient reflexivity.

Conclusion

This has been an attempt to suggest the close links that exist between social work, social development and globalisation, with an illustration situated in India. The concept of social development is problematic in the current context of cultural plurality, and it needs to be redefined in a manner acceptable to marginalised communities so that it will be compatible to the well-being of societies. This has to be undertaken when the current global values of equality, individualism and homogenisation, fostered by global structures, challenge the values of the local cultures (Oommen 2002), and there is the need to balance the two aspects in practice and policy. This calls for considerable reflexivity on the part of social workers if we are to contribute to a better future.

4 Changes in social policy and the social services in Senegal

Fatou Sarr

(Trans: Andrew Stafford, University of Leeds)

Introduction

This chapter offers an analysis of how social work in Senegal has changed in recent years as a consequence of globalisation and the resultant retreat of the state from tackling the social problems of its citizens. The structural adjustment programmes initiated in the 1980s have been accompanied by restrictions to employment, increased poverty and growing exclusion from the fruits of growth for the majority of the population. The state's poverty policies offer little, for it does not intervene in the 'new poverty' which has emerged as a consequence of the structural adjustment programme itself.

The decline in the economic situation in Senegal coincides with development of new social problems. These include problems associated with the armed conflict in Casamance, in the south of the country (1982), the increase in refugees and returnees from Mauritania (1989), Liberia and Sierra Leone (1990) and Ivory Coast (2002), and the social consequences of catastrophes or large-scale accidents such as a fire in an ammonia factory (1995), and the sinking of the *Joola* with 1863 deaths in 2002. Finally, in Senegal there is a continuing problem of violence on women and children.

The archaic structures of social intervention inherited from the colonial period are totally incapable of facing up to the situation in which we now find ourselves, because the colonial model was inoperable from the start and not in any way adapted to cope with the training of social workers.

Social policy and the inapplicability of the colonial model

After World War I, France decided to replace the old economy of pillage in its colonies with an economy integrated into capitalism (Coquery-Vidrovitch 1979, p. 58). Edmond Giscard D'Estaing in 1932 (cited in Audibert 1977) made clear the desire of the colonisers to bring the productive forces in the colonial domain to a higher level of development. Hence the ratification in 1937 of the Geneva Convention outlawing forced work, and promulgating a labour code for the indigenous population, with collective agreements, salary increases, a policy of mass healthcare and increases in schooling and social services, though this has been qualified by Marseille (1976) as 'social clothing' tied tightly to a demanding requirement of social returns. These developments were not only economic but had, as a central aim, social and political stability, what Coquery-Vidrovitch (1979) describes as a 'political view' of social problems, considered as just one element within imperial policy.

France was obviously preoccupied with answering the following question: 'how do we reconcile the need to kickstart and develop the agricultural production which exists already (or which could be created), such as mining, forestry and present or future industries, with the double obligation of maintaining the indigenous society in good order and of insuring repopulation ?' (Audibert 1977, p. 191).

Let us not forget, not all social policy is necessarily progressive, and certainly not its colonial version. France never tried to install a social policy with the aim of helping development for African populations; it was set up to serve only the interests of France.

The Brazzaville conference (30 January–8 February 1944) is where the new orientations in French colonial politics were defined, and where the idea of helping Africans, at least in part, first emerged, implementing social laws which up until then had concerned only the colonialists. The elements of social policy put in place were inseparable from the economic programme. The areas that were addressed corresponded to the areas of intervention highlighted by colonial policy, especially public health and regulations at work.

On 15 December 1952, the first code of employment was set up; but it was not until 1958 that we see the beginnings of a social security system. Thus, in Dakar a pension fund was created by the French West African Institute for Foresight and Pensions (IPRAO). But the funds could offer only the most minimal of social protection for employees (unemployment and invalidity benefits). Rural populations were not included, nor were the majority of urban people working in the informal economy.

Child and maternity benefit were tied to civil marriage declarations, and the rules of marriage favoured monogamy based on the Western model of the family. Rights for the natural family made no provision to include the extended African family (Lucrèce Guelfi, quoted in Audibert 1997).

In fact, family protection measures actually served as instruments in the policy of changing family structures, and women seem to be the central element in the colonial project. Indeed, prevention and care programmes, found at the level of social centres for maternal and childhood protection, were aimed exclusively at women.

Colonial social services and social protection

During World War II, the colonial social services were initially aiming to counter the effects of the war on colonialists' families. It was only in 1946, after Brazzaville, that minsterial instructions stipulated the conditions for the organisation and the activities of the social services within the French Union, set up under the auspices of the regions's Governors (Audibert 1977, p. 254).

The first social service structures saw the light of day in French Equatorial Africa (AEF) in 1948, under Governor Cornut Gentille. For French West Africa (AOF), we have to wait until 1952, when the Governor General Béchard, hostile to the idea, stood down.

In Senegal the first team of social workers, integrated in 1955 into the social affairs cabinet, was restricted to emergency assistance (help for the needy) and to looking after social centres whose principal activities were knitting lessons, sewing, family economics and sanitary education.

With independence in 1960 social policy sent the responsibility of looking after the bulk of people's social problems back to communities. Statutory outlines were designed for emergency interventions which targeted the weakest in society, such as the disabled, widows and orphans; but there was no global approach to social problems. Social action programmes followed the logic set in motion by the colonisers.

The leaders in social affairs, with the job of instigating and promoting social services, were given no specific support for two decades, lost as they were in the Ministry of Health, and so continued to intervene within the colonial logic. Until 1975, social services were implanted exclusively in urban areas, and social centres, the central elements in the running of the Social Action programme, were stuck in their colonial ways of thinking, continuing to target only young girls and women (Fall 1980).

This failure to innovate incited the other ministries (Health, Justice, Education) to set up their own social services which had little coordination or collaboration with the leaders of the Social Action programme. Numerous small groups (associations, NGOs, private organisations, etc.) were set up in particuliar areas to tackle social problems. Thus, given the absence of a schema in which everyone is helped, it is difficult to speak of a policy of social action (Fall 1980).

At the end of the 1970s, the perceived failure of development and the worsening of social problems led African intellectuals to come together to decide on how economic and social development could get out of crisis, which lead to the Lagos Plan. Following this there were attempts by certain African countries to reorient their social policy and social services towards a perspective for development (Sewa 1983). In Senegal, a new ministry of social development in 1982 brought together the appropriate ministries—human development, women's issues and Social Action programmes—to remove the divisions in social intervention; but soon after, in 1988, Senegal was forced to return to its previous policy by the structural adjustment programme.

Structural adjustment programmes, globalisation and social exclusion

Up against difficulties linked especially to the loss of foreign assets and to debt that went from 10.8 billion CFA Francs in 1963 to 87.2 billion in 1980 (Dia 1988), Senegal now finds itself obliged to sign agreements with the IMF and the

World Bank to allow the setting up of a structural adjustment, the principal measure of which will be the disengagement of the state from social sectors.

Backed by the slogan 'less state means better state', the government is set to give up defining its own vision of what it does in social policy and to place itself within the guidelines of the World Bank and the IMF, which emphasise reductions in internal demands, the opening out of the economy to the outside and the balancing of internal and external accounts, as the conditions for a return to growth and for the progressive eradication of poverty. But this technocratic vision (Lautier 1995), which links increases in productivity to economic growth, and stipulates that growth, as if it were something which permeates society, is supposed to allow a reduction in poverty, has shown its limits. This period has been mainly characterised by the failure to provide cover of essential needs. Growth in GDP in Senegal went from 3.2% on average across the 1980s to 0% between 1990 and 1994 (World Bank 1996).

During the 1990s, the problem for the state was above all how to maintain a balance in budgetary, monetary and fiscal matters, as required by the international economy. But despite all the measures put in place, the social situation and living conditions did not get better. Liberalisation and privatisations have not produced a rate of growth and poverty is not about to be eradicated.

The search for ever-lower production costs and new market shares have dictated their logic, leading to massive job losses, closures and restructuring of businesses. The years 1980–2000 were marked by salary freezes in the public sector, recruitment freezes and voluntary redundancy schemes. The rate of annual growth in the number of state employees was on average 4.4% in 1970–1979, 4.6% in 1980–1984, but it went into negative figures during the adjustment period, going from −0.8% in 1985–1992, to 0.3% in 1993–1994.

Between 1970 and 1979, the number of state employees went up by 2100 every year and with the Plan for Economic and Financial Recovery (PREF) between 1980 and 1985 it fell back to 1900 annually. At the start of the 1990s, with the setting up voluntary redundancy programmes the trend was reversed. Between 1985 and 1992, the numbers of state employees went down each year by more than 400. Overall, the number of state workers per 1000 inhabitants went from 10 in 1980 to 8.3 in 1992 and 7.9 in 1995.

The Institute for African Economic Development and Planning (IDEP), which carried out a study in 1992 on the social consequences of structural adjustment in Senegal, reckoned that the rolling back of the public sector in general, between 1985 and 1991, led to the loss of 4082 people out of a workforce of 11 277, a 36% redundancy level.

The budget for health went from 9.2% in 1970, to 6% in 1980 and 4.6% in 1995, which leaves Senegal well below the 9% expected by the WHO. With the decline in healthcare, we have in effect gone from 404 818 inhabitants per hospital in 1988 to 494 000 in 1995, or more than three times the norm set by the WHO.

In the social housing sector, the state has given way to private developers, taking away any hope for the middle classes of finding decent housing. Only 11% of requests for housing are successful in the whole country. For the 30 000 new households every year in Senegal, public and private investment in housing combined amounts to 930 new places to live, whereas the state had set a target of building 2000 every year for both sectors combined.

The redistribution of wealth is also a problem. The poorest 40% of people have 11% of household income, whereas the richest 20% control 58% of national resources. In 2000, public expenditure on Basic Social Services (SSB) was around 11.2% of the national budget, well below the 20% objective (MEFP 2000). The budget for this expenditure represents 18.1% of GNP, whereas the norm is at least 25%.

The growth in poverty sees the emergence of new problems: armed conflicts, children living on the street, child abuse, sexual exploitation of children, Aids, etc. The rebellion in the south of the country has led to 15 000 families becoming uprooted (Sarr 2001). Social services in the region are not able to meet the needs of orphans, abandoned children, victims of mines and of a range physical and psychological traumas; it is community organisations on the ground like Kagamen (a local group for mothers and children set up by women) in Ziguinchor, who have thought to create a place where people can come to before developing a strategy for fostering with families in Ziguinchor town.

With the development of conflicts in the sub-region, there has been an influx of Senegalese repatriated from Sierra Leone, Liberia and most recently Ivory Coast. The situation for the children of 60 000 refugee families, in the river valley since 1989, is a cause for deep concern: not to mention the exclusion from the education system, these children are up against problems of nationality and are practically nationless and not entitled to basic social rights. The social services in the various counties which exist in this region have one single social worker, and a budget of less than 500 US dollars.

With sex tourism, paedophilia has seen a massive increase throughout the country, and there exists no professional approach to the question, nor any structures maintained by the state. Organisations do remarkably well in setting up social help and advice, but it is a very limited operation.

In 2002, with 1863 victims in the sinking of the *Joola*, there was the grave problem of looking after the psychosocial well-being of those 64 who escaped and of the families of the victims traumatised by this totally new type of tragedy. Overall, social services are not in a position to take on new social problems, and the reason for this can be found in the policies as well as in the rigid nature of the training.

The limits of professional training

Training for social workers, begun in 1964 and conceived within colonial logic, and which concentrated on women and on changing the family, continued until

1968. Teaching covered family finances, health and the classic models of social intervention.

With the university crisis of 1968, the state stopped all training for a period of reflection. This led to the option of starting up professional colleges in order to unblock the university, perceived as a source of conflict, and to offer other possibilities to school-leavers with 'A' levels.

In 1970, when the National College of Social Workers and Specialised Teachers (ENAES) was founded, recruitment was aimed at A-level school-leavers, and training benefited from the creation of an option to become a specialised youth worker to tackle the new forms of urban delinquency that had arisen. This has happened because, in the 1970s, drought and the crisis in the groundnut oil industry, the country's main production, led to a huge migration of rural populations to urban areas with all the perverse effects of an urbanisation which is too fast and badly regulated.

But 30 years on, youth work has failed to live up to the task. In 2001, 400 000 children were living on the street (UNICEF), with nearly 900 minors in prison (Sarr 2001). However the accommodation in detention centres run by the Ministry of Justice is hopelessly empty despite their modest capacity (35–40 children per centre). Their initial training based on repressive prison regimes has not prepared them to welcome children who are used to having a life of freedom.

In the early 1980s, social workers at the ENAES realised that they had to break with the colonial model; hence the partnership with the School of Social Services at the University of Laval. This realisation came from the trainers who saw how the urban situation was being transformed too quickly. There was a huge rural migration to Dakar, where, in 0.33% of the country's surface area, there lives nearly one-third of the entire population. The teaching team propose an inversion of the training model with training being moved into the real world so that students would gain a better understanding of the social problems.

This new approach required more expertise in terms of education and training, for which the University of Laval offered its help. The cooperation with the School of Social Services allowed ENAES to have qualified permanent tutors with Master's degrees or a PhD. Many trainers have benefited from courses in their field. This has increased the range of the colleges, which train social workers in 13 countries of the sub-region.

However, the decision makers' lack of vision and apparent failure to understand what is at stake has led to the end of cooperation with the University of Laval. Responsibility for this failure can be mainly attributed to the Senegalese authorities for their stubborness in retaining a director who, because he had not been part of this process, deployed methods that were decried by his colleagues and who did not appear to respect the commitments made to the School of Social Services. Confronted with the decision by the Minister of National Education to remove the director from his job in order to end the stalemate and to allow cooperation with the University of Laval to continue, the Minister for Families, Women and Children, who has a close relationship with the Prime Minister and the President of the Republic, successfully requested that the

School be linked to her Department and the director was allowed to continue in his position.

This situation has harmed the overall policy for training social workers. It has caused the break up of a training team that took 20 years to achieve a dynamic in coherent training.

The Senegalese state has not yet managed to establish a clear vision to define a social policy which conforms to the real concerns of the people. The neo-liberal option, which the government has clearly been following since 2000, does not show any perspective for an improvement of the situation, as the brief return to a Ministry of Social Development shows; this Department has been emptied of its content, to become but an instrument to manage extreme poverty in line with the strictures set by the IMF and the World Bank. Let us not forget that the concept of social development as formulated by the instigators of the Lagos Plan and based on a state vision of society is incompatible with the neo-liberal route which has removed from the state its role as the defender of the right to public service and to citizenship itself; because, as Alain Supiot (1999) puts it, the state is reduced to a walk-on part, without any real control over the economy, subordinated as it is to a logic which passes it by: 'on the one hand there are structural adjustment plans imposed by the Bretton Woods institutions, and on the other the informal economy which allows the majority to survive and over which it has no control'.

Analysing the new approaches and practices in a globalised context and the question of citizenship

Confronted with the weakening of the state's social role, people are going to become the main agents in tackling their own problems, which will be carried out in a logic of solidaritity. We are seeing the emergence of new players whose mutual care for each other stands in contrast to the logic of state intervention.

From the logic of state intervention to mutual care

In traditional Senegalese societies, economic relations did not pass through a market of capitalism but through networks of solidaritity and mechanisms of helping each other out, which allowed for the circulation of goods and products. So in African custom-based societies there was the development of numerous institutions whose role was to look after individuals with respect to certain objective threats recognised socially as such: illnesses, old age, financial destitution, loneliness, overwork, etc. These institutions, often known as traditional social security, stand out in that they do not divide material from moral or social security. They arrive at technical solutions jointly when confronted with difficulties and uphold jointly the individual's rights.

In this logic of traditional solidarity every family needing to solve a problem could rely on a contribution from other people, and if this failed, then on collective help. In urban areas and in a context of poverty and shortage of resources, in order to respond to social and cultural demands, communities set up solidarity funds in anticipation of events as unpredictable as births or deaths; for, despite the poverty, social logic forced them to face up to their obligations. These solidaritity funds, which at first were meant to help out with certain needs (such as ceremonies for families), now became useful for problems of an economic nature.

With the crises of the 1980s, women now decided to use the money not only for social or food expenditure but also for investment in production. To do this, there needed to be a break with traditional ways of doing things where the individual was subordinate to the collective. When the group decided that the money should be spent on buying eating utensils, a bag of rice or clothes, no-one could pull out. The use of money for things not envisaged for everyone's use was out of the question.

Women managed to make collective organisation an instrument to help an individual's interests, when they decided that money accumulated collectively could act as investment and be controlled by the recipient. They put in place a mechanism which was able to offer to each of their community members the necessary resources to allow economic activity to start. They produced a model able to give people a real autonomy in collective and individual control over their destiny. This model was original for several reasons:

1   The model developed by the women satisfied the double requirements of offering each member the possibility of having an economic activity whilst at the same time being able to offer help with unforseeable problems: deaths, accidents, illnesses, etc.
2   The structures put in place, whilst they continued to provide the solidarity which came from their traditional culture, were able at the same time to evolve in a new context.

By modifying the mechanisms by which traditional structures of solidarity operated, the women laid the basis for real social change using two fundamental principles: negotiating the world of the individual with that of the collective, and that of the economic with the social. Women proved that, despite social differences, in a context where a salary is fairly uncommon, mutual support was possible, in which each member of the community was offered the means to survive and a large category of the population given permanent help, allowing social integration to take place.

Two studies, by Madeleine Diop (1993) and Maïmouna Sourang (1996), have made an assessment of two social services in Senegal by using the Dutrenit scale,[1]

---

1   The Social Integration Index (DIS) is a scale of assessment devised and realised by Jean Marc Dutrenit in 1986. It is designed to measure the progress made by people who are not integrated but who want to get on in society, so it is applicable to all those targeted by social work (Dutrenit 1989).

in order to measure social participation and the level of integration of the users of these structures.

Madeleine Diop has shown that the classic range of activities in the social centres inherited from the system used by the French social services, which amounted to giving house-running training to girl's and which is a model of intervention privileged by social workers, has not led to social integration. The inappropriate content in this training for real needs did not help its beneficiaries to obtain the necessary skills to carry out their responsibilities and affirm their leadership role where they were working. However, above all, the low level of social integration of its users is linked to their difficulties with access to economic resources (Diop 1993).

Maïmouna Sourang's study (1996), using the same scale to assess the experiences of a building society (CEC) benefiting the women users of a social centre, shows that these building societies, which are adaptations of the traditional practice of mutual help, increase social participation for women within the community and therefore also their social integration.

The conclusions of the studies bear witness to the inapplicability of the traditional training model for social centres and to the low level of encouragement towards integration; they also reinforce the hopes placed in the deployment of mutual help by women living amongst the people.

The mechanisms put in place go beyond ethnic or class divisions, which proves that the ways and means of African mutual aid displays models which lay the basis for an alternative to the Western model.

Social policy in the context of globalisation and the question of citizenship

Social policies are designed so as to have an institutional response to those needs which are based on the right to universal public services and which guarantee protection against risk and economic insecurity. They aim to guarantee social redistribution and protection, principally by way of transfers of social services, so as to redress the imbalances produced by the market.

In a context where poverty affects 54% of households, the social policy to be implemented cannot be reduced simply to programmes of help. It cannot be about producing social aid, but managing to arrive at a situation in which communities are able to produce satisfactory living conditions. The problem is no longer simply to warn the individual of the possible dangers of life, but to find ways for each citizen to face up to their needs, whilst accepting their social responsibilities.

In this way of thinking, the state would guarantee at least the minimum of well-being and economic security; it would set in motion a range of social rights, implying a new rationale in opposition to that of the free market. Thus, social work has to procure more independence and autonomy for its clients; but in order to understand this idea, it must develop a vision of social policy which is free of all forms of alienation; this presupposes a redefinition of social policy and efforts to adapt training and qualifications.

With the changes in how mutual help is organised, we can see the possibility of a redefinition of social policy, one which is no longer based on a vision and on values which set the individual against the collective or the economic against the social, but rather on their dialectical interaction.

Hope in these women's ways and practices of mutual aid is pertinent, because they allow each individual the conditions for social integration by his/her being actively involved in the life of the community and thus avoiding exclusion.

Vuarin (1999), who has studied mutual help practices in Mali, recognises their interest but questions their ability to construct an alternative to the Western model of social protection. For him, 'it is the integration or the exclusion of the weakest in the people's way of providing social protection which constitutes the criterion of global efficiency'. These systems will reach their modern objective of universality of protection only if everyone is socially covered widely, in general and with integration. For him, a large number of beggars is an indicator of the model not working.

However, to understand the ways and means of African mutual aid, it is necessary to leave behind the paradigm of social protection as practised in the welfare state. It is not possible to make comparisons, because the rationale underpinning African ways of mutual help are different from those forming the basis of the Western system of social protection. The Western model of social protection is based on full employment and on dependency, with which to offer a minimum level of security to the excluded, but it relies on destroying social relations other than salaried labour to avoid social exclusion. The model of African solidarity is based on a positive reciprocal arrangement and on autonomy, which allows for maximum integration of the majoritity of the poor thanks to the maintenance of social links. We are encouraged to say that a new paradigm is being put in place which values solidarity and integration over the logic of state intervention and exclusion.

Just as the West starts talking again about a social and caring economy, about the need to reinvent collective society, about recontructing social links in order to avoid falling into the situation where societies are reduced to a set of completely isolated individuals, fearing loneliness and the insecurity which can bring about the catastrophes such as that during the heat wave of summer 2003 in France (where it was more the lack of human warmth than the heat which was to blame), it is the time to look critically at the French model of protection.

Just as questions are being asked of the Western model of social work and ways of renewing the profession's practices are being discussed, it is a good time for social work in Third World countries to set out their specifications. And here the example of Latin America is very instructive. Here there has been a move to reconceptualise social work (a move inspired by the experiences of Paulo Freire in Brazil and in the education methods used with the working and peasant classes), with the creation in 1975 of Latin American study centres for social work (CELATS). The experiences of social work in local community kitchens have since been taken up in Quebec and elsewhere (Legault 1991); and our working hypothesis, now we have made the link with ancient practices, is that they have their origins in Africa, and that it was slavery which exported them to that continent.

Social workers in the South can, as they think about the situation in their own country, set up exchanges and partnerships with countries in the North, in which everyone can profit from the experience of others. We believe that an analysis of mutual help practices is part of this, and the model of social work to be put in place can only bear fruit if it takes stock of these solidarity networks, even if they are constantly changing. This requires an approach based on a concrete knowledge of changing contemporary African society. This is the main point of our study.

Conclusion

The sinking of the *Joola* was the worst catastrophe in human navigational history. Officially 1863 died, but, in reality, we will probably never know the exact number who disappeared. For the journalist Abdou Latif Coulibaly it was caused by lack of equipment and serious professional error, and was above all political (Coulibaly 2003). The sinking of the *Joola* showed that there was a general failure: the way the tragedy was handled has allowed us to see just how poor social services are in Senegal, because it was not so much the state's intervention which allowed Senegalese to survive in the face of this unparalleled catastrophe, but the traditional structures of solidarity.

The official structures for social intervention were totally incapable of looking after the psychosocial well-being of those who survived and of the families traumatised by their loss. Nassardine Aidara's (2003) work describes the suffering of a father who lost his four children in the disaster, and going beyond this, he shows the glaring lack of social services in Senegal. The people supposed to answer the helplines, without any training at all, merely added to the frustration of those they were supposed to help. The emergency services, operating in such a serious situation, did nothing but turn away the parents who came looking for information or to collect the victims' bodies, with totally unacceptable insulting comments. But where were the professionals working in the social services?

An association led by a social worker tried to offer help, with an appeal to colleagues to help her, but managing the situation was the responsibility of the official state structures; and the heads of these structures are totally removed from the profession and therefore incapable of taking the appropriate measures. We need to add to this the non-qualified status of social workers for this type of intervention, caused by a lack of adequate training.

This tragedy is an historic moment for Senegal to look lucidly at the multiple failures in state-provided services. It will also be, I hope, an opportunity to rethink social policy and the training offered to social workers.

5 New arenas for social intervention in France: addressing integration, social control and racialisation

Abye Tasse and Manuel Boucher
(Trans: Andy Stafford, University of Leeds)

Introduction

Since the birth of modern society and the extension of the division of labour which accompanies it, there have been many professional or voluntary workers committed to working with marginalised groups: helping the poor, the disabled and the old, as well as bringing the excluded back into society. By applying their abilities and their commitment, these social agents tried to respond to the deleterious consequences of industrialisation. At this time, none of these social agents were able to benefit from a recognised status or qualification appropriate to their job.

Within industrial society, social work slowly began to be considered as a necessary activity for maintaining social cohesion, but it was still marginalised for many years. So on the scale of 'acceptable' and desired jobs, for a long time social work was not valued, and was at best considered a professional career by default. Thus, the uninitiated who went into the various jobs in 'social work' did so mostly not out of choice but by chance, usually because their aim of finding a more valued job had not worked out, while others went into it simply out of family tradition (Vilbrod 1995).

Since then, the situation has changed and social work is no longer located on the wider fringes of social organisation but right at the heart of a social service society.[1] Now that social work is associated with professions which are backed up

---

1   The conflation of the different statistical sources (DREES, INSEE, CNAF, DARES, MSA, etc) regularly carried out by the Ministry of Employment and Solidarity estimated the number of social workers (maternity helpers, home helps, youth workers, female social workers, playgroup workers, medico-psychological helpers, nursery helpers, specialised technical helpers, advisory workers for social and family economics, etc.) at around 600 000 in 1992 and 800 000 in 2001. It is to be noted, however, that out of 800 000 social work posts about half are maternity helpers and that home helpers, whose number has grown in recent years, represent about a fifth of these posts. The main sectors where social workers operate in 1998 are in establishments designed for the disabled, the infirm, and the aged, in creches, with members of the public, and in local councils and in the Ministries and organisations working on social protection.

by national diplomas, people choose to go into the social sector, not as a last resort, but actually to have a career. Nevertheless, even if professional social work is now recognised, it has still had to go through several painful phases and still experiences major upheavals which weaken the professional standing of social workers. Thus:

- Their world of work is split between a number of professions and jobs.
- They have to evolve within a 'polycentred' world, where there is a multiplicity of employers working on a plethora of targeted problems and receivers of help.

In the context of the fragmentation of social intervention and of decentralisation, and the expansion of both the modes of action and of the categories of the population at risk, today's social workers have difficulties in getting recognition for their capacity to intervene and therefore have doubts about their legitimacy as 'social regulators'.

Working at the forefront of social inequalities, many social workers also have the unpleasant, even horrible, feeling of being simply 'tools' and of having to respond to 'urgent' social problems without the real possibility of providing a genuinely optimistic outcome for the people they work with. So this situation ends up bringing them back to their previous role of social pacifiers, which is rejected by the majority of social workers. In fact, whilst sections of them have to deal with the huge task of helping the 'new' poor, the old debate about the role of social work in 'keeping people happy' comes back to question contemporary realities and the meaning of social work. Indeed, what does social work cover today? How has it changed? What is it made up of? Has it fragmented, or ossified or simply become more complex? What is its real role in modernity? Furthermore, and outside its transformations, is social work still there, above all, to maintain social peace by neutralising conflict (Boucher 2003a) in a world which is more and more unequal, or, conversely, has it become indispensable for helping people prosper in society and for allowing individuals in difficulty to become more integrated as human beings (Dubet and Wieviorka 1995) within an information society? And if so, what conditions are needed to do this?

It is the aim of this chapter to try to answer all of these questions, on the one hand by setting out the changes in social work so as to better understand what is at stake, and on the other, by considering the conditions that are necessary if social intervention is not to be purely and simply an instrument of social pacification but rather a lever for individual emancipation and social integration (Wieviorka 2001, pp 9–20).

The development of social work

Historically speaking, it is a commonplace to say that social work first proved popular with religious people and with believers wanting to distribute charity, and then with lay militants wishing to socialise and re-educate the 'socially inept' or 'delinquent youth'. As François Dubet underlines, 'religious faith became a sort of social faith' (Dubet 2003, p. 233). Thus, the engagement in social and educational work first derived from confessional conviction or from the need to have the social order respected.

As time went by and modernisation occurred, especially in the second half of the twentieth century, this vision of social work, made of three parts—altruism, security and equality of opportunities—was transformed. With the birth of scientific concepts (Durkheim 1998) and of political concepts of 'solidarity', and with the aim of confronting the destructuring effects in society's fabric and avoiding a revolutionary uprising of the working classes (Donzelot 1984), social work became an indispensable sector at the heart of modernity.

In a 'Welfare State' (Ewald 1986) which tries to redistribute riches and to organise social protection (Hatzfeld 1989) in order to compensate for the social inequalities generated by a society of capitalist production (Bell 1979, Touraine 1969, 1973), social work actually becomes central. It is now considered as indispensable in any attempt to prioritise social regulation within individualist and competitive society.

The increasingly professional, complex and technical world of social work

After the early period, we can see the increasing rationalisation and 'professionalisation' of the social sector. Models of social action as mutualist, philanthropic, catholic and defined by solidarity slowly gave way to another form of socialisation, that of the professional: the social worker. Social workers wished to break from the old models of 'Lady Bountiful' on the one hand and institutions for young offenders on the other by promoting an educational relationship. The social worker now operated principally in three domains help, assistance and educational action and saw her/his action as going beyond 'total institutions' (Goffman 1968) and panoptical forms of control (Foucault 1975).

On the one hand, in terms of help and social assistance around the time of World War I, this meant the first social workers benefitted from a state diploma (1922, for the visiting nurse; 1932, for the social helper), with the role of the social helper (Le Bouffant and Guélamine 2002) being to oversee the setting up of a social service. On the other, with respect to youth work (Dréano 2002) which was carried out by specialists (1967) working within the 'maladjusted youth' sector defined by the Vichy government (Chauvière 1980), it involved working with young people who were either delinquent or potentially at risk. In the 1950s, workers' educational movements supplemented the influence of religion and of lay reactionaries in the history of militant social work, especially in the areas of local organisation and youth work.

During the 'thirty glorious years' [1946–1975—translator's note] social work continued to diversify and as a result was no longer associated simply with voluntary or charity work, with help or social control, but also with popular education, with prevention, child protection and socio-cultural youth work, with helping people progress and attain some degree of individual and collective emancipation. We are talking about a powerful moment in social structuring, in which, influenced by vindictive sociologists ready to denounce social work as 'policing' (Donzelot 1977, Esprit 1972[2], Meyer 1977, Verdès-Leroux 1978) and by well-known critical and engaged intellectuals (e.g. Foucault, Bourdieu, Althusser, Marcuse), social workers developed a hypercritical discourse on their work (Lascoumes 1977). During this period of 'politicisation', François Dubet stresses that social workers were 'colonised' by a set of theoretical models which they did not really understand, and 'what (in fact) they were looking for was the "secular" meaning of their activity in the theoretical works' (Dubet 2003, p. 240) of critical sociology and psychoanalysis. Thus the meaning of professional practices was interpreted via the prism of sociological, psychological and philosophical theories.

These years of the 'grande critique', between May 1968 and May 1981, are also the years of social work's golden age as a profession (Dubet 2003, p. 241). The core of that profession by then comprised three essential elements: vocation, social control and emancipation.

Rationalising social work

However, the increasing professionalisation and complexity of social work (Chopart 2000) has not led to a democratisation of the sector. On the contrary, this period of greater professionalisation and diversification of the social sector coincided with institutionalisation, specialisation, homogenisation (even if social work was never completely homogeneous) and the 'canonisation' of social work. Since then, social work has been organised into large areas of intervention, with varying degrees of prestige, divided into segments and all but impervious to each other.[3]

Despite waves of dissatisfaction during this phase of professionalisation, linked to a feeling that they were not being sufficiently recognised, social workers began a period of 'technical euphoria'. They moved away from militant beliefs, henceforth rejected by a majority of social workers, and then reaffirmed their 'professionalism': that is, mastering the skill of a one-to one relationship with people. In reclaiming the 'professional secret', so precious to traditional social workers, they wanted the relationship with service users to be defined as a specific professional task (. . .), different from merely popping round for a chat (. . .), or merely getting bogged down in day-to-day life' (Dubet 2003, pp 239–240). Social workers now felt that they had a role in society, as the fully-fledged representatives of the

---

2   This number of the journal condenses all of the criticisms made against social work at the time: essentially, that it is an institution of social control.

3   Indicative of this is the social and medico-social branch of the 'Contrat d'études prospectives' [Agreement on future plans—translator's note] (December 2002), a non-profit organisation, which covers seven sectors (child and adolescent disability, adult disability, senior persons, childhood and adolescent difficulties, adults and families in difficulty, the new-born sector and also training) and then 64 different types of establishment.

'universalist model of conflict', whose job it was to ensure respect was given to the secular republican order that is necessary for guaranteeing equal opportunities. Social workers felt answerable to a twin project:

• That of social integration.
• That of individual and collective emancipation.

Fragmentation of the social sector

The end of industrial society has seen a deep transformation of the social sector as it has become an institution and it has led also to the collapse of the universalist beliefs held by the Republic's 'foot-soldiers'. Indeed, social work is at the heart of all major socio-political change and is always transforming itself in line with the new stakes that arise out of societal transformation.

Whereas professional social work once corresponded to the institutionalisation of the idea of 'social treatment for social questions', in a post-industrial society, the social work sector now sees itself being swamped by a plethora of new posts whose function is to educate those left behind by 'the big changes in the social question'. Some then speak of the 'deprofessionalisation' of social work (De Ridder 1997).

Since the beginning of the 1980s, social, political and cultural changes—such as the rise in mass unemployment especially amongst young people, impoverishment of many families, immigration, political and administrative decentralisation and globalisation—have led different institutions and public services to respond in very different ways to social emergencies. Here we enter the age of large-scale operations (urban projects, income support, etc.), of the 'socially needy' and of social engineering. The state itself is no longer the sole interlocutor, no longer the sole backer of social workers. The professionalisation of social work, which was based on the clinical model of helping very specific populations, during a glorious period of growth, now came up against its limits. Since the late 1970s and early 1980s social workers have had to deal with new populations (new poor in the cities and rural areas, immigrants, asylum seekers), for whom the old models of social intervention are no longer appropriate, which were aimed at well-known categories of 'social cases' but which now had to be dealt with on a massive scale. Robert Castel (1995) no longer talks of the invalid population, but instead of 'supernumeraries', in other words of 'able-bodied, disabled' according to social and economic factors. For social workers, it is now no longer a question of repairing but of managing the effects of 'long-term disaffiliation'. In the face of this, the classical model of help once again becomes centrally relevant, whilst new spheres of intervention develop exponentially, especially those of mediation and social insertion (Autès, 1999).

The new world of profits

Nevertheless, these emerging modes of intervention coincide with social work's entry into the market sector. By moving from the logic of work to the logic of the market, social workers now have to negotiate contracts and advertise projects in order to get a share of the market and in order to satisfy their political masters who only support them on condition that they recognise and above all do not publicly challenge their new authority.

In fact, since the first wave of decentralisation (1982), the social work sector has had to respond to the injunctions of local political masters who want to make sure that the social regulation work they finance looks like value for money. Outside the language of the benefits of 'local democracy' and of diversification in public action, decentralisation actually limits the amount of professional autonomy for social workers. The development of the logic of politics and institutions is in practice to the detriment of professionalism which is still badly understood by local politicians. Indeed, as François Aballéa has underlined, attempts to provide a code of practice for social work is seen, at least initially, by the new 'bosses' of social intervention (at both 'département' and 'commune' levels [or in the UK at both county and municipal levels—translator's note]) 'as a reticence to collaborate but also as a sign of lack of discipline and of a rejection of authority' (Aballéa 2002, p. 23). In these conditions, the employers challenge the logic of professionalism, considering it a corporatist means of defence, and then move towards a system of 'social interveners' rather than social workers.

A professional model under threat

In fact the social work field now has to confront various tensions brought about notably by the change from one model to another.

The first model, that of certified, qualified and agreed levels of professionalism within the state (youth workers, social workers, etc.), was the main set-up within industrial society. Here, despite the diverse range of situations in which their intervention had to take place (institutions, specialist prevention, disability, etc.), these workers were backed up by qualifications guaranteed by the state. As the work of Michel Chauvière shows (1998, pp 45–52), canonical professional social work between the mid-1960s and mid-1970s benefited from a historical conjuncture which was very favorable to its development and its bid for recognition (diplomas for early training were agreed, there was recognition and increased sophistication in the training schemes, and expansion of the social sector supported by a political and administrative system).

But now the stirrings of a communication society (Dubet and Martuccelli 1998) coincided with the development of a second model (De Ridder 1999), no longer linked to the 'logic of qualifications' (or collective identity), but to 'the logic of competence' (hence individualisation, atomisation). Access to new posts in social intervention is not now necessarily dependent on a diploma, but linked above all to individual ability, and according to experience and practical skills, that is to a very precise social need in any one sector or terrain. In fact, with the end of industrial society and the development of mass 'marginality', traditional professional social workers did not know how to, or were not able to become, the uncontested experts of 'the new social question'.

Social work thus becomes a polymorphous hierarchical space at the centre of which we find the traditional jobs carried out by qualified staff who have worked for a number of years in the traditional sectors, but who are now on the periphery of the 'emerging jobs' in rapid expansion which are carried out by a myriad of social agents who have more often than not a very low level of studies behind them.

Of course, the competence model has not completely replaced the qualifications model. We can see that, despite considerable evolution in the sectors of social maladjustment, of disability, of child protection in particular (since the 1982 law on decentralisation, social intervention has been managed at the 'département' level), the qualifications model remains dominant. Furthermore, traditional social workers even manage to be involved in the coordination of the 'new jobs' in social intervention (as those in charge of urban projects, of projects concerned with social reinsertion, as coordinators of cultural or social policy at municipal level).

That said, this qualifications model is no longer hegemonic. For certain social theorists such as Philippe Estèbe (1998), decentralisation and urban policy (Anderson 1998, Anderson and Vieillard-Baron 2000, Bachmann and Leguennec 1996, Donzelot and Estèbe 1994), which have grown unceasingly since the 1980s, are a symbol of social work's decomposition. The culture of conflict in the social work of the 1970s has been replaced by the 'optimistic' utilitarianism of urban policy. Rather than the traditional social worker, local politicians prefer in fact to employ as project leaders people with a much looser culture of professionalism, or as social mediators people with uncertain career paths, and often 'young working class people who swap social violence, whether real or presumed, for the vague promise of promotion in society via youth work'.

Thus social work as a unified profession is in competition with jobs whose contours are badly defined. The rational and code of practice aspect of social work is regressing towards an 'emotional level of legitimacy' linked to a practical and territorial conception of social action[4].

For the public powers that be, the state and the different groups covering the various terrains, it is now all about satisfying a huge range of needs and wants which are no longer necessarily linked to a list of well-established social jobs. For

---

4   In practice, it is above all in urban social intervention directly linked to the fundamental changes of decentralisation that the ability model is the most visible. The groups in each locality (wards, groups of wards, housing associations, local and regional council, etc.) have to look after a multiplicity of concrete problems which they did not have to look after directly before. Since decentralisation, all local forms of politico-institutional systems have had to deal with multiple local difficulties (helping weaker populations to integrate, educational failure, integration for immigrants, urban violence, housing for the homeless, etc.).

these people who represent authority in the public sphere, it is a question of responding efficiently to social insecurity, exclusion and violence on their doorstep. So, given the apparent desocialisation taking place, they concern themselves with 'resocialising' by bringing in a whole set of different mechanisms and initiatives. It is all about innovation in the ways of doing things (Madelin 2001, pp 81–91; Ravon 2001, pp 68–80), using new agents (coordinators, project leaders, social facilitators, women's liaison officers, social mediators, etc.). In managing a society based on exclusion, there then appear, alongside the traditional jobs, new managers such as those responsible for urban development programmes, lots of little social intervention jobs working in home help, safety, in social insertion and mediation. Jean-Noël Chopart talks of a 'hierarchisation' in social intervention. The people carrying out these new tasks are recruited using the following two principles:

1   A recruitment logic aimed sociologically across the different generations, ethnicities or places where people live.
2   A logic of technical specialisation for each sector.

Dissolving references to a code of practice

The creation of hierarchy in social intervention is particularly visible in the social treatment of insecurity. There is in fact a wide range of procedures, and agents who can help with local insecurity, especially in 'urban policy', to short-circuit the process of racialisation of these urban areas as well as the exponential development of insecurity and violence, France has set up a socio-urban policy so as to supply extra help with which to contain unrest to those areas where the consequences of social fragmentation are felt the hardest. However, this space in which security is 'co-produced' has its limits, especially in the appropriate ways of intervening, in the reasons for intervening, in the ways to provide representation, and how to deal with identities of professionalism which have historically looked very different, and are even in opposition, antagonistic to one another. However, to illustrate how this confrontation occurs, we will look at only two emblematic cases: local mediators and youth workers engaging in specific forms of prevention.

Ways of intervening for mediators and youth workers

With respect to mediators, and picking up on an old idea of sociologists from the Chicago School (Cloward and Ohlin), which emphasises the advantage in recruiting 'indigenous leaders' to fight against delinquency and urban violence (Wieviorka 1999) in the area in which they live, local politicians have recently created a mass of local agents for each district. They are barely trained and have no professional identity. In fact this emergence of social mediators largely employed for their 'ethnic capacities' coincides with the call by mayors for there to be more 'visible security' in the wards. By their 24-hour presence in the community, local agents are there, above all, to reduce feelings of insecurity (Robert 2002). Of course, mediators do not only have the role of 'police auxiliary'; they also have to talk to young people, so as to reduce tension in the housing estates and prevent potential trouble exploding. However, they also have to pass on information, if possible by giving names, about how people feel and about people considered to be dangerous. Thus their work of mediation is intimately linked to that of social control.

For their part, prevention officers, who for a long time have had to deal with greater levels of suffering, want to be considered part of a specific field of youth work. Specialised prevention in fact has its own history; it has an ethics, a code of practice which gives rise to distinct modes of intervention (interministerial directive of 4 July 1972). So the prevention clubs develop forms of action appropriate to them (anonymity,[5] freedom to join, etc.). What characterises specialist prevention is deep personal investment and the refusal to abide to some kind of routine youth work. To succeed in creating relations built on trust for the long term, youth workers invest themselves personally and often go well beyond the call of duty to uphold their humanist and lay convictions. If they do not deny being, or indeed want to be considered as, agents of social regulation, their work cannot then be divorced from a code of practice. They refuse to be simple agents of a security policy and informers telling on young people.

In this context, prevention specialists consider the mediators as 'Canada Dry' youth workers, a sort of political puppet, there solely to maintain the peace and certainly not to help people in difficulty. But youth workers are aware that their work too has an element of social control. Conversely, in opposition to the agents working in housing areas, they believe that they have much more autonomy with regard to politics and above all that they are protected by a history, by an ethics and by a code of practice.

Now, paradoxically this form of intervention and safety management, which the local agents on the estates carry out, is widely contested by the mediators themselves who aspire to more diversity in their ways of working. In doing 'the coppers' work', mediators are not only getting the impression that they are heavily criticised by young people and social workers but also have very low self-esteem. Consequently, despite appearances (uniforms, walky-talkies, links to the local police), local agents refuse to consider themselves as a form of surveillance but as 'do-gooders'.[6] They see themselves as professional agents whose first objective, like other qualified social workers, is to help young people in difficulty get out

---

5 Anonymity means that the youth workers must agree not to relay to the outside anything that is said by someone who has not agreed to its being repeated. That said, even if specialist youth workers say they are using an agreed code of practice, unlike social workers, they do not enjoy the right to 'professional secrecy'. Consequently, when there is a court case, youth workers working in prevention have to say everything they know about a situation like any other citizen before the law. So, as far as the youth workers are concerned, this means that they have to explain to the young people with whom they came into contact that 'they are not allowed to tell all, but nor to hear everything'.

6 Cf. A. Coulon 1992 *L'Ecole de Chicago*, Paris: Puf.

of trouble. In fact, contrary to what many qualified social workers think, the majority of agents working on the estates would like to be trained so as to become part of the 'team' of established social agents.

Acting in a risk society

It is clear that the erratic social experience of today's social workers suggests that social work is part of a new type of society. Indeed, their arenas of social intervention are part of the 'risk society'.[7]

Within a radical modernisation process (individualisation, rationalisation and social differentiation), this type of society (Ascher 2001) is defined above all by the refusal to leave any area of life uncontrolled and therefore by the desire to rationalise and control the future which this society is itself producing (Le Breton 1995, Peretti-Watel 2000). By 'institutionalising doubt', it then becomes a question of controlling and containing undesired events, threats and dangers (Beck 2001, 2003, pp 27–34). We are talking about 'a reflexive society' (Giddens, 1994) in which, in order to face up to the uncertainties which have become more and more unbearable (disenchantment with the world) since the end of the era of fatalism (Weber 1967) and the beginning of modernity (Touraine 1992), the setting up of a policy of 'risk management' and the precaution principle[8] have been favoured. Indeed, 'the risk society' (Peretti-Watel 2001) fears any move towards social deregulation, thereby bringing the concept of risk[9] close to that of social order. In many cases, risk management is conflated with attempts to socialise disorders found in the 'target populations' classified as such (Mansanti 2001, pp 111–132).

However, we agree with the thesis (Boucher 2003b) that risk society is not characterised by the decomposition of social control (Cusson 1983) but by its diversi-

---

7   In the risk society, sociologists studying those people involved in social regulation refuse more and more to speak of social workers, who remain attached to the image of a professional social action based upon a relationship and developed as part of industrial society, and preferring to use the term 'social interveners' which includes all those agents involved in the 'socialisation of risk' who implement a set of policies and agreements.

8   This is the principle according to which a lack of certainty, given the scientific and technical knowledge of the moment, must not impede the adoption of those effective and adapted measures which aim to warn of the risk of grave damage. Furthermore, the principle of precaution is a strong part of the notion of responsibilisation. Indeed, contrary to the principle of solidarity in an insured society, which used to protect above all against damage to property or person, the principle of precaution does not question the protection but tries to find the person responsible for the damage to bring them to justice. Not knowing for certain not only excuses nothing, but it also must incite more prudence (see Ewald 1996, Kourilsky and Viney 2000, Ewald et al. 2001, Hunyadi, 2003).

9   From the low latin *risicus* or *riscus*, from the latin *resecare* (to cut), the etymology of the word is disputed by those who think that it comes from the Spanish *riesgo* or the Italian *risco* and which meant first a fleet of menacing ships and by extension anything representing a danger, and by those who favour the Roman derivation of *rixicare* which means to argue, evoking the idea of combat and thus the notion of danger. Whatever our uncertainties on the origin of the word *risk*, today risk most often represents chance, hazard, a potential danger, an inconvenience which is more or less predictable and which we try to avoid.

fication and recomposition.[10] We are witnessing as the majority in an integrated society the attempt to contain social disorders by the development of a set of disparate logics of interaction (integration, assistance, repression, insertion, mediation, strategy, subjectification) which link motivations to the system and to the person. Thus, a revived form of social control is based on the development of a logic which traditionally was operated by specialist institutions (police, school, religion, social help, associations) or by more classical ones (family, ethnic and cultural communities, social group), whether already established or newly emerging with, but also associated to the logic of social agents in evolution within these institutions or having an 'interest' in cooperating with them. Social control or regulation happens then through a paradoxical combination and alliance of those logics which guarantee the reproduction or the maintenance of the social order with those that ensure the development of a person's freedom.

In this dynamic of the recomposition of social control, social interveners are key agents. In fact, the majority of new and old social interveners (youth workers, social workers, community helpers, mediators, trainers), whether employed by the state, by politico-institutional structures (local groups) or by social organisations (local voluntary associations), all orient the thrust of their actions towards populations 'at risk', who must be helped, accompanied, educated, looked after, 're-qualified', even contained, managed or controlled. The new space of social intervention is thus made up of a multiplicity of social agents who develop a wide range of conflicting ways of working, typically with an idealistic point of view, who compete in constructing social regulation when other logics want to respect individual freedoms, or who favour social control and pacification when the agreed logic is one of above all respecting the rules and social order.

Conclusion

In conclusion, we have seen how social work and social intervention are linked by a common process: the disqualification of professional and transversal action in favour of social intervention which is both protean and instrumentalised. Indeed, now that the social work sector has become more complex and, since the end of industrial society, its usefulness in maintaining social order and cohesion no longer doubted, one question remains none the less central: how to give back a meaning to the whole social intervention sector so that it is not limited to helping, to 'risk management' and to the ethnic neutralisation of social disorders?

---

10 See the remarkable analysis by Robert Castel describing transformations in the medico-psychological field which, leaving behind the 'ghetto of the asylum', had developed in the 1960s and 1970s a form of social psychiatry and psychoanalysis centred on the subject. He shows that following this period, in the early 1980s we moved to a post-disciplinary period in which social management was organised through a multiplication of those agents involved in social regulation and through a diversification of the modes of intervention (social work, expertise, health work, management of populations at risk and even 'therapy for the normal') (Castel 1981).

To maintain its emancipatory, individualising and integrationist action, social intervention cannot indeed be reduced to an opaque market made up of a multiplicity of social agents, experts or technicians working towards a policy of social pacification. However, the intrusion by market forces, by liberal politics and those of security, chips away on a daily basis at the ethics and code of practice of social work, which, beyond the suffering this causes to social workers, undermines the very existence of social work understood as an essential element of democracy.

It is not a question however of rejecting the changes, the diversification and the democratisation necessary to the social sector. But this process of change should not then be carried out 'from below', that is by undermining the qualifications process, by deprofessionalising and racialising the field of social intervention. Beyond its corporate nature, is it not desirable in fact, in being a social worker or 'authentic' social intervener—that is someone working towards integration rather than maintaining order—to implement a range of different logics of action (service, integration, relation) but equally to maintain certain principles? For example:

- A personal ethos (philosophical, religious and political beliefs and convictions) which is necessarily humanist and respectful of an individual's complexity.
- A professional ethos.
- A true code of practice

Indeed, social work or social intervention must be defined only by reference to an ethos and to a code of practice[11].

Thus, to reject the logics of the market, of instrumentalisation and of segmentation now taking place in the arena of social intervention would not be impossible but would need the implementation of two types of action.

The first requires a logic of 'reconflictualisation' of the sector by the social agents themselves. It is then up to social interveners to change the system (bottom up) and not the opposite (top down), by redrawing these boundaries of conflictualisation. Very concretely, to develop a logic of conflictualisation would require social interveners to give priority to spaces of negotiation and mediation rather than pacification, in which the thoughts and views of everyone (social workers,

---

11 François Aballéa underlines that the ethos of professionalism is defined by those collective values which are the basis of individual action of social workers: 'autonomy not dependence, education not help, structural responses not short-term solutions, desire for a durable solution not just rapid response, providing access to rights not just helping people with them, social insertion rather than institutional solutions involving ad hoc solutions or sectioning, encouraging people's participation rather than a passive use of services which are lent out, an attempt to make people responsible rather than giving individual protection, voluntary participation rather than passive administration, etc.' (Aballéa 2002, p. 20). The agreed levels of independence in national and international codes for its part is linked more specifically to those principles and values which act as a guide to implementing action (equality of treatment, rejection of discrimination, neutrality, professional discretion, requirement to provide funds, a respect for a person's wishes, autonomy with regard to the employer).

local groups, local ward committees, local landlords, companies, local associations, etc.), those directly or indirectly affected by social questions, could say what they think and then come together to find humane solutions to problems. As Michel Wieviorka underlines '. . . conflict sets up an opposition not between enemies . . . but between adversaries who could stabilise their relations by institutionalising them, by putting in place rules, negotiating procedures which allow a link to be maintained between agents standing in opposition to each other' (Wieviorka 2002, pp 14–24).

The second action requires the affirmation of a drive towards 'reprofessionalisation'. This would involve professionals in the social sector requiring a redrawing of benchmarks, set by the training colleges and professional bodies, with the continued professionalisation and development of qualifications that also provide a bridge between the two (to fight against discrimination), so that social interveners having particular capacities get proper training qualifications. Indeed qualifications always seem to be crucial in producing people capable of combining basic skills with independent action, which, for the moment, seem to be the only real guarantee of respect for the complexity of those people in need of support. This guarantee would also be a measure of how autonomous professionals are when confronted with the numerous temptations to instrumentalise those representatives of the social order whose job it is to maintain the peace in society. Is it not with these conditions alone that social work and beyond it requalified and reprofessionalised social intervention can avoid being conflated with the logic of social pacification and social control, and to be linked instead to a logic of democratisation in social regulation?

6   Globalisation, neo-liberal managerialism and UK social work

John Harris

Introduction

The trend towards economic globalisation, defined simply as the openness of national economies to trade and financial flows (Mishra 1999, p. ix), resulting in 'greater mobility of capital, investment, production processes and the new forms of technology (particularly information technology) that enable this increased spatial freedom' (Clarke 2000, p. 203) is now the macro-context within which national welfare regimes, and hence social work, operate. It has been argued that the relationship between national developments in social work and this macro-context does not result in straightforward and unilinear responses to globalisation (Harris and McDonald 2000; McDonald et al. 2003); 'glocalisation' may be a more accurate term, according recognition to the mediating role played by the national level in the processes that are taking place, particularly with regard to social work (Harris and Yueh-Ching 2001). However, this mediating role is played against the pressures exerted by globalisation in the direction of promoting labour 'flexibility', depressing wages and weakening social welfare arrangements or, put more baldly, the generation of increasing inequality (see Hills 1995, for data on inequality in the UK context).

Against this background, although an element of political choice about welfare regimes remains, national strategies are increasingly constrained by globalisation (Beyelar 2003), with an ongoing debate about the extent of choice and the degree of constraint that exist. On the one hand, the role of the nation state is seen as having been reduced to devising strategies that can only hope to shape the pace, timing and effects of globalisation (see for example, Yeates 2002). On the other hand, the analysis of the impact of globalisation is regarded as having fallen prey to a substantial degree of overgeneralised assertion that amounts to 'globaloney' (see, for example, Carroll 2002).

There may be endless debate and a voluminous literature about economic globalisation and its impact but one thing is clear: globalisation is currently dominated by neo-liberalism (Clarke 2000; Jessop 2002, pp 113–118), with its emphases on free markets and the associated economic rights of the individual. As a consequence, there is a broadly similar trend, regardless of the political persuasion of national governments, of global capitalist developments moving social welfare regimes in a neo-liberal direction (Barns et al. 1999; Deacon et al. 1997; George 1998). Mishra argues that one of the key factors allowing neo-liberalism to occupy a dominant position in the globalisation discourse is the perceived lack of an alternative, given the collapse of state socialism, following the demise of Communist Party governments in Central and Eastern Europe, and the retreat from social democracy in Western European countries (Mishra 1999, Ch.1). It is certainly the case that 'there is no alternative' is a constant refrain in the out-pourings of advice to nation states, and in the monitoring of their performance, from global organisations such as the Organisation for Economic Cooperation and Development, the World Bank, the World Trade Organization and the International Monetary Fund. Directly and indirectly, these organisations are involved in promoting privatisation, downsizing government and scaling down social welfare around the world (Deacon et al. 1997; Mishra 1999, p. 8). What are presented by these organisations as the impersonal forces exerted by the global market are seen to cry out for the commitment to competitiveness from nation states, demanded by neo-liberal ideology. As a consequence, for those govern-ments that are enthusiastic proponents of neo-liberalism, globalisation is not sim-ply a 'fact of life' to which they must develop social welfare responses; it is a source of legitimation for the restructuring of social welfare regimes, including the reshaping of social work:

> . . . globalization is not simply a market-driven economic phenomenon. It is also—and very much—a political and ideological phenomenon . . . Thus globalization must also be understood as the transnational ideology of neoliberalism which seeks to establish its ascendancy world-wide.
>
> (Mishra 1999, p. 7)

Enthusiastic proponents of neo-liberalism have argued that one aspect of the impact of globalisation has been the introduction of a new model of manage-ment in the public sector (see Osborne and Gaebler 1992, for the most well-known example). Flynn (2000, pp 27–28) raises the possibility that whilst there are differences amongst professional cultures and national ways of managing services, there may be pressures on governments that transcend these differences and that may lead to similarities in managerial solutions. One of these pressures is exerted by capitalist enterprises; as companies transform themselves, public organisations are under pressure to change in similar ways and, in any case, governments have seen the efficiency of the public sector as an important ele-ment in national competitiveness. Although Flynn concludes that claims of homogenisation are exaggerated and there is 'no single form of managerialism that suits all circumstances' (p. 43), it is nevertheless increasingly the case that the 'solutions' to the reordering of welfare regimes are looked for somewhere within the corpus of neo-liberal-inspired managerialism.

The neo-liberal dominance of globalisation, and the neo-liberal-inspired managerialism it has spawned, have had a particular resonance in the UK, as the culture of capitalism has colonised social work. In seeking to understand how this happened, it is first necessary to take a brief step back into the era before neo-liberalism.

Before neo-liberalism: social work and the post-war welfare state

In the UK, the welfare state has been the direct source of social work's institutional position and authority. Social workers implement legislation on behalf of the state, as an arm of social policy. The law sets out the rights, duties and responsibilities of social workers, on the one hand, and of service users, on the other, in areas of life that have been accorded official recognition as socially problematic by the state. On the basis of constructing social problem categories through legal definitions, the state decides who social work's clientele will be and what should be provided for them by social workers. Accordingly, social work is the operational embodiment of the state's intervention in individual citizens' lives (Harris 1999; White and Harris 1999). Social work's institutional affiliation to the state is so close in the UK that Jones coined the term 'state social work' to describe it (Jones 1983).

Traditionally it was argued that what underpinned social work's institutional locus in the post-war welfare state was the welfare regime's distinctiveness from the market; the social services provided by the welfare state were depicted as driven by a very different dynamic. In contrast to the competitive cut and thrust of capitalist markets, social democratic analysts represented the welfare state as a source of collective obligations towards, and mutual care for, the citizenry (see, for example, Marshall 1981). An alternative interpretation of the dynamic driving the social democratic welfare state is to see it as legitimating capitalism, ameliorating class conflict through its responses (to some extent) to demands for social justice. Marshall appeared to recognise the importance of the legitimation function of the welfare state when he argued that the inequalities of the market had to be constrained by the state in order to promote social stability, thus balancing the socially divisive effects of market-based inequalities by the integrative experience of social solidarity. Thus he regarded the citizen's social rights to welfare state services as a means of stabilising capitalism and regulating, at least to some extent, its impact on people's lives (Marshall 1950). These ideas lay at the heart of what is usually referred to as the post-war cross-party political consensus on the centrality and distinctiveness of the welfare state in UK society.

Social work joined the post-war welfare state somewhat belatedly and in the shadow of its major pillars, the National Health Service and Education and Social Security. However, from the end of the World War II the dominant professional interests saw their struggle to secure a legitimate position for social work in the UK as linked to its incorporation in the welfare state (Jones 1999, p. 48). The range and responsibilities of social work grew through its fragmented location in different departments of local government, with administratively discrete, legislatively specific and professionally specialised services for children and families (Children's departments), for people with mental health problems and learning disabilities (Mental Welfare services under the auspices of Medical Officers of

Health) and for older people and people with physical disabilities (Welfare departments).[1] It was not until the early 1970s that social work broke out of its position, as a dispersed collection of roles and practices located in separate social work services, and was transformed into a central and systematically organised element of the welfare state (Clarke 1979, p. 127). This was achieved through the production of the Seebohm Report (Cmnd 3703 1968), commissioned by a Labour central government, and the subsequent implementation, by a Conservative central government, of its recommendations for the restructuring of the departments providing social work into single social service departments at local government level.

The Seebohm Report reflected the overarching social democratic assumptions of the post-war welfare state. It contained a commitment to universal services, which were regarded as the antidote to the Poor Law legacy of social work. Universalism was regarded as the basis on which social work could be transformed:

> We recommend a new local authority department, providing a community-based and family-oriented service, which will be *available to all*. This new department will, we believe, reach far beyond the discovery and rescue of social casualties; it will enable the greatest possible number of individuals to act reciprocally, giving and receiving service for the well-being of the community.
>
> (Cmnd 3703 1968: para. 2, *author's emphasis*)

The universalism underpinning the Report was complemented by an equally strong stress on the comprehensive nature of citizens' entitlements to social work services (Webb and Wistow 1987, p. 64): 'One single department concerned with most aspects of 'welfare', as the public generally understands the term, is an essential first step in making services more easily accessible' (Cmnd 3703 1968, para. 146). The Report's implementation, following the passing of the Local Authority and Allied Social Services Act (1970), consolidated and strengthened social work's position in the post-war social democratic welfare state on the basis of, at the least rhetorical, commitment to providing services that were universally available and comprehensive in scope.

Enter neo-liberalism

The election of the first Thatcher government in 1979 marked a turning point in the fortunes of the UK welfare state and social work. As Leonard notes, Western governments

---

1   Wherever there are references to specific organisational, legal and policy arrangements, the versions described throughout are those pertaining to England and Wales.

urge us to come to terms with the fact that the competitive life is nasty and brutish and that we are immersed in a life or death struggle for economic survival. In this struggle, the old ideas which ruled the modern welfare state—universality, full employment, increasing equality—are proclaimed to be a hindrance to survival. They are castigated as ideas which have outlived their usefulness: they are no longer appropriate to the conditions of a global capitalist economy where investment, production, labour and consumption are all characterised by flexibility, transience and uncertainty.

(Leonard 1997, p. 113)

From 1979 onwards, the Conservative governments embraced this creed enthusiastically and set about subordinating social welfare measures to the creation of conditions that would be conducive to international competitiveness in the global economy, seeing the interests of business as the same as the national interest (Flynn 2000, p. 33). Capital controls were abolished and attention was turned to deregulating business, weakening industrial relations safeguards and lowering rates of taxation on corporate profits and upper incomes in order to make the country attractive to global capitalist investment. The Conservatives' dominating neo-liberal vision was of a deregulated, weakly unionised, flexible, low wage, low taxation economy in which the state would spend a decreasing percentage of national wealth on public expenditure, providing the individual entrepreneur and the global corporation with open markets for their products (Lee 1997, pp 107–8). Three principles were paramount in the direction mapped out for public services: limiting expenditure; the pursuit of efficiency, economy and effectiveness; and the intrinsic superiority of the market in the provision and delivery of welfare (Spicker 1995, pp 96–7). A fundamental incompatibility was perceived between the market economy and social welfare provision and, in the cause of reviving economic growth, taxes were lowered, the goal of full employment was abandoned and the economy was deregulated (Mishra 1993, p. 23). The Conservative reappraisal of the welfare state was thus linked to maintaining the conditions necessary for business profitability in order to avert capital flight and to attracting new investment from multinational corporations and international finance capital. Neo-liberal managerialism was central to implementing this process of reappraisal and reform, as Conservative governments sought to reposition the UK as a player in the global economic context. This brand of managerialism was to have significant consequences for the restructuring of social work.

After the first Conservative government was elected, the critique of the public sector was intense, with ferocious attacks on the welfare state on ideological and economic grounds. Welfare provision was depicted as: too expensive for the state's tax base to support; squeezing out private sector investment; and undermining (through its demands for taxation support) entrepreneurial and managerial incentives. In attacking the welfare state as economically mismanaged, dependency-inducing and needing to be trimmed, if the UK was to succeed in the global economy, the Conservative government saw itself as beginning to correct the failings of the post-war social democratic consensus, in which social work was considered to be deeply implicated. The welfare state's fiscal and legitimacy crisis (O'Connor 1973; Offe 1983, 1984) was focused into a sharp neo-liberal attack, which was characterised by an ideological commitment to privatisation and the extension of market principles (Taylor-Gooby and Lawson 1993, p. 1). This critique of the welfare state predisposed Conservative governments to take a sceptical view of social workers and local government social services departments (Jones and Novak 1993; Loney 1986, p. 142); social work became a metaphor for what was considered to be wrong with the welfare state (Midgley and Jones 1994, p. 118).

Despite the Conservatives' antipathy to social work, in the first two Thatcher administrations, from 1979 to 1987, what in retrospect look like fairly cautious moves were made to cut back budgetary allocations to the personal social services and these were largely thwarted by local government. In addition, the Conservative central government was faced with massive Labour Party gains in local government elections in the early 1980s. These 'urban left' Labour local authorities experimented with new forms of decentralised provision, which were more responsive to service user needs, as an attempt to develop policies and provision that would win the support of local people and that could be adopted nationally on the return of a Labour government. This brief period of experimentation was curbed by a severe reduction in the grants made from central to local government and limitations on local government powers to raise any consequent shortfall in expenditure through local taxation. (The Rates Act [1984] made it illegal for local government to set taxation rates above a level determined for each individual local authority by central government.) Having reduced the scope of local government's financial independence, the Conservatives actively pursued their policies through the Audit Commission and, in the case of social work, the Social Services Inspectorate. The Audit Commission, set up in 1983 following the Local Government Finance Act (1982), encouraged the emergence of a strong management culture (Kelly 1992) in social services departments. It reinforced moves towards neo-liberal managerialism by suggesting that generic expertise in accountancy and management was powerful enough to question any area of policy and practice (Cochrane 1994, p. 127). By this means, the Commission extended its role to broader judgement of performance in using resources, captured in the phrase 'value for money', thus moving beyond an emphasis on accounting. In pursuing value for money, it promoted the virtues of the three 'e's:

Economy means ensuring that the assets of the authority, and the services purchased, are procured and maintained at the lowest possible cost consistent with a specified quality and quantity.
Efficiency means providing a specified volume and quality of services with the lowest level of resources capable of meeting that specification.
Effectiveness means providing the right services to enable the local authority to implement its policies and objectives.

(Audit Commision 1983, p. 8)

In tandem, from 1985, the Social Services Inspectorate took on the role of ensuring the implementation of central government's policies in relation to social work (Day and Klein 1990, p. 27). The Conservative government's monitoring of local authorities' compliance with central government policy and its constraints on local government expenditure constricted the freedom to pursue policies at local government level which were substantially different from those of central government:

> The more the balance of power shifted towards central government in the 1980s, the more it was able to insert its own values, methods and language into the new management practices and the more difficult it became for local institutions to shape new methods into their own image and for their own purposes.
>
> (Burns et al. 1994, p. 85)

After the Conservatives won a third term in the 1987 election, the attempts at shaping policy through financial control and monitoring policy implementation at the local level were augmented by a radical legislative programme aimed at the following.

- Further limiting expenditure.
- Breaking up public provision.
- Increasing the scope of commercial sector operations.
- Bringing in business management principles to what remained of the public sector.
- Reducing the power of welfare state professionals.

(Jones 1994, pp 190, 205)

Jessop argues that this initiative by the third Conservative government was a key aspect of the neo-liberal political project.

> . . . successive Conservative governments pursued a distinctive neo-liberal strategy intended to marketise social relations and create an enterprise culture so that individuals could operate in (and embrace) a market-oriented society. Such a strategy clearly cannot be confined to the (expanding) market economy alone; it must also be extended to the whole ensemble of social institutions, organisations, networks, and norms of conduct which regularise economic relations. This all-embracing tendency is especially clear from 1986 onwards when a near-fatally drifting Thatcher regime rescued itself with a wide-ranging radical programme to re-invigorate civil society as well as regenerate the economy and restructure the state. . .This extended key elements of the neo-liberal accumulation strategy and also supplemented them by an ambitious hegemonic project for the wider society. What had previously been hesitant and halting accompaniments of economic regeneration were accelerated and given a more coherent ideological justfication . . . For

the public sector, it involve[d] privatisation, liberalisation, and an imposition of commercial criteria in any residual state sector.

(Jessop 1994, pp 29–30)

This added twist to the Conservative programme encompassed fundamental changes in the arrangements for local government services (Audit Commission 1988, p. 1). Shortly afterwards, as part of these wider changes, social work's future was set out. It was to take a different form and to be placed in a different context shaped by the Children Act (1989) and the National Health Service and Community Care Act (1990). Of these two Acts, it was the National Health Service and Community Care Act (1990) that became the primary vehicle for accomplishing the transformation of social work in the direction sought by neo-liberalism. The promotion of a new policy direction in community care, embodying a market framework, was integral to the Conservative government's radical reform of the welfare state and the reduction of Social Services Departments' role in service provision (Baldock and Evers 1991, 1992). The role of the state as a direct provider of services was to diminish, to be replaced by the roles of enabler, subsidiser and regulator; an overarching concern of the Conservative government in the late 1980s and early 1990s was to move social work as close to market conditions as possible. Although the initiative was seized originally in the sphere of community care, the restructuring of social work that ensued had ramifications across the board.

As elsewhere in the reform of the welfare state, the Conservative government's starting assumption for the introduction of market mechanisms into social work was that capitalist enterprise is more economical, efficient and effective than the public sector in providing services. This neo-liberal assumption stems from the belief that competition produces efficient services in which prices decrease whilst quality increases, as a result of the market system requiring service providers to compete for contracts. The radical changes in social work were marked indelibly by the encapsulation of this belief in a 'quasi-market' arrangement (Le Grand 1993), with cash-limited budgets, purchaser–provider splits, contracting out, the use of independent agencies and more widespread use of charges. The welfare state became primarily a funder of social services, with individual service user budgets given to (or, more commonly, recommendations for expenditure from those budgets made by) a social worker and the allocation of those budgets between competing suppliers. The introduction of quasi-markets in social work, initially in the sphere of community care for adults but later developing in a range of other services such as foster care and children's homes, was significant for two main reasons.

First, marketisation undermined the sense in which social services had represented a counterbalance to market values during the post-war consensus on welfare discussed earlier:

Marketisation may be seen as one among many examples of the New Right's antagonism towards the decommodifying aspects of the welfare state. It is intended to challenge the, albeit limited, extent to which the social services intrude on market values and threaten their reproduction by promoting citizenship rights and needs-based priorities.

(Walker 1989, p. 216)

Second, marketisation was intended to move the provision of social services outside the state. The Conservative government achieved this intention by stipulating that 85% of the funds transferred from central government's Social Security system to local government for community care services had to be spent on the independent sector (Department of Health 1992, Annex C, para. 3). This was consistent with the concerns of the White Paper *Caring for People* (Cm 849 1989), preceding the NHS and Community Care Act (1990), which stated that one of the key objectives of the reform of community care was to promote the development of a 'flourishing independent sector' (Cm 849 1989, para. 1.11). This point was reiterated in subsequent policy guidance (Department of Health 1990), with social services departments being expected to make clear how they proposed to stimulate market activity where independent providers were not available. The Conservative government saw promoting a market as essential to the development of competitive cost-effective services (Social Services Inspectorate 1991a, b, para. 1).

The significant emphasis placed by the Conservatives on marketisation placed new responsibilities on social work in local government social services departments at a time when these departments had little or no experience of operating in a market context. However, they not only had to define their new role in the quasi-market but also had to engage in a corresponding process of substantial change in their internal organisational culture, shaped by neo-liberal managerialism. As elsewhere in the restructuring of the welfare state, this was a key component in shifting social work in line with market forces (Clarke et al. 1994; Pollitt 1990). Managerialism was regarded as a dynamic transformative process that could demolish the lingering welfare structures of the post-war social democratic consensus. It was the means through which the structure and culture of social work were to be recast (Clarke et al. 1994, p. 4). The neo-liberal model of management that was promoted regarded private-sector practices as applicable to the public sector and claimed to provide skills applicable in all circumstances, thus providing a management solution to any problem (Du Gay 2000, Ch. 4; Rees 1995, pp 15–17). Pollitt argues that the importation of managerialism involved embracing an ideology that justifies particular actions by reference to the 'right to manage' and 'good management practice'. The ideology's framework of ideas includes the following.

- Progress is achieved through economic productivity.
- Productivity increases come from the application of technology, including organisational technology.
- A disciplined labour force is needed.
- Management is a separate and distinct function that has the answers.

(Pollitt 1990, pp 2–3)

The adoption of this strategy of marketising and managerialising social work by the Conservatives was part of wholesale neo-liberal changes in the welfare state in response to the demands for competitiveness in the global economy. It was a strategy inherited by a Labour government.

Neo-liberalism and modernisation

By the time New Labour came to power in central government in 1997, the context within which social work operated and the content of social work itself had changed fundamentally as a result of the Conservatives' programme of reform. New Labour accepted this neo-liberal legacy and set about its 'modernisation'. Rhetorically New Labour was at pains to distance itself from its 'old left' past and from the Conservatives' neo-liberalism. It did so by depicting itself as the 'Third Way' (Blair 1998). This phrase was meant to capture the ideological indifference of New Labour, presenting itself as steering a middle course through any of the issues that it had to confront (Hall 1998; Jameson 2000; Powell 2000). For example, *Modernising Social Services* acknowledged difficulties in relation to eligibility and equity in market-based social services but stressed that New Labour did not take an 'ideological approach' to service provision (Department of Health 1998, Ch. 7). However, there are substantial areas of overlap between the Conservative governments and New Labour in terms of: the primacy accorded to globalisation; the restructuring of the economy and society that is seen as required in response to its impact; and the changes required in established practices and ways of working as a basis for capitalism's future prosperity, in particular the imperative towards low costs and highly flexible forms of working. Four cross-party themes can be identified: the primacy of economic competitiveness; the subordination of social policy to the needs of a competitive national economy; the limited or reduced scope envisaged for government intervention or direction; and a central concern with control over public expenditure (Clarke et al. 2000, p. 13). In this reading of New Labour, it represents a readjustment of neo-liberalism, rather than its replacement:

> New Labour under Blair has embraced most of the neoliberal legacy of Thatcherism and has extended it into new areas. It has also taken the first steps on the road to a routinization of neoliberalism. Thus more emphasis has been given to securing the operation of the emerging neoliberal regime through normal politics, to developing supporting policies across a wide range of policy fields and to providing flanking mechanisms to compensate for its negative economic, political and social consequences.
>
> (Jessop 2002: 266)

One of the key elements of neo-liberal continuity between the Conservatives and New Labour is the representation of globalisation as an uncontradictory, uncontrollable, unitary phenomenon, to which UK society must adapt in ways required by global capital (Hall 1998).

This neo-liberal continuity is also evident in New Labour's stress on the need for 'modernisation' as a shorthand term for bringing the public sector, including social work, into line with the modern practices of globally fit capitalist enterprises. New Labour's drive for modernisation has intensified pressure on the public sector, for example through the introduction of its 'Best Value' regime. Four principles underpin Best Value:

- Challenge (why and how a service is provided).
- Compare (with others' performance, including the use of performance indicators in benchmarking exercises).
- Consult (local taxpayers, service users and the business community in setting performance targets).
- Competition (as the means to efficient and effective services).
  (Department of the Environment, Transport and the Regions 1999)

These four principles emphasise the neo-liberal ethos of 'Best Value' as placing 'everything up for grabs'. There is no assumption that a particular service should be provided, there are no assumptions that services that are provided have to continue to be provided in the same way as previously and there is a driving dynamic of saving money. As well as absorbing the cost of the additional processes associated with the 'Best Value' regime, local government services like social work have been expected to make efficiency savings. Thus, under New Labour's 'Best Value' regime, the neo-liberal drive for efficiency has continued and been intensified by forcing services like social work into a 'business performance' mould, with an emphasis on achieving managerial results defined by central government's performance targets (Waine 2000, p. 247). By this means, private sector-style entrepreneurialism and modern commercial practice are harnessed as core components in challenging and transforming the shape and role of public sector services such as social work (Newman 2000).

As well as bringing social work within the general ambit of the 'Best Value' regime, New Labour has set in train a more specific set of changes. The *Quality Strategy for Social Care* (Department of Health 2000) exemplifies the desire to see local government deliver New Labour's agenda for social work: 'Delivering high-quality social care services is essentially a local responsibility. The Quality Strategy will set a national framework to help raise local standards, but this will only be achieved through local policy and implementation' (Department of Health 2000, para. 18). Elements of the design of the quality system were set out in the *Quality Strategy* and included national service frameworks, national standards, service models, and local performance measures against which progress within an agreed timescale could be monitored (Department of Health 2000, para. 26). The *Quality Strategy* moved New Labour into the micro-management of performance in social work by setting out a system through which standards would be set and monitored for individual social services departments.

As the preceding discussion has implied, New Labour has placed greater emphasis on direct regulation as one of the key strategies for undertaking its neo-liberal modernisation of social work. The implementation of New Labour's specific initiatives for particular service user groups is inextricably intertwined with, and evaluated by, external audit, inspection and review. This high level of regulatory activity suggests that whilst the Conservative governments placed their faith in local management having a constraining impact on social workers' discretion to undermine the neo-liberal agenda, New Labour has adopted a more hands-on approach to its active promotion. In effect, civil servants and central government ministers are dictating New Labour priorities at the local level in an attempt to ensure that social workers are delivering the detail of the neo-liberal agenda; the intertwining of policy and regulation results in detailed stipulations about the management of practice. The proliferation of managerial control since New Labour came to power has resulted in a high degree of uncertainty and instability, as local social services departments are judged by the different means and methods used by different inspectorial agents. The pressures of being constantly accountable, inspected and regulated are thus amplified by changing demands and indicators. New Labour's surveillance and regulation through audit and inspection is combined with competition through rating systems and league tables (Hood et al. 1999), which encourage social services departments to find ways of improving their performance so that they stand out from the run of the mill. There are performance assessment indicators and league table comparisons between social services departments (see, for example, Department of Health 2000). Such processes incorporate constant repetition of neo-liberal imagery of capitalist businesses and the presentation of such enterprises as superior to public services. Regulatory mechanisms imbued with this imagery have become a powerful means of monitoring performance.

Concluding comment

Given the lack of an immediate alternative, noted at the beginning of the chapter, capitalism is now self-legitimating, seen as the only system capable of delivering economic growth and consumer goods (Mishra 1999, p. 3). Within this self-legitimating system, globalisation is represented as driven by uncontrollable forces and as being good for everyone. This representation of globalisation points inevitably towards neo-liberalism.

Neo-liberal-inspired managerialism claims to have the solutions to any social or economic problems. In pursuing those solutions, politicians and managers see themselves as having the right to claim authority and power over social work, premised on the exercise of managerial control. This is not to suggest that neo-liberal managerialism has a single or fixed character. It is flexible and contingent, shaped by the national context in which it is located. In any country that embraces it wholeheartedly, there has to be *motive* and *opportunity* (Hood 1991, pp 104–5). For example, in the UK, the Conservative governments had both motive and opportunity. Their motive was their commitment to neo-liberal-driven reform of the welfare state. The opportunity was provided by an economic crisis, the high degree of centralisation of the British state and the lack of a written con-

stitution stipulating the limits of central government powers over local government. These three factors provided the opportunity for Conservative, and later
New Labour, governments to be highly interventionist in pushing neo-liberal
managerialism into social work, as part of the progressive promotion and facili-
tation of globalisation: 'What began earlier as a national project under neocon-
servative governments has now become generalized as part of the economic
agenda of globalization' (Mishra 1999, p. 51). Accordingly, globalisation has
become the context of the welfare state, and hence of social work. In pursuing
globalisation-friendly strategies, neo-liberal managerialism has a clear direction:
'. . . social domains, whose concern is not producing commodities in the narrower
economic sense of goods for sale, come nevertheless to be organised and conceptualised in terms of commodity production, distribution and consumption'
(Fairclough 1992, p. 207).

   In following this strategic direction, the interests and approaches of capitalist
businesses are seen as the key to demonstrating how things need to be done in
public services like social work (Flynn 2000, pp 33–4). Far from being a neutral
trend and a set of techniques for increasing efficiency, neo-liberal managerialism
represents a power struggle by politicians and managers against institutions and
people seen as thwarting their purposes and intentions; a key aspect of which is
to cuts costs, an aspect wrapped up in the Conservatives' language of 'doing more
for less'/'achieving value-for-money' and New Labour's commitment to 'modernising' social work through the application of managerialism's distinctive and
valuable expertise. The impact of that power struggle on social workers in the
UK, has been to place them in the front-line of retrenched services, working
under increasingly controlled conditions and experiencing increasing levels
of stress (Carey 2003; Harris 2003; Jones 2001b). There is every reason to believe
that the dis-identification and cynicism (Fleming and Spicer 2003) and informal
communities of coping (Korczynski 2003), which have been identified in other
contexts where workers experience strain, are part of the responses of social
workers. Such reactions are examples of some of the ways in which neo-liberal
managerialism has changed social work in the UK.

Part 2

Neo-liberal globalisation and its impact on social workers and clients

7 The neo-liberal assault: voices from the front line of British state social work

Chris Jones

Introduction

Since 1999 I have been talking to state social workers about their work. I had a number of reasons for doing this research, but one, which was close to my heart, was that I felt we needed to hear the voices of front-line workers who for the past 25 years have too often been vilified and silenced. They have much to say and their perspectives should at least figure in shaping our assessment of the impact of neo-liberal thinking on British state social work. Quite coincidentally, as I was preparing to give my first talk based on the research, the *Guardian* newspaper ran an unprecedented 2-day series covering more than 30 pages about the work and experience of public service workers. Putting aside the question of why this newspaper should give such unprecedented coverage to this issue at that time, its opening comments happen to reflect my own views as to why we should take note of social workers and the broader significance of public welfare services for providing a useful vantage for looking at society more widely:

> Over more than 30 pages today and tomorrow we have constructed a mosaic of voices. They are men and women who are often talked about but heard only rarely. They are the voices of people who work in our public services— people who, in some fundamental sense, work for the public good. Why are we giving so much space, not to an election or a Budget, a royal death or a foreign war but to Britain's public services and the people who make them work? At the most elevated level, because a civilized society is judged on how it provides for its citizens. Decent public services—schools, hospitals, rail-ways—are both prerequisites for and measures of a decent nation. They say something about who we are and how we take care of each other.
>
> (*Guardian* 20 March 2001, p.1)

I would contend that state social work provides us with a particularly sensitive measure of 'decent nationhood' and 'civilised society'. This is because state social work has historically engaged with and been immersed in the lives of some of the most marginalised, disadvantaged and impoverished people in British society. The manner in which they are treated, and their plights understood, tells us a great deal about the character and morality of a society, especially its elites. The account that follows will more than suggest that Britain, at the beginning of the twenty-first century, under a new Labour government which professes to be concerned about poverty and inequality, cannot be considered to be a decent nation, at least not on the test suggested by the *Guardian*.

To date I have interviewed just over 40 front-line practising social workers in local authority social services departments stretching across the north of England. In addition to these interviews I have now presented my finding to a number of meetings of state social workers in England, Wales and Scotland where I have encountered something in the region of a further 500 state social workers, many of whom have further enriched my research. Their response has been overwhelming.

The majority of the social workers I interviewed have been in post for 8 years or more, which, in state social service departments, makes them unusual. In Pithouse's (1998) terms these social workers warrant the title of veteran practitioners. They are unusual in the sense that they have not followed a common career trajectory within British state social work agencies whereby qualified social workers tend to move out of front-line practice after about 5 years and travel upwards into managerial positions or out of state social work altogether. I wanted to talk to this group in particular as I thought, rightly as it turned out, that they could offer some interesting perspectives on the manner in which state social work had changed over time. However, not all the social workers I spoke to were veterans, and over the past 18 months I have spoken to some more recently qualified social workers and a smaller number who after many years of state practice moved into the voluntary sector. All had much of value to say.

Stress and unhappiness: the realities of neo-liberal social work

The manifestations of stress and unhappiness in today's local authority social services departments were various, serious and pervasive. Social workers talked of how commonplace it was to see colleagues in tears. I heard stories of social workers throwing their papers onto the floor and walking out, of people locking themselves in rooms or just disappearing from the office for hours on end. Going sick, for some time each week or month seemed routinised in many agencies and was one of the most cited examples of a stress survival strategy. A surprising number of the long-serving field workers I met had recurring and serious health problems, which had resulted in extended periods of absence. Many spoke of being emotionally and physically exhausted by the demands of their work. Social workers talked of being completely 'wrung out' by Friday night and how their personal and social lives had become stunted as a consequence.

In one moving interview I was told by a social worker of how resentful she was because sheer exhaustion meant she slept through her favourite Friday night TV programmes. Weekends for many seemed little more than recovery times for another week. To date, I have not interviewed *one* state social worker who was prepared to recommend their job as a career. Most wanted to get out of social services departments and were actively looking for jobs in the voluntary sector, or were looking to leave social work altogether (See also Audit Commission 2002). The government has been compelled by staff shortages to acknowledge the recruitment crisis. In 2001 the Department of Health launched a 3-year advertising initiative at a cost of £1.5 million in order to raise the profile of social work in the hope that it would attract more recruits. By January 2002 government ministers were claiming success for the campaign (*Guardian* 2 January 2002). But what is meant by success? The recruitment problems persist and employment agencies continue to flourish as they provide stop-gap cover. Perhaps ministers are referring to the dramatic increase in overseas recruitment, especially from southern Africa. According to the *Guardian* (2 Feburary 2003) 'almost half of Zimbabwe's social workers now work in the UK . . . [which] threatens to cripple the African country's welfare system'. For those working in state social work the campaign was little other than an outrageous attempt to portray state social work as a rewarding career. State social workers are remarkably clear on this point: the job has become awful and many know it.

What became clear in the course of the research was that most of the negative stress and frustration came directly from the agency and not the clients. Clients were a cause of considerable anxiety but it was a quite different form of stress to the aggravation caused by agency and government policy. The majority of social workers with whom I spoke generally regarded their clients' demands for support as reasonable and in some instances they even commented on the modesty of the requests given the levels of need. Even so the pressure on agency budgets was such that many of these requests, whether it was for respite care or help in the home, were not capable of being met. It was these kinds of agency constraints which stressed social workers greatly.

There were a number of interconnecting elements which the state social workers regularly referred to, and here the perspectives of the more experienced workers were particularly helpful as they could track the changes over the years. The issues, which were raised time and again, included anguish over the growing intensity of bureaucracy and paperwork (which 20 years ago was estimated to occupy 30% of a social worker's time compared with 90% for a community care social worker today); speed up of the work; the prevalence of poor and often aggressive managers; limited contact with clients; inadequate budgets and growing poverty and inequalities.

They also complained that professional support and concern had largely disappeared from their workplaces and that divisions with management were more stark. They did not feel cared for and many times I was told of the battles social workers had had to fight to secure some minimal protection when they went out on home visits such as mobile phones (bearing in mind the increase in violence against social workers). The social workers felt that they were no longer trusted or acknowledged for their skills and abilities.

I was also given many accounts of seemingly endemic organisational change within state agencies which never involved any consultation with those who actually attempted to provide, let alone use the services. The extent of such top-down control was extraordinary. And of course I was regaled by talk of budgets, and not only their appalling paucity to meet the needs of clients, but also the manner in which budget management and control had become the key concern of the agency, stripping out its welfare ideals in the process. This was no series of disjointed factors, but as the state social workers reported, an interconnecting series of processes which created a new working environment within state social work. All of which gave rise to new types of highly regulated, more mundane and routinised relationships with clients which could not be described as social work, at least not in the terms that they understood it.

Such changes are not trivial developments within British state social work. For example:

> We are now much more office based. This really hit home the other day when the whole team was in the office working at their desks. We have loads more forms which take time to complete. But we social workers also do less and less direct work with clients. Increasingly the agency buys in other people to do the direct work and we manage it.

Doing less direct work is a consequence of reducing the role of the state, as dictated by the neo-liberal project. Moreover, reducing the welfare state has been much more than a measure of economy, it has also been considered a moral necessity which apparently does 'good' for those in need as welfare dependency saps their very humanity (Jones and Novak 1999). Thus it is not so surprising to note the waves of legislation (including the 1990 National Health Service and Community Care Act) that have resulted in social services departments doing far less in the provision of services, and far more with respect to gatekeeping, rationing and policing services. This has had enormous implications for shifting social work practice and frustrating social workers. After all social work has direct work with clients as its focus and raison d'être. This is how one community care social worker explained the difference:

> Being a care manager is very different from being a social worker as I had always thought of it. Care management is all about budgets and paperwork and the financial implications for the authority, whereas social work is about people. That's the crucial difference.

Social workers are still seeing clients, but in the state sector at least, the nature of that contact has fundamentally changed. With some important exceptions (in some specialist teams it would seem), the contact is more fleeting, more regulated and governed by the demands of the forms that now shape much of the intervention. Much of this comes from the new regulatory focus of the agencies, but above all from financial constraints, which leads to state social workers doing ever more assessments to see if those who are referred to social service departments meet the ever-higher eligibility requirements. I was told by social workers how their managers advised them not to form any sort of relationship with those they were assessing as this would make it more difficult to make an assessment (with no resources or services offered!) I was recently informed by one social worker working with older people that he was criticised by his manager for getting to know his clients and spending too much time with them. The implications of these injunctions cannot be underestimated for if social work ever had any claim to be an effective welfare intervention it was due to the therapeutic potential of the relationship created between the social worker and client. This, it would seem, is now actively discouraged in many state social work agencies. Instead, I was told that social workers were expected to be speedy in their assessments, limit the contact with the potential client and get in and out quickly; this apparently reduces expectations. I was told how:

> Our [social worker's] contact with clients is more limited. It is in, do the assessment, get the package together, review after a spell and then close the case and get on with the next one as there were over 200 cases waiting an assessment.

I was listening to social workers describe their work as if they were in a factory. This was how one social worker described the experience:

> I now work much harder than I have ever worked in my life. You are expected to work at a much faster rate with no breaks. It is no wonder that so many social workers are off with stress and on long term sick. It is appalling and it is going to get worse now we have all these league tables that are beginning to drive things.

This child protection worker captured some of the bewilderment felt by state social workers, a sort of madness in the system, when she explained aspects of the duty system in her agency:

> Everyone closes things as soon as they possibly can, but you know that 3 weeks later it is going to come back again. It's a complete nonsense.

And this community care social worker said:

> Social work is more and more about numbers with managers wanting to hit so many targets which involves turning cases over quickly. They want a case in, sorted and pushed out. We have many unallocated cases so there is great pressure on everyone to take the maximum number of cases. I think this emphasis on turnover is cosmetic, to make it seem that we are giving a service to the public. But we don't give anything. We have nothing to give.

Even if the agency has something to give, it is now commonplace that this no longer directly involves the state social worker who has made the visit and undertaken the assessment. Rather the front-line worker is removed from the crucial meetings where decisions are made concerning the allocation of resources as this social worker explained:

> I feel so deskilled because there are so many restrictions over what I can do. Yes I go out and do assessments, draw up care plans, but then we aren't allowed to do anything. I can't even go and organise meals on wheels for somebody without completing a load of paperwork, submitting a report to a load of people who would then make the decision as to whether I can go ahead and make the arrangements. I just wonder why I am doing this. It's not social work. Many of my colleagues in the adult team are looking to get out of social work altogether. They say they don't want to take this garbage any more. That's how they feel. The will to do social work is still there. They are still committed to work with people in distress. That heartfelt warmth has not gone away, but the job is so different.

That the job is so different was a recurring theme and the paperwork and form filling was always mentioned. The social workers I met were not, in principle, opposed to all paperwork, and some of the paperwork regarding children in care (looked after children) was welcomed as it ensured that recommendations were more likely to be acted upon and children in care would be more regularly reviewed and less likely to drift. But the social workers felt that the excess of paperwork indicated not only a concern with vulnerable children but also a sense that they, the social workers, were not to be trusted. This perspective was fairly typical:

> I don't have a problem with the LAC forms. But then we also have to fill in initial assessment forms, comprehensive assessment forms and lots of other forms, many of which don't make any sense to me. I don't know what happens to all these forms, but I think they are government driven and its considered to be proof of what we are doing.

No change with New Labour

Interestingly, most of the social workers in this research project felt that the onslaught of regulatory intrusion had accelerated since 1997 with the election of the Blair government. This comment was not unusual:

> I voted for Labour in 1997 and like all my friends was really excited to see the Tories defeated. But my life as a social worker has been no better as a consequence. They don't seem to like social workers any more than Thatcher's lot. They don't have any real feel or concern for poverty and how people have suffered in these sorts of areas for 20 years.

What troubled many social workers was that the Labour government had not identified a woeful lack of investment over years coupled with growing social polarisation and inequalities as underpinning the difficulties confronting social workers and their clients. For a government which prides itself on having an evidence base to its policies, its hypocrisy is quite breathtaking when it comes to its analysis of poverty and the poor. Underinvestment over decades in services directed at the most vulnerable and disadvantaged in society has quite simply been devastating, yet the inevitable tragedies which follow and which occasionally make it into the media are treated as no more than agency or professional failure.

Labour have embraced the notion of 'failure' with the same enthusiasm as the Tories and continue to make policy based on a notion of failing schools, teachers, hospitals, prisons, local education authorities and so on. The government has also similarly embraced the neo-liberal assumption that the problems of the poorest are essentially the consequence of poor parenting skills amidst that section of the population. There is a striking congruence in the neo-liberal position on both clients and social workers with both being problematised and seen to be in need of close control and supervision. And it is getting worse as state welfare agencies latch on to the potential of information technology (IT) for controlling both clients and social workers. I recently discovered social workers in one agency confronting computers which interrogated them about late returns and warning them of the need to improve their conduct! It will be of no surprise to find managers asking for social workers to be tagged in the same ways that young people and children deemed to be 'at risk' are now being electronically monitored.

The neo-liberal justification for more harsh interventions (or neglect) relies heavily on portraying the victims as 'nasty' and distasteful. This is one of the most evident shifts from the earlier social democratic period (see Jones and Novak 1993). As this social worker noted, this has not changed with the advent of New Labour:

> I was talking to a youth justice worker last week and she told me how much she had loved her job until the recent changes. Now she hates it as they do less work with the kids, have got to be more concerned with disciplining them and have to work with police officers and the like. It seemed to her that it was all based around a punitive approach and that Jack Straw [Labour minister] was as bad as Michael Howard [Conservative minister]. Both seem to hate youngsters and seem more concerned with criminalising the kids who are seen to be of no use.

As for social workers, the breaking down of complex tasks into compartmentalised tick box forms was seen by many as reflecting the government's lack of respect for, and trust in social workers. This was how one described it:

> Governments believe that social workers can't do the job; therefore you turn it into a job that you do in boxes and you tick the boxes and do the job.

In no small part, successful social work seems to be a matter of ensuring that the data required to meet the various performance indicators are submitted on time and processed through to the appropriate central government department. The provision of such data alongside keeping in budget have become the twin imperatives against which social workers' performance is measured and monitored. What actually happens to or with clients seems to be accorded a much lower priority. This reality was well demonstrated in the comments made about supervision. One children and families social worker aptly described supervision as a 'bingo session' as all her manager required was numbers and dates. The extent to which this has become the norm was further illustrated by a senior social work manager who reported at a university seminar how they were delighted to have received an improved rating for their work with young people who had left the local authority's care. They could now honestly say that they had nearly 100% contact with all their care leavers. But what this performance indicator did not reveal was that the contact comprised a single telephone call from someone unknown to the young person merely checking out that they were still alive.

It is salient to note that these changes—the more mechanistic, time limited and regulatory contacts with clients—have been taking place at a time when inequalities in Britain have been deepening. As was noted earlier, the gap between the rich and the poor has widened significantly over the past twenty years as both the rich have got richer and the poorest have become poorer. This trend has not been reversed by the election of a Labour government in 1997 (CACI 2003). One of the most significant factors which explains why state social workers experience greater distress and poverty amongst their clients follows directly from Labour's infatuation with waged work as the solution to social exclusion (Jordan 2001). David Blunkett, when he was the Labour government's minister for Education and Employment, described this policy approach as a move 'from the welfare state to a working state' (*Times* 15 March 2001, p. 4). But, as John Hills has observed many of New Labour's labour market oriented 'new deal' initiatives means that a

> Substantial proportion of benefit recipients—pensioners, lone parents with pre-school children and some of the long-term sick and disabled—will continue to have their living standards determined by benefit levels, however successful other measures are. Where these continue to be linked to prices, those dependent on them will continue to fall behind the rest of the population. In terms of the numbers living with low incomes relative to the average, it has been suggested that this effect could swamp all the positive effects of the other initiatives.
>
> (Hills 1998, pp 31–2)

Hills's predictions have proved correct. The 2003 Rowntree report on Labour's impact on poverty since 1997 noted that 'greater employment, or "work for those who can", has made a real contribution to reducing poverty' but for those dependent on the main state benefit (income support) which would include the vast majority of social work's clients, their prospects have not been enhanced. This is almost entirely due to the reluctance of the government to raise the level of this core benefit in line with incomes, which means that this benefit is far below 60% of median income which is the government's poverty level (Rowntree 2003, p. 4).

The numbers involved are considerable, with an estimated 15 million people in the population who by virtue of age, illness, special needs, childcare and other caring responsibilities are in no position to enter the waged labour market. Included within that number are the vast majority of state social work's actual and potential client populations. Little wonder then that state social workers report that the hardships and inequalities which they experienced under Thatcher's social policy agenda have persisted under New Labour. Moreover, as the children's charity Barnado's noted when launching its latest campaign in November 2003, in order to 'highlight the fact that despite having the fourth largest economy in the world the UK has one of the highest levels of child poverty of all industrialised countries with 3.8 million children (1 in 3) living in poverty' (Barnado's 2003, p. 1).

It was not surprising then to find social workers reporting that one of the most significant changes over time was that their clients were now on the whole more troubled and distressed and in greater need than before. This is further exacerbated by the eligibility criteria now in use which also means that it is increasingly only those in severe difficulty who are considered suitable for some kind of service. According to this children and families worker:

> Many of the clients are more stressed than ever and certainly more stressed than when I started as a social worker 20 years ago. They have such grotty lives with no hope. Most of the kids we work with have no hope and I see the situation getting worse and worse. It seems that society has no need for them anymore. No one seems to care and the government just wants them shoved aside. So some of the families are in terrible downward spirals where I agree that their kids need to be taken off them but if you go back you can see if something had been done earlier then this could have been avoided.

And on top of this, they talked of the ghettos which had emerged—those 'sink' estates where their clients tended to end up. This child protection worker puts it clearly:

> Most of our time is spent on a massive sprawling council estate on the out-skirts of the city. It's got a crappy shopping centre and there is nothing there for the kids. There are lots of families there who are totally entrenched in poverty and all that brings with it. They are really struggling and in a mess. They really need some help. What they need is some money but of course nowadays nobody's actually offering what they need. Nobody is offering them jobs, any type of support or access into social networks that might get them out of the place. All they might get is a social worker who will go round to their house and ask a lot of questions—a bloody cheek many of them think—and because there are no immediate child protection needs they will get nothing.

Social workers also talked of their sense that the state welfare system had given up on so many of their clients. Social work in its struggle to gain acceptance after World War II made so much of its rehabilitative purpose. Armed with variants of neo-Freudian psychology and casework methods, social workers promised much in terms of its potential to break into cycles of deprivation and lift families and individuals out of their cultures of poverty. Their claims, especially through the 1950s and 1960s, were often outrageously audacious and when they failed to be realised probably contributed to the undermining of governmental trust in the capacity of social work. But entwined in that audacity was a welfare vision about the possibilities of helping people and families who for generations had been castigated as the residuum and for whom a place in the common humanity had been denied on account of their alleged flawed biology. The rehabilitative ideal in state social work seems lost and forgotten now. It is no longer part of either the rhetoric or the practice.

Transformed social work

There is an historical weakness and fragility to state social work (see Jones 2001a). This has many facets but probably the most important relates to the historical lack of respect accorded to clients who over the years have been cruelly dismissed as the residuum, the undeserving poor, problem families, the underclass and now the socially excluded. This fragility has, I would argue, contributed to local authority social service managers being particularly compliant in accommodating the neo-liberal agenda. The veterans I spoke with supported this assessment, and many went on to claim that their middle and senior managers seem to relish the managerial ethos of neo-liberalism. I was told that many seemed impatient to boss them around and how you could tell who of them had been on the MBA courses because their vocabularies changed and they bounced around the departments talking about 'can do' organisations and the like. In many of the agencies I visited the depth of the divisions between the front-line practitioners and their managers surprised me and has been subsequently reinforced at recent meetings with social workers. If a 'them and us' culture is a measure of proletarianisation than I have no hesitation in describing British state social workers as being thoroughly proletarianised. I heard no positive word about managers. I did hear of some sympathy:

> The first line manager's job is a horrible job. It's a shit of a job. I wouldn't want to do it. It is an incredibly pressurising job but so many of them behave like bastards even if I can see why, but oh, some are so horrible.

I heard that they had lost touch with the welfare ideals of social work:

> It seems to me that many of the senior managers have no feel for social work anymore. They are managers, professional managers who have little feeling for the clients.

That some were bullies:

> Much of the stress at work is fear; social workers are scared of their managers, scared of all the monitoring stuff. We get no help and if we can't manage our work then we are told that we are poor time managers. There is no solution offered. Most managers now are only interested in allocating work irrespective of the pressure on us the social workers. We will be blamed for the problems which are due to a lack of resources. This is the attitude of quite a few of the managers who are also being pressed by the senior management group to take on more and more work. The pressure is always downwards.

That management could not be relied upon to support you:

> I wouldn't trust the managers to protect me, but I do cover myself.

> There is a kind of macho sense around that you don't look for help in your work. The idea that you might need a bit of space after working on a particularly difficult case has gone right out the window.

This social worker represented many I spoke with:

> I can't see how you can do social work unless you've got some sensitivity and awareness about the impact of life events on people. I find it amazing that this agency which is supposed to be highly attuned to this and highly aware cannot actually recognise the needs of its staff. I just find it really hard to get my head around that.

So what do we have?

All is not well in British state social work. The signs of stress are everywhere. Local authorities are finding it hard to recruit new staff, especially in the south-east of England where the turn to overseas social work labour is most apparent. There is an extraordinary movement of social workers into employment agency work, which needs some investigation. Many social services departments only manage to get by with high numbers of such temporary workers. Haringey in London, the site of a social work tragedy in 2000 involving the murder of a young girl, has something in the region of 40% agency staff. Similarly, applications for places on social work courses have plummeted by 60% in recent years. All of these are indicators of an occupation in crisis.

This crisis in British state social work, which is very much the consequence of the sway of neo-liberalism, is above all else a reflection of neo-liberalism's view of the poorest, who are deemed to have no contribution to make to society or its economy. Once this significant section of society is cast as inadequate failures and seen only to be worthy of consideration because of the financial burdens they impose through welfare dependency or nuisance, then it follows that the degradation of clients will lead to the degradation of social work. This ultimately is the message from the front line of state social work in Britain at the beginning of the twenty-first century and highlights that the precondition for progressive and humane social work is respect for clients. Nothing less.

8 Through the eye of a needle: the challenge of getting justice in Australia if you're indigenous or seeking asylum

Heather Fraser and Linda Briskman

We are always both starting over and continuing

(Galper 1980, p. 6).

Introduction

This is by no means a golden era for social work, if there ever was one. Injustice, however it is measured, is at an all time high, especially if one considers the current treatment of indigenous people, and asylum seekers in Australia. Ever more inventive are the victim-blaming tactics of the new right, which ordinarily assumes poverty and injustice are self-inflicted. Inviting other Australians to join with them, they encourage social workers to shake off the 'bleeding heart' stereotype by (re)adopting the view that resource-poverty is a manifestation of personal deficiency. Yet, many social workers refuse to do so. As we will explain in this chapter, many do not conform to the agendas of the new right, no matter how much they are encouraged to do so. Instead, they find ways to resist. Sometimes alone but often in concert with others, many social workers refute archaic assumptions about those who are not faring well under global capitalism and instead look for, or are at least amenable to, new forms of political participation.

In this chapter we note some of the historical context of the Australian welfare state before highlighting two examples of people who are highly susceptible to injustice and resource poverty. They are (1) Indigenous Australians (Aboriginal and Torres Strait Islander peoples); and (2) people who have recently arrived in Australia to seek asylum from oppression in their countries of origin. After tracing the current treatment of both groups, we consider what some of the 'old' radical social work texts might still teach us as social workers. By critically analysing some of the more progressive actions that Australian social workers have taken with respect to these groups, we aim to highlight some possibilities for change. Asking ourselves 'Where might we go to from here?', we consider what a radical/progressive guide for practice might look like now that we have moved beyond modernity. Apart from urging social workers to tackle injustice through whichever modes of practice in which they are engaged, we find inspiration from, as well as the need for, 'new' sites of protest and new forms of political participation.

The consolidation of the Australian welfare state post-World War II

As with so many other Western nations, the period after World War II signals the emergence of the welfare state. Housing for returned soldiers is prioritised and incentives are given to women to return to their 'natural' roles of wives and mothers. Pensions are provided but only to those deemed to be 'deserving'. Single mothers do not fit this bill. Nor do the able-bodied unemployed. Stigmatised and often ostracised, these groups frequently suffer some of the same treatment levelled at people with disabilities, who at this point, are locked up in institutions.

Indigenous issues are largely buried from middle Australia, with many displaced Indigenous Australians tucked away in relatively isolated church-run missions, or on government reserves. While some are employed in low-paid jobs, many are unemployed. Most are not free to move around as they wish or marry whomever they choose. Instead, they remain infantilised under the strict control of 'protectors' whose permission they must get to visit family members. Assimilation policies emerge to replace 'protection policies' that deny indigenous people the right to their culture, spiritual beliefs and family life. Governments and churches colluded in removing indigenous children from their families in order to 'take the Aboriginality out of Aboriginal children' (Dodson 1997). Through calculated social engineering the foundations of White Australia are reiterated. Many, especially those who arrived through subsidised packages, still call Britain home.

In Australia and elsewhere, the 1950s and 1960s are dedicated to nation building. State subsidies are given to those thought to be showing entrepreneurial spirit through the development of primary and secondary industries. No mention is made of Aboriginal rights. Under exclusionary clauses in the Federal Constitution, Aboriginal people are not counted in the national census until 1967, nor is the federal government permitted to legislate on behalf of Aboriginal Australians. Similar to today, most indigenous people are poor, and at the bottom of the socio-economic ladder on a range of indicators including health, education and employment. In non-indigenous society wealth is polarised but poverty—particularly poverty experienced by working-class, heterosexual families—is tackled through rational planning activities orchestrated by a so-called benevolent state.

In a country largely inhabited in south-eastern cities, the growth of the suburbs becomes a blueprint for town planners. With little knowledge of or interest in community consultations, these professionals and others are charged with the task of devising plans that will help this 'new' nation to grow. For people who are not white and middle class, few attempts are made to cater for their needs. What this means is that the meagre provisions that they sometimes receive, such as some of the early housing programmes, are often ill conceived and irrelevant.

While still tied to Britain, mainstream Australia aspires to have a classless society, one where people can have a 'fair go' and perhaps work towards owning their own homes. Yet, this is not meant for Aboriginal people who are still classified by many as inferior, if not subhuman. Nor is it meant to apply to newly arrived migrants from non-Anglo backgrounds. Their task is to carry out most of the dirty, heavy and dangerous work that their white working-class counterparts hope to shun. Their role is not to complain or make demands but to show gratitude for being permitted to remain in this 'lucky' country. Not surprisingly, the health of non-Anglo people, even narrowly defined, is anything but enviable.

However, with the global introduction of television and Australia's participation in the Vietnam War in the 1960s and 1970s, many people are shaken from complacency. The conscription of young Australian men to the fight with the United States against communism, as well as the draft dodgers who refuse to go to war, prompts many to rethink their alliances. As well, both the women's movement and the anti-war movement challenge the ways people think about themselves and society. For more than a few, street protests become part of everyday life. Across diverse groups, coalitions form. Groups who might never have imagined sharing anything in common before now find reasons to put aside some of their differences so that they can work together on specific campaigns. Once marginalised calls for justice now get more attention and indigenous issues, as well as those affecting non-British migrants, start to get more airplay. Some social workers are central players in this struggle.

The campaign slogan 'It's Time', heralds in an ambitious reform platform. Led by Prime Minister Gough Whitlam in 1972, a radical federal Labor government comes to power. This is the time to review the old order, including whether the long-standing White Australia immigration policy, which was initially enshrined in the Immigration Act of 1901, should continue. So too, it is time to embark on a series of new ventures that place human need before the accumulation of private profit. Equal pay and the provision of affordable public childcare finally gain recognition. More and more women enter the paid workforce and some attention is given to their working conditions. So-called 'protection policies' that apply to women, as well as the assimilation policies imposed on indigenous people, are called into question. In this climate of change, indigenous issues can no longer be ignored. The 'Tent Embassy' that indigenous people set up outside the Federal Parliament in 1972 draws attention to the fact that so many Aboriginal people remain in 'real' terms, 'citizen-minus' (Dodson 1996, p. 193) in their own land.

Over this decade and the next, the Australian welfare state incorporates the newly emerging community health movement, and the policy of multiculturalism unsettles the long-standing monocultural identity that many have held. From many quarters, the myth of lucky country is exposed as inequalities based on class, gender and race are recognised by growing numbers of people. Yet, for some, including some in social work, there is great distrust of the welfare state for its capacity to cover over class inequalities, with the belief that it is largely designed to subvert any revolutionary inclinations that the 'dangerous classes' may be entertaining. For others, however, the welfare state represents a series of partial victories on the part of working-class people and their allies, who win benefits through their political agitation. Still others, using critical analyses, see the welfare state as a combination of the two positions and view its utility not in the relative crumbs that it distributes but as a stepping stone for oppressed people to pursue their own goals.

The rise of economic 'rationalism' and the celebration of the individual

At the political level, the rush towards progressive politics is, however, derailed in 1975 when the Senate blocks Whitlam's federal Labor budget. In a now well-documented scandal, the Governor General responds by collaborating with Queen Elizabeth II to sack Whitlam and install in his place, the Liberal (read Tory) opposition leader. In amongst the protests and the growing fears of government instability, the electorate is persuaded to retain this new government. For conservatives, this event signals a return to all that is good and proper. 'Fiscal restraint', as it is now termed, becomes the Liberal government's new aim and the provision of social services is drastically curtailed. Although the women's movement make some important gains, including the installation of income support for sole mothers, and the trade union movement brokers some better deals for (largely Anglo, male) workers, the next decade can be remembered for its attacks on unemployed people and drastic cuts to social programmes.

In the early 1980s, a more cautious Hawke Labor government comes to power, renouncing Keynesian economics for monetary policy. Yet, multiculturalism is expanded and more ethno-specific services and benefits emerge. These programmes are made available for the wide range of people arriving in Australia, including the many asylum seekers who arrive by boat from places such as Vietnam, and who, at this point, are treated with a degree of respect. In state education policies and in some schools of social work, structural analyses are used as a matter of course to understand social problems. Across the three tiers of government (federal, state and local), some equal opportunity officers are employed and human rights processes instituted.

By the early 1990s Michael Pusey (1992) writes of the attempted take over by right-wing think-tanks and their insinuation in federal and state bureaucracies as 'economic rationalism'. With its top-down, work-intensified processes that are now referred to as 'new managerialism', economic rationalism becomes embedded in both the private and public sectors. Over the next few years—in the face of many academic critiques of science—formulas are used to determine how much funding public utilities (such as hospitals) should get. At this point, it is not a case of post-Fordism but, rather, a reiteration of Fordism as human services of all kinds are 'standardized' and 'streamlined', a trend that continues to the present day. Social workers become caught up in the impact of new managerialism on their organizations and practices.

During the 1990s, opposition to capitalism weakens. The Hawke and Keating Labor governments that hold power from 1984 to 1993 embark on activities that are now termed Third Way. Always known to be an argumentative bunch, left-wing groups in Australia start to fracture in ways that they had not before.

Growing numbers of people on the left, especially young people, have little faith in party politics. Fewer people elect to join trade unions. There is a backlash against feminists, especially those 'femocrats' who occupy senior positions in the bureaucracy. Manufacturing dries up and unemployment rises. In universities, education is commodified and sold to overseas students. New currents of academic thinking also surface. This is not surprising given, as Galper (1980, p. 6) argues, '. . . each successive period of political development has required new definitions, formulations, and understandings of the major political tasks facing [those who are] leftist [in orientation]. . .'. Yet, the new formulations that he has in mind are hardly in step with many of those now promoted.

With the advent of post-modern ideas, the grandeur of revolution is challenged, and 'dualisms' such as powerful/powerless, oppressors/oppressed and care/control are not just scrutinised but also discarded. As some go further to reject the very notion of a collective, many other academics and students start to shy away from any analyses that evoke notions of class. With the sidelining of class analyses comes the marginalisation of structural feminist analyses, as both tend to be seen as 'old hat'—analyses that 'totalise, homogenize and suppress difference'.

In contrast to other disciplines that 'play with' post-modern/post-structural ideas in the 1980s, post-modernism arrives quite a bit later in many Australian schools of social work, if it 'arrives' at all. For some educators who are basically liberal humanists, these new ideas provide a more fashionable way of dismissing the utility of radical/structural social work texts. For others who might be more radically inclined, there is a new climate of tension, particularly at conferences, when radical social work ideas are used. This provides an extra incentive for approval seekers to stop mentioning radical texts. Other responses are for people to oscillate between almost apologetic and/or aggressive stances. This is no heyday for radical social workers as references to rights, as well as any mention of oppression, are increasingly disparaged as old-fashioned, modernist mind-sets that either straightjacket individual 'agency' or reflect the West's fantasy of superiority.

Meanwhile, economic fundamentalism grows, as does the 'Hanson phenomenon', and the resurgence of hard-line racism. This phenomenon is attributed to the rise of the One Nation Party with Pauline Hanson, who was elected to the federal parliament in 1996, at the helm. Hanson's anti-immigration and anti-indigenous rights stance appeals to many Australians, particularly in rural areas, who feel they are not being given a 'fair go'. Right into the new millennium the story of major industrial restructuring, one that involves flexibility on the side of workers but little responsibility on the side of employers, is now well established across the Western world. Renowned for its profitability but not for its ability to feed, house, educate and serve its citizenry—nor its capacity to engender health, harmony or happiness across society—global forms of 'casino capitalism' have become entrenched.

For all the changes that have taken place, Harold Throssell's (1975) argument still applies about the Western world's reverence for competition and acquisitiveness;

that a capitalist social order is not meant to meet the needs of all but those who consume the most resources and accumulate the most wealth. Yet, what is different is that the legitimating discourses of capitalism are now so embedded in mainstream thinking that alternative ways of organising society become difficult for most people to even imagine. Indeed, the tenacity of capitalism is impressive. With its architects able to ensure that it mutates sufficiently to accommodate new desires and interests, contemporary forms of capitalism appropriate leftist ideas and practices and package them into marketable lifestyles. Most of all it is able to convince a lot of people that, with modifications, it can be a system that works for 'everybody'.

Moving beyond the structural/post-structural opposition

Understanding that global capitalism will never work for everybody, some social work academics and practitioners reject 'binary oppositions', or the tendency to split related phenomena from each other. Similar to the way Leonard (1984) refuses to split materialism from psychology, and Fook (1993) refuses to dichotomise casework from community work, many reject the structural/post-structural opposition. Mostly their aim is to articulate radical ideas in ways that do not privilege the experiences of able-bodied, white male heterosexuals. Some attempt to do this so as to resuscitate some of the 'old' radical ideas that are still relevant but are on the brink of extinction (see for instance, Ife 1997, Leonard 1997, Mullaly 1997). Other attempts are made by people who participate in the 'narrative movement', a movement that seems to appeal most to practitioners. What both groups share is the refusal to adopt an antagonistic relationship to 'modernist ideals' such as community, citizenship and rights (Yeatman 1994). Blending vocabularies and reworking some of the constructs, they make a point to refer to the struggles of subgroups of people who are often ignored. As a result, they tend towards more tentative, negotiated plans and explanations (see Leonard 1997).

For many of the people in these groups, recognition is given to the potential for theorising to '. . . become debased into mere verbalism in which radical rhetoric accompanies oppressive practice' (Leonard 1975 in Bailey and Brake 1975, p. 47). The main aim of theorising, therefore, is not just to avoid the nihilism of uncritical forms of post-modernism and the paralysis that comes from endless deconstruction, but also to suggest some ways forward. Appreciative of the power of language but hardly convinced that language determines all aspects of life, they refuse to ignore the importance of materialism (see Ife 1997, Mullaly 1997). Yet, rather than suggest that material factors determine lives, or to rank class as the highest form of oppression (as some of the earlier radical social work texts tend to do), they talk about the ways class, race, gender and so on mediate culture and thus, human experience. Often legitimating popular texts in similar ways to academic ones, some try to appeal to a new generation of progressives, especially younger people who are internet savvy, raised on diets of 'infotainment' and are concerned not just about social justice but also environmental issues.

From the mid-1990s onwards, these critical post-modern ideas, ideas that might otherwise be described as reworked structural ideas, develop more currency in Australian social work. Drawing on post-modern constructs, social workers also begin to challenge the inherent conservatism in the Australian Association of Social Workers' Code of Ethics (Briskman and Noble 1999). Without so much reverence for 'received ideas' and 'authoritative voices', post-modernism allows for greater latitude in application. Granted, these ideas can seem unduly verbose and at times, more than a little timid, particularly in comparison to the more authoritative, polemical declarations uttered by radicals in the 1960s and 1970s. Yet, the flip side of this means that these ideas have the capacity to accommodate different manifestations of heterosexism, racism, classism and so on. This means that those who use them can avoid the charge of erasing some of the differences similarly classified individuals can experience. This is important given the cultural sensitivity predominantly white social workers need to show towards Indigenous Australians and recently arrived asylum seekers.

Indigenous rights and Australian social workers

In the early 1990s, the federal Labor government launches a 10-year reconciliation process that aims to resolve some of the effects of Australia's domination of Aboriginal and Torres Strait Islander peoples, who comprise some 400 000 people, in a general population of around 18 million. International pressure helps to precipitate this work, as do years of local indigenous advocacy. Such advocacy is needed because, in mainstream society, there is still little knowledge or understanding of how different groups of indigenous people have been treated. Whether one considers the attempts to eliminate them as a distinct group of people, the dispossession, the level of police surveillance and incarceration, or the calculated neglect of rural and regional Aborigines, the colonisation of indigenous people can be seen as violent, callous and uncivilised. As Markus (1995, p. 144) states, 'In the treatment of Aboriginal people the full force of Australian racism is apparent'.

Designed to be an independent, statutory body, the Council for Aboriginal Reconciliation is set up for 10 years with full funding from the Commonwealth government. One of its tasks is to distil a framework '. . . through which unresolved issues of reconciliation can be resolved' (Council for Aboriginal Reconciliation 2003). To do this, much energy is expended trying to engage community groups around Australia, as well as consulting with local businesses and government officials. Similar to reactions made about other government-led inquiries and Royal Commissions, many indigenous people remain skeptical about the process, whereas others hold great hopes about what it might achieve.

However one views the reconciliation process, there is little dispute about it raising community awareness. Reconciliation groups flourish in the suburbs, as organisations and communities find ways to engage with indigenous issues. In many parts of Australia, some of them surprising, credence is given to previously silenced indigenous voices. As 'ordinary people' discuss reconciliation, many participate in a spectacular art display referred to as the Sea of Hands, and the Walk for Reconciliation that takes place across the iconic Sydney Harbour Bridge.

Similar to a number of protests that are now designed by actors and artists, the Sea of Hands is created in 1997 by a coalition of community groups who call themselves Australians for Native Title and Reconciliation (ANTaR), with the help of Artists Against Racism (AAR). Essentially it is a visual petition, otherwise known as a 'citizen's statement', that is used to mobilise non-indigenous support for native title (land claims) and reconciliation. Apart from being the biggest public art display in Australia, it is an eye-catching, media-attracting event that testifies to the strength of support that exists in the general public. The same may be said about the walk across Sydney Harbour Bridge. And although neither campaign is radical, in the sense that they require 'militarism' and direct opposition to the state, they are radical in so far as they build alliances across diverse groups, many of whom do not feel comfortable with orthodox protest methods.

In the same year, a year that coincides with the first national reconciliation conference, the *Bringing Them Home* (1997) report is launched. Based on a national inquiry conducted by the Human Rights and Equal Opportunity Commission (HREOC), and resulting from many years of lobbying by indigenous groups, this landmark report exposes past and present child removal practices that become known as the 'stolen generations'. The report confronts social workers, churches and government bodies with the evidence of complicity in genocidal practices. Included in it is evidence of the laws, policies and practices instituted throughout Australia that attempted to eliminate the Aboriginal race by assimilating indigenous children into white society. For many Australians, including many social workers, this is the first time they have heard of the extent of these practices and many react with bewilderment and great sadness.

During the next 10 years indigenous voices are increasingly legitimated through mainstream media. Community awareness is raised through music, film, theatre and art. Pressure is placed on the Prime Minister, John Howard, to say sorry for the wrongs of the past. The opening ceremony of the 2000 Sydney Olympics includes a band Midnight Oil, singing about the need for a treaty while wearing black shirts that spell 'sorry'. Such acts are important because they capture attention of the 'mainstream'. With more airplay, indigenous issues make their way into popular culture, dense academic texts recede, as do the searches for singular 'truths' based on white notions of historiography and anthropology.

Many social workers are part of this popular, collective movement to redress the legacy of colonisation of indigenous people. As a result, more attempts are made to understand how social work, as a profession, can prevent being part of child removal practices. Drawing from the work of Ruth Frankenburg from the United States, some start to acknowledge the privileges they enjoy from being white and/or non-indigenous. Social work conferences often herald indigenous themes or apply the overarching theme of social justice to this constituency.

Not renowned for its activism, the Australian Association of Social Workers (AASW) finally incorporates indigenous peoples into its Code of Ethics in the late

1990s. Symbolically, this is important. Yet, it may also be seen to be tokenistic, given it falls well short of the recognition given to the Maori people in New Zealand through their bi-cultural social work code (Noble and Briskman 1996). In 1997 the AASW then supports the national peak body, the Australian Council of Social Services' (ACOSS), to unreservedly apologise to indigenous people for the forced removal of their children. Calling on the federal government to follow suit, this coalition also recommends that a national compensation fund be established. Perhaps because of the debates that ensue about Aboriginal sovereignty, the AASW then joins a diverse range of organisations in the community services sector in October 2001 to release a statement entitled, *Achieving Justice for Indigenous Australians* (Australian Association of Social Services 1991). In this one-page statement, indigenous oppression is reiterated and four major strategies are announced. They comprise: (1) reviewing policy approaches used in the community sector to ensure that they are rights based; (2) continuing their engagement with the Council for Aboriginal Conciliation; (3) supporting the introduction of an Aboriginal Treaty; and (4) working with indigenous people to create genuine employment and training opportunities.

In many agencies where social work is practised, policy and procedural changes are instituted so as to recognise the needs of indigenous people and to work more closely with indigenous organisations. While there is much work still to be done, these changes are important. So are the press releases and government submissions that the AASW makes. For instance, in March 2003 the AASW works in partnership with the National Coalition of Aboriginal and Torres Strait Islander Social Work Association Incorporated to produce *Submission to the House of Representatives Standing Committee on Aboriginal and Torres Strait Islander Affairs, Inquiry into the Capacity Building of Indigenous Communities* (AASW 2003b). While it may be criticised for the social capital perspective that is used to underpin it, the submission recognises the need for indigenous self-determination through equitable access to resources and ownership of programmes.

Showing more radical promise is the media release that the AASW puts out in the lead up to the 2003 Sorry Day. Here, the association again commits itself to Aboriginal reconciliation before recognising the historic role social workers played in the 'Stolen Generations' (AASW 2003a). Thus, it recognises the potential tension underlying current relationships between indigenous people and social workers.

Human rights discourses are gradually entering Australian social work (see Ife 2001). For some who subscribe to radical social work, however, human rights might be seen to be a trumped-up version of liberal humanism: that it, along with the reconciliation process, serves to 'whitewash' oppression, with the true extent of indigenous disadvantage shrouded in glossy marketing materials and supported by high profile sports people and media personalities. From this perspective it is possible to point to the Council for Aboriginal Reconciliation's (2003) framework that gives priority not to land rights but to '. . . better approaches to Indigenous self-governance'. . . 'Indigenous employment strategies'. . .'improving access to banking and other financial institutions'. . . and lending support to 'best practice conferences' (Council for Aboriginal Reconciliation 2003).

Yet, from another radical social work perspective, more credence might be given to the context in which the Council for Aboriginal Reconciliation has had to operate. For in the face of the federal government's lack of support for reconciliation and its own major funding cuts, the ongoing call for its sponsoring body to formally apologise might be seen as strong. Continued calls for a treaty (including land entitlements) might even be seen to be radical; as might the suggestion that it produce a 'yearly report card on the progress of reconciliation'. Finally, its condemnation of the federal government for '. . . abrogat[ing] its leadership role in the broader reconciliation agenda' (Council for Aboriginal Reconciliation 2003), might also be seen to be bold.

After 10 years of a Howard Liberal government, the modest demands of the original reconciliation process are in jeopardy. From this government there is no interest in indigenous sovereignty and self-determination. Instead, it pursues a programme it calls 'practical reconciliation'. From any kind of progressive standpoint, 'practical reconciliation' offers Indigenous Australians practically nothing. For all the rhetoric that surrounds the idea of 'practical solutions', this watereddown version of reconciliation threatens the underlying notion of rights and replaces it with recycled notions of charitable welfare; where 'self-reliance' is enforced to prevent the problem of 'welfare dependency'. Unless social workers retain a 'critical consciousness' (Leonard 1975), there is a danger that they will unwittingly implement policies in the spheres of health, child welfare and juvenile justice that will collude with these prevailing ideologies.

While most indigenous people reject practical reconciliation, its underlying assumptions resurface, especially on radio talk shows, where opportunities are taken to reiterate the hopelessness of the 'Aboriginal problem'. Homogenised as one group of people and largely represented as substance abusing and ungraciously relying on 'hand-outs', indigenous people are again subject to the kinds of assaults on their character with which they are long familiar. Yet, with the benefit of education, greater insight, not to mention a semblance of decency, many people, including most social workers, have not fallen prey to these diatribes. Rather, most continue to supplement any formal knowledge they have of indigenous oppression with material they glean from responsible media, internet, and other popular sites. As they do so, many reject the Prime Minister's denial of what he refers to as a 'black armband history' and continue to call for a national apology.

Seeking asylum in Australia today: the terror of detention

Although contested, there is some justification for non-Indigenous Australians claiming that they are unaware of the past wrongs inflicted on indigenous people. However, such a denial cannot be made where the current treatment of asylum seekers is concerned. It cannot be made because the laws, policies and practices inflicted on asylum seekers are very widely publicised. Whether it is from the wide variety of media that publish stories about the conditions facing asylum seekers (both inside and out of detention), or the damning reports handed down from international bodies and other outspoken critics, Australians have been, and continue to be, bombarded with evidence of what is now being seen to be among the worst policies in the world. The question is, how did this happen?

In 1992, following the arrival of Cambodian asylum seekers by boat, the Labor government introduces the policy of 'mandatory detention' for 'unauthorised arrivals' (Jupp 2002). Apart from the responses made by refugee groups, there is scarcely a murmur. Ten years later when a highly developed, for-profit, private detention regime is elaborated through the policy now dubbed, 'the Pacific solution', sections of the media, international human rights bodies and refugee advocates express outrage at the human rights abuses they see occurring. Located mainly in remote areas of Australia and in 'underdeveloped' neighbouring countries such as Papua New Guinea and Nauru (that are paid millions of dollars to accept Australia's asylum seekers), these facilities are said to deter 'people smugglers'. What they do, however, is cause physical and mental harm to the men, women and children who are incarcerated for years on end as they await the uncertainty of their legal processes or deportation.

Meanwhile the Australian public is led to believe that those fleeing despotic regimes may be terrorists. Fuelling this are the growing fears of Islam infiltrating the nation, as most of those arriving in Australia by boat are from Afghanistan, Iran and Iraq. Amidst these fears, neither the federal government nor the general community is moved to any significant degree when 353 asylum seekers die at sea on route to Australia in 2001.

However, when the well-known *Tampa* incident occurs in the same year, emotions shift and indifference turns to anger. This incident occurs when the captain and crew on a Norwegian vessel rescues a sinking boatload of refugees and then defies Australian orders to turn back from Australian waters. For days while the federal government uses the Australian military forces to intervene, the asylum seekers are left in the burning sun without medical assistance. With the media coverage that ensues, many people across the political spectrum start to feel ashamed. This shame intensifies when New Zealand's government demonstrates compassion by offering a safe haven to many on board.

Following the *Tampa* incident another scandal unfolds that involves the federal government and a boat full of refugees. Referred to as the 'children overboard affair', this involves the Prime Minister John Howard and members of his cabinet holding press conferences and using popular talk shows to tell Australians how asylum seekers have thrown their children overboard so that they could land on 'our shores' (see **http://www.truthoverboard.com/**). Declaring that 'we don't want people like that here', many people's hearts and minds harden once again to the point that the Howard government is able to use the issue to be re-elected.

The 'children overboard' incident is shown to be fabricated through the national inquiry that later indicts those involved. Despite this finding, and the raft of reports that substantiate the severity of harm caused to the children and their parents in detention, many of whom are so desperate they self-harm, public opinion of asylum seekers fails to be swayed enough to reverse government policies. To many refugee advocates, including many social workers, it remains a puzzle as to why a relatively small number of people seeking asylum in Australia are perceived to be such a threat to national security and border integrity. Not only is it alarming to think of how popular anti-asylum seeker discourses have become, but that they can be used for electoral success.

For most of those fortunate enough to be deemed refugees, the reward is Temporary Protection Visa (TPV) status that denies basic rights such as family reunion and social security provisions. Not allowing for full participation in society, this temporary status does not allow for people to plan for the future. Which is why many people experience TPV status as a form of 'secondary detention' (Marston 2003). With some regimes, such as Afghanistan, now deemed by the federal Australian government to be safe, despite reliable evidence to the contrary, those on TPVs live in fear of being returned.

A national anti-deportation alliance is formed but cannot prevent the first round of deportations. Many refugee fears are substantiated. For instance, Amnesty International tries to locate one man forcibly returned, following the inability of his friends in Australia to make contact with him (Shaw 2003). The federal government of Australia, especially the immigration minister, Phillip Ruddock, is not moved. Instead, he offers small financial incentives to detained Iranians in the hope that they will 'give up and go home'. Most reject the offer.

To maintain support among progressives and to engage the previously uninformed and/or disinterested the arts community searches for new ways to draw attention to the plight of asylum seekers. Through art, theatre, song and literature, the stories of oppression, flight, incarceration and uncertainty are told. Examples include a play in Melbourne in 2002, *Kan Yama Kan*, which is performed by refugees, and the release of a book of anecdotes from detention centers (Austin 2003). These popular forms of representation combine with the powerful documentaries and investigative journalism of those in the mainstream media. Among many of the audiences are social workers, and not just those who work with asylum seekers.

Given the stories that they hear, including those told by service users on TPVs or colleagues who work with them, many social workers are perplexed by the events they see unfolding in Australia. While the detention centres mean that most do not come into contact with asylum seekers who have just arrived, there is anger and despair at their treatment. Some of this is generated by the stories they hear from those granted temporary visas (see Kenny et al. 2002).

As many asylum seekers and formally recognised refugees are not eligible to use a good number of social services and supports, growing numbers of social workers struggle to provide assistance without it being recognised as part of their work. Appreciative of the relative privileges that they enjoy, and compelled to take action, many social workers support (largely unfunded) refugee agencies (see for instance, Hotham Mission Asylum Seeker Project (North Melbourne) website (**http://www.hothammission.org.au**). This is often done out-of-hours, as are much of the contributions made to social action campaigns. Yet, on the legal front social workers are not nearly as active as they might be. Partly this is because of the secrecy of the federal department that deals with detainees' claims but it is also due to the complexities of immigration law, and the legal system more generally.

So, even though the social work profession in Australia does not tend to engage in 'serious' advocacy and activism in its own right, social workers are among those who volunteer their time, join large-scale protests and instigate protests on a smaller scale. For instance, in 2002, many Australian social work academics put an advertisement in a national newspaper calling for the end of mandatory detention. Two other social work academics take the unprecedented step of reporting suspected child abuse (of the systemic kind) of children in a South Australian detention centre to that state's child protection service (Davies 2002). The authors of this chapter also challenge their own university in 2002, when a group of their colleagues put forward a proposal to join a for-profit, private prison operator to deliver educational services to people in detention. With support from many other staff and the student union, as well as the wider community, this leads to the withdrawal of the proposal that would have seen the university profiting from people's misery (Briskman and Fraser 2002).

A code of practice for radical/progressive social workers

As we have suggested, Langan and Lee's (1989, p. 15) question, 'How should radical social work respond to the now worsening problems of poverty and state repression?' continues to be very relevant. To social workers who are interested in social transformation and looking for some 'ways forward', we modify ideas from a range of 'old' radical texts to offer this draft code of practice (see Galper 1975, 1980; Leonard 1975, 1984; Ragg 1977, Simpkin 1979, Throssell 1975). We do this not as a final declaration but to open up discussion with progressive social workers across the world.

1   We regard our primary obligation as the welfare of all human kind, across the globe, not just to those in our immediate vicinity.
2   We understand the contradictions inherent in delivering social work services in a capitalist society. We know that the state can be both oppressive and supportive.
3   We never claim to be 'apolitical' or 'neutral' and we define social justice in political, material and global terms, not just psychological terms.
4   We respect the need for resources and decision-making processes to be fairly shared, and we realise that this will be hard to achieve given the current social order.
5   We recognise the importance of language and try to show sensitivity through the words that we use. However, we realise that we might 'get it wrong'.
6   We value processes as much as 'products' or 'outcomes', and we are—at the very least—skeptical of using violence to deal with conflict.

7   We define power in possessive and relational ways. This means that while we are wary of calling anyone 'powerless', we are also aware of the way dominant groups can exercise power over people who are oppressed on the basis of race, gender, class, ability, age, sexual orientation and geographical location.

8   Because we strive to live in a society where people are able to exercise their human rights, we try to democratise our professional relationships as well as our personal ones.

9   We do not see financial profit as the primary motive in life. Thus, we do not uphold the tenets of global capitalism nor do we value paid work over that which is unpaid.

10   While we appreciate the importance of group bonds, we are wary of the way nationalism can be used to deride and exclude others. In so doing, we seek to work with people from diverse backgrounds in equitable—and culturally sensitive—ways.

11   We value education for the ways it can be used to develop critical consciousness.

12   We respect the need for oppressed groups to sometimes 'go it alone'. Yet, we do not presume this will always be their preference. Instead, we are open to providing support/resources to oppressed groups in a manner that they suggest will be useful.

13   While developing knowledge that will be useful to social transformation, we speak up whenever we can about acts of unfairness that we see, using all sorts of media to broadcast our observations and ideas.

14   We recognise the potentially conservative nature of all methods of social work and strive to radicalise all forms of work that we undertake. As we do this, we avoid individual acts of heroism or martyrdom, preferring instead to work in collaboration with others.

15   We do not see ourselves sitting outside society, nor as liberators of 'the needy' or 'the downtrodden'. Rather, we try to use the benefits derived from our professional status to work against the exploitation of individuals and groups.

16   We try to do all this in everyday, reflexive ways, without posturing as self-appointed experts.

17   Given the obstacles that confront us, we realise that fatalism, cynicism and despair may set in. To prevent this we try to keep our sense of humour, have fun with others and incorporate self-care activities into our lives.

Summary

While asylum seekers and indigenous people are by no means the only oppressed groups, they have experienced, and continue to experience, some of the worst forms of deprivation, surveillance and bigotry in Australia. While both groups are subject to the systematic denial of their human rights, neither group has the financial resources to sustain lengthy forms of legal recourse. And even if they were able to do so, neither would escape the fact that they are, as classes of people, subject to some of the worst conditions produced by global capitalism.

Whether it is with indigenous people, asylum seekers or any other group of oppressed people, social workers are political actors. Radical/progressive social workers do not just know this, but they refuse to become swept up in activities that negate the politics of our work. As Leonard (1984, p. 15) writes, 'Where mainstream practice want[s] to close issues off and wrap them up in a technical and professional blanket, radical social workers [ask] awkward questions'.

Finally then, it is not as though we have embraced every aspect of the old radical texts. We have many criticisms of the works produced, particularly in relation to the way they tend to prioritise class over all other forms of oppression, using male pronouns as they speak with such certainty about the revolution, that revolves around white, working-class male workers. That said, we maintain that there is still much to learn from these texts. Not least is the need to create solidarity with others; build counter-systems; and creatively respond to injustice through a range of micro- and macro-practices (Leonard 1975).

9 Compromise, collaboration and collective resistance: different strategies in the face of the war on asylum seekers[1]

Ed Mynott

Introduction

On Thursday 28 August 2003 Israfil Shiri walked into the offices of Refugee Action in the centre of Manchester. It was not his first visit. Israfil was an Iranian asylum seeker and Refugee Action was the voluntary organisation responsible for providing help and arranging accommodation for asylum seekers who had been 'dispersed' to Manchester by the Home Office. In front of a member of staff Israfil poured petrol over his body and set fire to himself. He was rushed to the burns unit of nearby Wythenshawe Hospital in south Manchester where, on 3 September after several days in agony, he died.

Israfil's story is a shocking one. Equally shocking, however, is that it went unreported by every single national newspaper in the UK.[2] Any national newspaper could have discovered from the press release issued by the Manchester Committee to Defend Asylum Seekers that Israfil had told his friends he was planning to kill himself to prove that the government cared more about animals than people fleeing torture and persecution; that he suffered from a complicated medical condition and since his application for asylum was rejected over a year previously, he had been refused any medical treatment, had been made homeless from his council flat and had received no benefits or support; that before he committed suicide Israfil was in great pain due to his illness and was terrified of being sent back to Iran. He had lost all hope.[3]

---

1 This chapter relies not only on direct experience but also draws on the ideas and insights of other political activists, academics and researchers. As a discursive piece it is very lightly footnoted but I feel the need to record my debt to others. For a more academic treatment of some of these issues from a similar standpoint see Cohen et al. (2001) and Hayes and Humphries (2004). The views in this chapter are none the less my own and do not necessarily represent the views of the Greater Manchester Immigration Aid Unit or any other organisation mentioned in this chapter.
2 The incident was mentioned some weeks later by a sympathetic journalist in a comment piece in the *Guardian* newspaper.
3 Manchester Committee to Defend Asylum Seekers. Death of young destitute asylum seeker from Iran following setting himself alight. 3 September 2003.

Israfil's last desperate act was felt perhaps most strongly by his fellow Iranian asylum seekers in Manchester who responded by setting up their own Iranian community organisation to try to make sure that any of their fellow nationals who might be gripped by the same desperation could be stopped from making the ultimate sacrifice. No doubt it was also felt strongly by other asylum seekers. However, Israfil's desperate act affected other groups too: those activists who campaign for political solidarity with asylum seekers; those workers in the voluntary sector whose job is to support and advise asylum seekers; and those workers in the public sector whose job is to provide, or deny, resources of one kind or another to asylum seekers. Not for the first time did they note with outrage the contrast between the daily clamour of mendacious stories about asylum seekers and the sudden silence when desperation drove an asylum seeker to commit suicide. This time the manner of Israfil's death gave their outrage a bitter edge. But it also raised questions: could it happen where I work? Could I be in danger? As a political activist and someone who now worked advising immigrants, including asylum seekers, I was not immune from these thoughts.

The first time I had visited those offices of Refugee Action, 2 years before Israfil killed himself in them, I was still an academic researcher. I had walked up the renovated tiled staircase of an otherwise anonymous old building and interviewed one of the staff. A year later and now a volunteer worker with the National Coalition of Anti-Deportation Campaigns I discovered the back entrance, hidden in a side street. Escorting an asylum seeker to an appointment we rang the bell before the locked door was opened by a security guard with a clip-board. Once satisfied that we should be let in, he led us through the bowels of the building into an ancient service lift (complete with retractable iron grill) and took us up to the offices where two-dozen or so people waited on plastic chairs before seeing a member of staff.

The journey from academic researcher to practitioner has since taken me via the Citizens Advice Bureau to the Greater Manchester Immigration Aid Unit. Now it is part of my job to see the immigrants and asylum seekers who fill our waiting room and advise them about how immigration law affects them; or what they can and cannot do if they have been made homeless and destitute by the government. It is my job to tell the lucky few that, yes, we can act as their legal representatives, while having to tell the rest that all we can do is advise them. To get a lawyer, they have to go somewhere else.

Both my experience as an academic and my experience as a practitioner have informed this chapter. But it is my experience as a political activist which shapes my concerns more than anything else. Hence this chapter aims to go beyond commentary on policy changes to a discussion of what can be done to resist the tide of inhumanity. In part this is about what can be done by asylum seekers and those (to use the jargon) who are 'subject to immigration control'. However, its main purpose is to provoke thought and discussion amongst those who campaign politically alongside asylum seekers or whose paid work brings them into contact with asylum seekers, whether providing or denying services to them. Is it really possible to resist or is it only possible to try to soften the blows for vulnerable people?

When does 'realism' become collaboration with an oppressive system and its agents? What is effective solidarity as opposed to well-meaning sympathy or angry gestures? These questions are approached here through a discussion of the experiences of asylum seekers and other migrants. The general political context of that experience makes up the first part of the chapter. But I strongly suspect that the themes of compromise, collaboration and collective resistance, which are dealt with in the second part of the chapter, will have a resonance in many other fields where practitioners and activists are grappling with the realities of capitalist globalisation and how to resist it.

The politics of asylum and immigration in the UK: a war on asylum seekers?

Is there really a war being waged against asylum seekers in the UK? Surely war is what was unleashed by the US/UK Coalition in its invasion and occupation of Iraq? We might describe as a war, the aggression of the Israeli state against the Palestinian people. We certainly can describe as civil wars the long drawn out hostilities which have killed millions in some parts of the world. Largely unreported in the West, the Democratic Republic of Congo, for example, has witnessed millions killed and millions more displaced in recent years. Similarly a dirty war in Algeria between the state and the Islamist groups raged in the 1990s leading to death and forced movement on a very large scale. But a war on asylum seekers?

Yet this powerful metaphor serves to capture the reality whereby a deep official hostility to asylum seekers has entrenched itself across the states of the European Union (although it is the UK which is the sole focus of this chapter.) Fortress Europe is an apt description of the vision cherished by Europe's political leaders of free movement for citizens within the territory of the EU while heavily policed or even militarised external borders prevent the entry of all others, unless their labour is to be exploited in the selfish interest of member states. The reality of migration is as ever, more messy, more desperate and disparate than the nightmarish vision would allow, but the vision and the policy informed by it are none the less chillingly real.

Naturally, both press and politicians use the alibi that they are only responding to 'legitimate public fears'. Such an alibi begs more questions than it answers. It supposes, whether naively or cynically, that the corporate news organisations and governments are the simple servants of an angry public opinion. Certainly, there is a great deal of evidence of popular hostility to asylum seekers, although that hostility is not universal nor without its own contradictions. The more fundamental question is how far this hostility is cause and how far it is effect. There are two factors to consider: first, the relentless outpouring of bile, myth and lies about asylum seekers on a daily basis by most of the British press; and secondly the existence for almost two decades of an official political common sense that part creates, part reinforces and part capitulates to this news agenda. Loudly proclaiming its determination to tackle supposed abuses of the asylum system, UK governments have delivered a stream of new legislation and policy changes which, while maintaining the need to distinguish between 'genuine' refugees and undeserving economic migrants abusing the asylum system, in practice makes life harder for all asylum seekers. Worse, this official political common sense lays the basis for a resurgence of racism which identifies black immigrants as a problem and opens up a space for the far-right to use opposition to asylum seekers as the key issue in mobilising a new and significantly wider circle of voters and sympathisers.

This is not the place to analyse the material conditions of working class people under capitalism and how competition, division and resentment can provide the soil out of which a popular racism can grow, inflamed by a news agenda hostile to asylum seekers in particular, and non-white immigration in general (see Ferguson and Lavalette 2004). Our task here is to recognise that governments have never been neutral, honest brokers in this process. Rather, they have implemented immigration controls which have been a key source of institutionalised racism, in the belief that this approach will undermine the more overtly abusive and violent forms of racism found on the far-right and in some of the news media. Instead, by accepting that certain forms of immigration are generally harmful and others are generally unproblematic (say, the Indian subcontinent versus the existing European Union states), and by accepting that tough measures have to be taken against unwanted immigration, official politics ensures that immigrants remain a 'problem' in the minds of a substantial (and, at the moment, growing) proportion of the public. In this way the institutionalised racism of immigration control bolsters popular racism instead of undermining it (see Miles and Phizacklea 1984).

This explains how 7 years of New Labour immigration and asylum policy, advertised as 'fairer, faster and firmer' by previous Home Secretary Jack Straw and more recently as 'tough as old boots' by his successor David Blunkett, has managed to create a much more harsh and inhumane system for asylum seekers while failing to prevent a steep rise in racist hostility to asylum seekers. From a purely humanitarian standpoint the one thing that Labour should have tackled has remained untouched: the culture of suspicion encountered by asylum seekers from the Home Office when it examines their claims. This culture of suspicion leads to many obvious candidates for refugee status or 'humanitarian protection' being initially refused and having to fight their way through the appeals system to have their claim accepted. Instead, the rise in the number of asylum claims has been met with a determination to 'crack down', take 'tough measures to deter abuse' and so on. The increased determination to do this was exemplified by Tony Blair's promise in autumn 2002 to halve the number of asylum claims being made, a promise which was kept. What this amounts to is a policy which has the following aims:

1   To make it as hard as possible for those fleeing persecution to enter the UK in the first place. The worst example of this was the imposition of a new visa regime on a refugee-producing country like Zimbabwe in late 2002. Entry is also made harder by the export of immigration officers to places like the French ports, where they check passengers on the Eurostar, and to Prague

airport, where they look out for Roma and seek to stop them coming to the UK because of their propensity to claim asylum from the extreme racism they face. Not the least result of governments' efforts to tighten border controls has been the growth of people-smuggling and people-trafficking. Irregular migrants (whether they seek work or protection) are driven into the hands of criminal gangs. Far from scrounging off the welfare state, migrants are paying thousands and thousands of dollars to be taken across borders.

2   To create a separate and inferior welfare system for asylum seekers: it provides benefits at 70% of subsistence level while 'dispersing' asylum seekers on a no-choice basis to towns and cities around Britain. These areas have been chosen because of the availability of cheap, usually privately owned and low-quality, housing.

3   To deny access to any form of welfare support to anyone deemed not to have claimed asylum 'as soon as reasonably practicable', i.e. within 24 to 72 hours of initial arrival. In summer 2002 Labour also removed the 'concession' whereby anyone whose claim had not been determined within 6 months was allowed to take paid work. This has led to most asylum seekers simply being unable to work legally. If you are not allowed to work or to claim any welfare benefits your choices are starvation, begging, prostitution or working illegally, thus opening yourself up to exploitation and criminal prosecution. All that matters to government is that they believe such hardship will stop people seeking asylum.

4   To restrict access to the judicial system so that refusals of asylum and decisions to remove (deport) from the UK are harder to challenge. The government calls this streamlining in order to deter abuse of the appeals system. In reality it is a denial of justice. In the context of both public and official hostility to asylum seekers, there has also been a disturbing tendency for the culture of suspicion to spread from the Home Office to the judiciary.

5   To declare, in the face of contrary evidence, that a given country is safe and therefore any asylum claim from that country must be unfounded. Alternatively, declare that although one part of a country may be unsafe, other regions within the country *are* safe and therefore people can be removed back to those safe areas. To try to strike deals with the governments of developing countries which allow the removal of asylum seekers back to their region of origin, if not their country.

Things can only get better

As one piece of legislation has rapidly followed another, it has become clear that the whole direction of Labour policy has been to retain the letter of the 1951 Refugee Convention but hedge around it with so many practical restrictions that it becomes more and more difficult to effectively exercise the formal right to seek asylum in the UK. Labour had already travelled quite a way down that road by 2004. Yet the proposed legislation currently before the British Parliament at the time of writing represents a qualitative shift toward restrictionism and repressive measures. Whereas in the past asylum seekers were treated as if they were criminals, the Asylum and Immigration (Treatment of Claimants) Bill literally criminalises the majority of asylum seekers.

The Bill threatens criminal prosecution and up to 2 years in prison for anyone who enters Britain without a passport. This will hit most asylum seekers. Because it is impossible to enter Britain legally in order to seek asylum, most asylum seekers have to pay people-smugglers (agents) to get them in. The Refugee Convention itself recognises that refugees often have to use false documents. Yet the new Bill specifically rules out reliance on an agent as a defence against criminal prosecution.

Added to this, the Bill gives government the power to electronically tag all asylum seekers from the moment they claim asylum. This criminalises people who have committed no crime, in the process lending weight to the racist smears and fevered imaginings of much of the press.

Further, the Bill *mandates* the Home Office and any immigration adjudicator hearing an appeal to declare that an asylum seeker who has arrived without a passport, or with a false passport, or passed through a supposedly safe country, is not to be believed. At the same time the Home Office routinely claims that an asylum seeker who has managed to flee using their own passport cannot be in any danger from their own government. Asylum seekers are damned either way. Those who have fled may have mountains of evidence about their persecution but it will do them no good. The law will automatically brand them 'not credible'.

And just to make sure that asylum seekers cannot use the legal system, the decision of the new Asylum and Immigration Tribunal will be final. Under the ominous heading 'Exclusivity and finality of Tribunal's jurisdiction' the Bill prevents access to any higher court to appeal or review decisions by the Home Office or an adjudicator. Such attempts to use higher courts are already difficult under the current system but the new Bill simply abolishes access to any other court. This is at the same time as the Department for Constitutional Affairs is making the provision of free legal advice and representation (commonly known as Legal Aid) much harder.

It is no exaggeration to say that this Bill comes very close to turning the Refugee Convention into a dead letter in Britain. It will be much harder for anyone to successfully claim asylum. An international convention which was created out of the bitter experience of two world wars and the holocaust has now been stamped on by a Labour government.

How much of this Bill makes its way onto the statute books will have become clear by the time this chapter is published. Yet the direction of government policy under Labour is clear. Labour shortages and fears about long-term demographic changes—fears which are common across European governments—have encouraged an opening up of legal routes for economic migration into the UK. The number of work permits issued each year, for instance, has increased by tens of thousands. At the same time the ideological and legal attack on seeking asylum has been relentless. What is common to both halves of the picture is a determination to reinforce immigration control. It is not true that globalisation has led to the free flow of people across borders. Rather, the UK state in tandem with its European Union partners, has sought to secure the interests of its own national capital by channelling flows of documented migrants through a rigid network of pre-entry, on-entry and after-entry controls; and this system of control is designed to be like a set of water pipes where the guiding hand of the state turns the tap on, off, or sets it somewhere in between, according to its own appreciation and preferences. This is what they mean by 'managed migration'.

But what about those who cannot access or wait for the rigid managed migration routes? What happens to those who are desperate enough to travel clandestinely and enter European states like the UK without documents? The history of the twentieth century, and not only in the UK, has been a history of ever more elaborate and harshly enforced immigration controls, apart from for citizens of European Union states within the Union. Only international conventions such as the Refugee Convention (1951) and the European Convention on Human Rights (1948) recognised that there could be imperatives which required states to put their controls to one side. These conventions were signed by states in the aftermath of the catastrophes of the first half of the twentieth century and brandished during the cold war as evidence of the superiority of one side over the other. One effect of the conventions was that the rights they bestowed on individuals could be invoked by undocumented migrants to stay the hand of the immigration authorities, even if only while their claim was being examined.

What has happened at the end of the twentieth century and the beginning of the twenty-first is that states have sought to ensure that, in practice, even their limited duties as parties to such international conventions are subordinated, and where necessary sacrificed, to the goal of immigration control with all its restrictions and racism.

So there is a general tendency for the UK state, in the form of the Home Office, to use a range of measures to make it harder to reach the UK in order to claim asylum; harder to exercise the right to claim asylum effectively; and easier to detain and remove people whose asylum and human rights claim has failed.

Exclusion from welfare provision

As already noted, amongst the measures which make it harder to effectively exercise the right to seek asylum are those which exclude asylum seekers from welfare provision. The effect of this exclusion is to make it more difficult to pursue a claim; and this exclusion from welfare is made worse by the fact that asylum seekers have no permission to do paid work. This is a condition of their temporary admission into the UK. Until July 2002 a concession operated whereby an asylum seeker who was still waiting for a decision on their claim from the Home Office after 6 months could apply for permission to work. Such applications were routinely granted. It is a mark of the political direction of the Labour government that this concession, introduced under a Conservative government led by Margaret Thatcher, was withdrawn suddenly and without any debate by the Home Office.

There has long been a link between immigration control and denial of access to 'public funds'. The link goes right back to the 1905 Aliens Act. According to this Act an 'undesirable immigrant' was someone who 'cannot show that he has in his possession or is in a position to obtain the means of supporting himself and his dependants' or 'owing to any disease or infirmity appears likely to become a charge on the rates or otherwise a detriment to the public.' Those who had been in receipt of 'parochial relief' could be deported (Cohen 1987, p. 21).

It was a strong feature of the agitation in the years before this Act that aliens were a burden on the British nation. This was a central element in the demonisation of the alien as a diseased criminal character sponging off the resources of the British people, exploiting their goodwill and generosity. Such demonisation recurred regularly throughout the twentieth century, finding in the illegal immigrant (black, of course) of the 1960s onwards the old demon in new form. As the issue of asylum has come to dominate in the 1990s and the new century, the racist virus has mutated until 'asylum seeker' and 'illegal immigrant' have become interchangeable terms of abuse.

The link between immigration control and access to welfare support remains in modern immigration law. Almost all immigrants given limited leave to enter or remain in the UK, whether as a visitor, student, spouse or whatever, must have 'no recourse to public funds'. Here public funds has a clear legal definition: essentially all non-contributory social security benefits plus public housing and homeless accommodation. This provision has always had a discriminatory effect on black communities for the obvious reason that such individuals or their family members are more likely to have restrictions on their leave to enter or remain in the UK.

Moreover, because of the link between immigration status and disentitlement to welfare benefits, those who may be identified by skin colour, language, 'unfamiliar' name or anything else, as 'foreign' and therefore potentially undeserving, are much more likely to be required to prove their entitlement. In the bad old 1970s this was often done by asking to see a passport. In our more enlightened times Home Secretary David Blunkett has been inflamed by undeserving asylum seekers and illegal immigrants getting medical treatment when they are ill and benefits when they are destitute. This is the openly admitted origin of the threatened national identity card system. If introduced, no amount of anti-discriminatory guidelines will prevent black people from being asked to prove 'entitlement' under circumstances and to a degree that white people are not.

There is a long history of linking immigration status with entitlement to welfare support. However as a result of the hostility to asylum seekers of the 1990s, further turns of the screw took place (see Patterson 2001 for a detailed account.) A Habitual Residence Test was introduced in the mid-1990s. This required anyone claiming public funds to show that they were habitually resident in the UK. Black people were disproportionately hit by the test.

However, the major changes in relation to exclusion from welfare support came in the sphere of asylum. The Asylum and Immigration Appeals Act (1993) curtailed housing rights for asylum seekers. In 1996 a distinction was made between port asylum seekers (those who claimed asylum immediately at their port of entry) and 'in-country' asylum seekers (those who claimed having been in the country for some period). In-country asylum seekers were excluded from all social security benefits and housing entitlement. Destitution followed as did legal challenges which established that under the National Assistance Act (1948), a classic piece of social democratic welfare legislation, local authorities had a duty to provide accommodation and support, even if only 'in kind'.

The new Labour government's response to this situation was to exclude all asylum seekers from the mainstream welfare benefits system and housing provision, establishing under the Immigration and Asylum Act (1999) a National Asylum Support Service (NASS). NASS has since become infamous among all those who come into contact with it for its gross inefficiency. Initially it provided financial support in the form of vouchers but after a long campaign led by the Transport and General Workers Union, Oxfam and the Refugee Council vouchers were replaced by cash support, albeit still at only 70% of income support levels. NASS is the only agency to which homeless asylum seekers can turn for housing but it offers housing on a 'no choice' basis, forcibly dispersing asylum seekers around the country. This NASS accommodation is sometimes local council housing but more often it is provided under contract by private landlords. Either way it is typically hard to let and quite often in a very bad state of repair. Asylum seekers are not legally tenants and do not have the rights of tenants. NASS, then, was set up to provide an inferior level of welfare support, with asylum seekers separated as far as possible from existing communities of whatever national or ethnic origin. As such it can meaningfully be termed an apartheid service. The development of NASS represents a new move into welfare provision by the Home Office and that is part of the explanation for why NASS is so infamously incompetent.

More significantly, we now have the very government department which exhibits such a 'culture of disbelief' in its examination of asylum and human rights claims, taking responsibility for those people's welfare support. Making NASS support conditional on having an asylum claim or appeal under consideration means that when the claim comes to an end, so does the welfare support (unless the asylum seeker has children). Destitution then becomes a handmaiden to enforcement action (arresting, detaining and removing people from the UK) in getting 'failed' asylum seekers out of the country. But for those who are not coerced into 'voluntary return' in this way, it can be months or years before they are removed, if they ever are. Some nationalities are, as a matter of course, not removed. At the time of writing this was the case for Iraqis and Zimbabweans. People of other nationalities may be fully cooperating with the immigration authorities but still waiting for months or even years in a state of destitution and without the right to work. If they are very unlucky they will be detained. This goes on until the authorities of the country to which the UK wants to remove them confirms whether they are indeed nationals of that country.

Yet this was not enough for the Labour government. Under Section 55 of its next piece of legislation, the Nationality Immigration and Asylum Act (2002), those deemed not to have claimed asylum 'as soon as reasonably practicable' were denied even NASS support. These asylum seekers are thus denied access to mainstream welfare support *and* the apartheid system of NASS *and* are not allowed to work to support themselves; but this time the exclusion takes place at the beginning of their claim and before any decision is made or appeal is heard. I am not the only caseworker to have the experience of an asylum seeker being denied support under Section 55 only to be granted full refugee status a couple of weeks later. By contrast, most asylum seekers denied welfare support face being forced into prolonged destitution for months and occasionally years before their claim is finally determined one way or the other.

Whether Section 55 in its current form is sustainable is an open question. Legal challenges have been made on the grounds that it breaches human rights. Those challenges will be decided, appealed and redetermined one way or the other, although the current judicial consensus appears to be that destitution per se does not breach human rights. The deep hostility to asylum seekers in most of the national press and the political determination of the Labour government to 'crack down' in every conceivable area makes it inevitable that a struggle will continue over these issues. What we need to do here is to look at the contradictions faced by those working in this area and the strategies which are open to us.

Contradictions facing welfare workers: compromise, collaboration and collective resistance

Most of those who work in health, social work, housing provision, education and other 'caring' professions are motivated by a genuine desire to help people and deliver the best service they can. Idealism may be tempered over time by a world weariness or, in extreme cases, by cynicism; but very few people enter such professions with the intention of denying services to vulnerable people, much less kicking them while they are down.

Yet it is a fact that professional workers (as I shall call them), whether state social workers or employees in the voluntary sector, are not free agents bound only by their conscience and the limits of their imagination. Every one of us operates under objective conditions which simultaneously empower and constrain us. These objective conditions are created by the general economic, political and legal situation outlined in Part 1.

In this context, professional workers who come into contact with people subject to immigration control (asylum seekers in particular) face a central dilemma: the thrust of immigration policy and law has been to exclude ever wider numbers of people from mainstream social provision by making entitlement dependent on immigration status rather than any assessment of need. As the tentacles of after-entry (or internal) immigration control have spread, workers involved in service provision have been brought into closer collaboration with the immigration control system. They have been conscripted into becoming immigration officers, and that is true both of the routine clerical workers who have traditionally had little autonomy in any modern bureaucracy to the 'professional workers' who by tradition and training expect to have much greater autonomy.

As entitlement to services has become linked more closely to immigration status, everyone involved in providing those services—from the secretary to the admissions tutor of a further education college to the receptionist of a hospital maternity department—is expected to adopt the gatekeeping role with respect to 'their' patch in much the same way that the immigration officer is the gatekeeper par excellence, guarding the national patch.

What does it mean to be conscripted into becoming an immigration officer? At worst, it means collaborating with immigration officers in their attempts to detain people and remove them from the UK. At best, it means denying a service to those who would otherwise be eligible due to their lack of financial means or due to other identified needs. Let me expand on each with some examples.

Let us look first at collaboration and what it can mean. By collaboration, I do not mean what is fashionably called 'partnership working' between agencies. I mean collaboration in the sense that those who give assistance to the forces which have occupied their country are collaborators. Nazi-occupied Europe (one thinks of France especially) provides the classic historical example; occupied Iraq provides the obvious current example. The collaborator's status as an insider enables him or her to provide information or assistance which strengthens the rule of the occupiers. In the current context, this kind of collaboration consists of gathering information about an individual's immigration status or their whereabouts and then passing it to the Immigration Service in order that they may act against that individual.

No doubt, many welfare workers will be shocked by this analogy. It is not intended to suggest that they are collaborating with fascism or that workers in the Immigration Service are fascists. It is to suggest that the Immigration Service—whatever the attitudes and values of individual officers—has the goal of enforcing immigration controls which are in practice racist. Moreover, whether one agrees that controls are racist or not, enforcement involves the deprivation of liberty from those subject to control, whether through the conditions attached to their permission to remain in the UK or, in extremis, through detention or forced removal.

By contrast the goal of welfare providers should surely be to identify needs and act in the interests of the service user or 'client'. It is not in the interests of the client to be detained or removed and it is, I would argue, a breach of professional duty to open a client up to that possibility by passing information to or collaborating with the Immigration Service. A clear example of this is where someone approaches a state social worker for a service and that person is not only denied the service but has their details passed to the Immigration Service or police to take enforcement action against them. At the very least a social worker can say: 'Let the Immigration Service do their job and I will do mine. My job is to provide a service not act as an immigration officer'. Naturally, a commitment to provide a service whatever the immigration status of the client is the ideal but achieving that will not depend on the individual moral conscience of the social worker (nor on their formal political views) but on the balance of forces within the profession, the local authority and the workplace between those who seek to deny services and collaborate and those who seek to provide and resist collaboration. The existence of legal duties on a local authority will always be cited by management and local politicians for why they must do certain things. In practice, those legal duties are open to some interpretation and whether or how they are complied with will depend on the balance of forces and the strength and nature of political, professional and trade union organisation amongst the social workers.

Now let us look at what is meant by denying a service to those who would otherwise be eligible due to their lack of financial means or due to other identified needs. This has become standard practice in the government departments which administer social security benefits or access to public housing. Application processes are designed to weed out the ineligible by asking questions about immigration status, often triggered by questions about length of time in the UK, or requiring the production of specific documents.

However, exclusion from services takes place in other more complicated ways too. In the sphere of state social work, local authorities have a duty of care to those categorised by the law as 'children in need'. This includes any unaccompanied asylum seekers under the age of 18 who arrive in the UK. However, how a local authority discharges its duties is open to interpretation. Young people under the age of 16 might be placed with foster parents while those who are 16 or 17 have often been transferred to hostel-type accommodation hundreds of miles away from the authority caring for them and the individual social workers who have official responsibility for them.

Another example of exclusion is those who have 'community care' needs unrelated to any destitution. This might include those with disabilities or those with sick children. Local authorities have a duty of care to such people but getting past the gatekeeping systems which declare that your immigration status makes you ineligible for any provision can be a formidable task. In my experience some of those who are eligible to receive a service (accommodation where the rent is paid for by the social services department, for example) have no chance of getting it unless a knowledgeable campaigner or adviser actually goes with them to the relevant office of the local authority and argues on their behalf: firstly, with the front-line worker who has been told to turn them away, and then with the local manager who has the autonomy to make a decision to provide a service or carry out an assessment which the department's internal systems appear to preclude. In some cases, even this is not enough and only a threat by a lawyer to seek a 'Judicial Review' of the local authority's decision will make it budge.

The issue of exclusion is illustrated sharply in the area of healthcare. This area is largely beyond the scope of this chapter but a brief visit illustrates well some of the dilemmas. The National Health Service was set up to provide free healthcare. In principle, that is healthcare provided to all within the borders of Britain, not just to British nationals. For many years, however, that principle has been eroded until we have reached the point where Labour government ministers at the end of 2003 were declaring their intention to get tough with foreign nationals (and asylum seekers of course) who were 'stealing' health provision intended for British nationals. Getting tough meant denying medical treatment to the sick, including those with conditions such as HIV or TB, in all but emergency cases.

This plan was immediately denounced by the British Medical Association, which declared the immorality of refusing to provide medical care to those who were sick. In practice, however, what is likely to happen is an intensification of the current system in hospitals whereby doctors will generally provide treatment if someone is ill while the hospital's administrative systems try to identify who is eligible for free treatment and who is not. The crucial factor in whether someone is able to access treatment is to what extent a gatekeeping system is operated, whether by clerical staff or by medical staff, which seeks to identify the immigration status of a prospective patient and then deem them eligible or ineligible for treatment. In practice, if a doctor undertakes treatment it is unlikely to be withdrawn. But whether a sick person gets to see a doctor or nurse in the first place depends on the approach of medical and administrative staff: how far they are willing or able to adopt the approach that the person in front of them is a human being who is ill and may need treatment, rather than a suspicious character who has the 'wrong' immigration documents and can therefore be left to bleed on the pavement. But this cannot be viewed simply as a choice made by an individual worker guided only by their conscience or principles. It will depend crucially on the balance of forces in a political and ideological struggle waged not only across society as a whole but especially within workplaces such as hospitals, schools, social services departments and so on. This point will be expanded on below.

Analogous to the issue of healthcare provision is that of social care to children 'in need'. One clause of the Asylum and Immigration (Treatment of Claimants) Bill which went through the British Parliament in early 2004 had gained particular notoriety. Under existing law, once a person's asylum claim has been refused by the Home Office and any appeals have been finally dismissed by the legal system, the financial support and accommodation provided by the National Asylum Support Service (NASS) is withdrawn. A dose of destitution is used to encourage such 'failed' asylum seekers to leave the UK voluntarily. However, an exception to this rule is made for any household which includes children under the age of 18. In such cases, NASS support continues until the family in question are actually removed from the UK by the Immigration Service. (Incidentally, migrants these days are rarely 'deported'. They are subject to 'administrative removal', a process which was adopted because it attracts no right of legal appeal.)

Under the new legislation, the presence of children in the household will no longer serve to prevent withdrawal of support and thus enforced destitution. (Remember, asylum seekers have no right to work.) Government ministers in their determination to show their tough credentials were clear what this could mean. Children who are put at risk by the family's destitution could be taken away from their parents and into the care of the state. This proposal caused considerable shock and anger. It is unspeakably inhumane, but even if it becomes law, it is eminently preventable. This is on the condition that the social workers who would be required to remove the child from a destitute asylum-seeking family organise themselves to refuse to do it. Organising collectively, preferably through trade unions, and invoking professional ethics, humanitarian principles and old fashioned solidarity (mix according to taste), they would be in a powerful position to make the policy and practice unworkable.

Initiatives to bring about this kind of resistance in fact began among the members of the Unison public sector union in the city of Leeds shortly after the Bill was published. Various factors will determine whether the initiative builds into successful resistance or peters out. One factor is the presence of activists within the relevant workforce who are able to coalesce the revulsion felt by social workers into a firm resolve to resist. Whether they are able to do that will depend on another factor: the attitude taken by the full-time officials and other caucuses within the relevant trade unions and possibly also professional organisations—in Britain this is the Unison public sector union and the British Association of Social Workers. Successful resistance will be made much easier if the union officials encourage efforts to refuse to take these children away from their parents, or are at least supportive; if they offer meaningful support to any of their members who come under pressure to take these children into care, or face victimisation for refusing to do so. Conversely, if the officials are lukewarm or block the efforts, successful resistance will be harder. The final factor in facilitating success will be the position taken by the elected local political leaders. The policies of social services departments are not only shaped by the law but the political positions adopted by the politicians who run the local council. In most of the British towns and cities where asylum seekers live, the councils are run by the Labour Party, and occasionally by the Liberal Democrats. It is quite possible to envisage a council leadership taking the position that it is not in favour of taking asylum seekers' children into care without much pressure having to be applied. It is also quite possible to envisage the kind of political campaign which could be run to encourage those who dragged their feet, whether through loyalty to 'their' Labour government or the sort of inchoate cowardice dressed up as respect for the law which is not uncommon among some local politicians. In either case the official support of a political leadership would broaden the front of resistance and make it much more difficult for any elements of management who were minded to try to enforce a policy of taking children into care.

Of course, it is true that not everything in the garden is rosy. Already, even before the Bill has become law, those of us working with immigrants and asylum seekers have heard of instances where social workers are offering the option of children being taken into care to families who are being denied welfare benefits. If resistance is not organised quickly, the new policy will be put into practice.

However, even assuming that social workers can successfully resist taking children into care, how do you deal with the original problem of destitution? (Answer: provide support under the provisions of the Children Act, which then brings you into conflict with immigration law.) Another comment frequently made by those familiar with the whole panoply of regressive measures in the Bill is that the assault on children will actually affect very few asylum seekers, even assuming the government chose to pick a fight over that issue. The other measures, such as preventing access to the higher courts, or mandating courts to find an asylum seeker's story 'not credible' because s/he has arrived without a passport, or prosecuting those who arrive without passports, will have a huge and universally detrimental effect on *everyone* who claims asylum. This is true but it misses an important point. If a group of workers could successfully resist the most high profile and noxious part of government policy, it has the potential to encourage other workers to refuse to act as immigration officers and, under the right circumstances, could even be part of changing the general climate of ever-increasing hostility to asylum seekers. Potential is not the same as actual, but the opportunity is there.

The issue of taking children into care is the sharpest expression of the dilemma faced by welfare workers. There are many others which there is no space to detail here. What I want to suggest instead are some principles which welfare workers could apply; or rather which activists could fight for within the profession and the workplace.

1   Immigrants and asylum seekers are human beings and deserve to be treated as such. This appears a banal proposition but if taken seriously it has consequences. Logically, I believe, it should lead to a questioning of immigration control and ultimately its rejection in favour of a human right to cross borders. However, even if one is not prepared to go this far, the principle should operate that while migrants are within a state they should enjoy equal treatment (the same rights and responsibilities would be the favoured Blairite expression). In so far as migrants come into contact with welfare-providing agencies it should be their needs which are assessed not their immigration status.

2   Welfare workers are not responsible for the policy, management or operation of the organisations they work for, state or voluntary. Independent collective organisation of workers is needed. This should not be the sectional and narrow trade unionism which is concerned only with terms and conditions, important though terms and conditions are; nor should it be a form of professionalism which focuses on the needs of service users while ignoring the wider material factors such as resources which constrain how needs can be met, if at all. Instead what is needed is what I shall call 'political trade unionism' which takes up the wider political issues such as the need to resist capitalist globalisation and the scapegoating of asylum seekers while also fighting for better conditions for its members and better services for the public, arguing that they are mutually interdependent.

3   Collective organisation is the only way to create the space within the workplace for workers to question managerial policies and practices which deny vital services to some of the most marginalised ('socially excluded'), even to the point of now threatening to rip children away from their parents.

4   It will not always be possible for an individual worker or team to provide a service because of the material or legal constraints which they face. However, workers should never be expected to act as another enforcement wing of the

Immigration Service. If expected to do so, they must have the support of their trade union in refusing. No-one wants individual victimisations or martyrs.

5   In order to overcome the tendency to view service users as mere victims—a tendency which arises from the professional–client relationship itself—efforts could be made to create solidarity between organisations created by asylum seekers and the organisations of welfare workers. (Any form of wider solidarity would, of course, be excellent.) This interaction would almost certainly take place outside the workplace but any solidarity would be extremely valuable in altering the balance of forces within a profession or a particular workplace in favour of those who seek to resist acting as immigration officers.

These principles are not exhaustive nor can they deal with every tactical issue which arises. A judgement can only be made on the ground about whether something is a necessary compromise or has crossed the line into unacceptable collaboration; and the line will not always be clear.

None the less the establishment or regeneration of this kind of political trade unionism among welfare workers and a simultaneous establishment or regeneration of self-organisation amongst migrants and asylum seekers would be invaluable. Locating this strategy within the creation of a broader and deeper movement against capitalist globalisation, which has the sympathy and increasingly the support of the majority of the world's population, could also serve to increase the confidence of welfare workers and migrants to resist what currently feels like a tidal wave of hostility, inhumanity and increasingly overt racism.

10 Educating for justice: challenges and openings in the context of globalisation[1]

Suzanne Dudziak

Introduction

It began one day in theory class, while discussing oppression in different contexts. I was talking about the anti-globalisation movement and the upcoming Summit of the Americas in Quebec City when one of the students spoke up and asked, 'Why don't we go?' Many reasons against the idea flashed through my mind, mostly related to keeping my job. But why not indeed! It was an opportunity for all of us to walk the talk; for me to test the boundaries between academia and activism and an opportunity for the students to put some theory into practice. And so it evolved over the next 2 months. We formed an affinity group that eventually included 21 people, mostly social work students, two economics students, an education student, a local community worker, a couple from another town and three social work faculty. And so we went to Quebec to live, act and learn together. The experience was profoundly transformative for each of us in different ways. On returning home, it also opened doors to further engagement on the local level.

This chapter explores the links between education and action in the interests of advancing a more committed and integrated social work practice. While educating for social justice is crucial to social work's mandate, it often does not occur in the classroom and even when some consciousness-raising does happen, it often does not lead to an engaged praxis beyond the classroom. This issue could be analysed from different disciplinary perspectives, including educational or psychological theory. My approach to this exploration involves an inductive and reflexive recounting of our experience and from a distinctly socio-political lens. In this regard, it is important to provide a context for situating our particular involvement. Thus, I offer a brief overview of Canada's involvement in facilitating economic globalisation and provide some background to our group before recounting and reflecting on our particular experience.

1 An earlier version of this chapter was published in the Fall 2002 issue of *Critical Social Work* (online at criticalsocialwork.com). I want to extend my thanks to Louis Barry, Jim Christopher, Jane Howard, Kate MacRae and Andrea Thoms, graduates and Quebec participants, for their ongoing comments and reflections on this topic.

The FTAA and the Quebec Summit

The Free Trade Area of the Americas (FTAA) initiative was launched at a first Summit of the Americas held in Miami in 1994. The FTAA proposes to establish free trade among all countries of the Americas, except Cuba, thus creating a regional economic block totalling 34 countries, with a population of 800 million and a combined GNP of US$11 trillion.[2] The FTAA builds on two previous agreements: the Free Trade Agreement (FTA) signed between Canada and the US in 1989 and the North America Free Trade Agreement (NAFTA) created in 1994 by Canada, Mexico and the US. Despite the 'free trade' label, all these agreements advance a global neo-liberal agenda that goes well beyond conventional trade issues to establish new rights for corporations and investors that effectively destroy the public sectors of nation states. For example, under the Chapter 11 of NAFTA, corporations can now sue governments. A number of US corporations have filed successfully for damages over Canadian government policies that allegedly limit their current or future value. As a result, Canadian public policy in the areas of health and the environment has already been seriously compromised. In uniting the economies of the western hemisphere, the FTAA proposes to go even further by negotiating away state-run services, including social services. The purpose of the Americas Summit in Quebec was to review a draft text of the agreement towards negotiating a completed agreement by 2005. Yet typically the text under discussion was not released to the public until *after* the Summit meetings. A major theme of the Quebec Summit to be addressed by government leaders was the issue of 'protecting democracy'. Again, the actions of the Canadian government belied their rhetoric as they sought to limit democratic dissent by erecting a fence 4 kilometres away from the building where the Summit meetings were being held. In erecting the fence, the government inadvertently provided the world with a very powerful symbol of how corporate globalisation operates against the public interest to exclude civil society. The fence itself provoked outrage among people, especially the Quebecois, whose city had been turned into a war zone.

The classroom

I am privileged to teach in a social work department at a small liberal arts university in New Brunswick that attracts students from rural communities all over Atlantic Canada. As they often comment, it is the smallness of the place and the sense of community that helps them to feel at home. Economically, we are situated in a marginalised region of the country, characterised by chronically high rates of unemployment and poverty, which, in turn, has attracted short-term

2   For further information on the Free Trade Area of the Americas and/or the Quebec Summit of the Americas, April 2001, the following websites are useful: **www.StraightGoods.com/FTAA** or **www.canadians.org**

investment by national and foreign capital. In his analysis of globalisation in the region, Workman (2003) states:

> Indeed, Atlantic Canada is a reserve pool of labour for North America, and this has allowed local governments to push for the establishment of call centres and other enterprises that are well known for their lower wages.
>
> (Workmen 2003, pp 105–6)

These conditions are a familiar fact of life for many students in our programme. Thus, the social work curriculum is oriented towards understanding and analysing forms of oppression from structural and other critical perspectives and is committed to social and environmental justice, building on the strengths of maritime communities and cultures.

In locating myself within this discussion, it is important to mention that I am a newcomer to Atlantic Canada and that my identity as a social worker was formed in and through practice rather than through formal education. As a white, middle-class teenager from suburban Toronto, I consciously identified that I wanted to be a social worker although I had known none. Unaware of the profession's code of ethics, I also consciously identified social work with social justice. Moved by conditions of poverty in Toronto's inner city and among Aboriginal peoples, social work meant social justice and so I set about doing it and opted to continue my post-secondary education by learning from those involvements.

After a number of years working in community development, I moved into the wider world of social movements and policy change through involvements with refugees from Chile and Central America. In the mid-1980s, I lived in Nicaragua and worked with peasant communities and the urban trade union movement during a period of revolutionary change. Only after some 20 years of activism did I venture into a faculty of social work and into the profession in a more formal way.

Thus, from my personal and political experience, organising for Quebec felt very familiar to me. However, as a newly minted academic, the challenge lay in doing so from within the institution of the university. For example, the Quebec Summit was planned for the third week in April, a traditional period for final exams in Canadian universities, including our own. Whether students could defer exams without penalty in order to go to Quebec became a public issue across campuses and in the national media. Tellingly, only one university in Canada came out in positive support of students' participation (our sister university in Fredericton, the University of New Brunswick). The administration at my university left the decision to reschedule exams or courses up to individual faculty and the social work department chose to do so.

Moving from the classroom to the street

Our preparation took on many facets. The initial group of interested students felt that it was important to spread the word about the FTAA and so they took responsibility for organising a public forum on campus to learn more about the issues of free trade/fair trade and the social, political and economic aspects of globalisation. This, in turn, attracted new students to the endeavour. Fundraising was an important element that brought in needed financial resources and helped to develop a sense of collectivity. Students sold pop, held bake sales and even made and donated a CD, based on a hip-hop music group they were part of! We also shared the tasks of finding accommodation, and organising food and cars.

In addition to practical tasks, our meetings also involved conscious attention to personal, group and political issues. Using group work skills, we engaged in rounds to facilitate team building, to reflect on our motivations and to process our fears and excitements. This helped several people to decide whether or not they wanted to venture to Quebec; instead, a few people opted to stay in Fredericton and organise solidarity events. In terms of political preparation, several students did some training in non-violence and brought back various exercises to share with the group. Similarly, a few people learned about 'street first aid' while others looked into legal and human rights issues. Several people also took on the task of monitoring the mainstream and alternative media. As a group, we opted to work by consensus so that everyone could voice their concerns and feel comfortable as a participant. We decided that it was important for us to operate on the basis of shared power and talents and to experience a sense of participatory democracy. Identifying important ethics and then finding ways to express them in political terms was an active, ongoing part of our collective process. All this preparation constituted a necessary, rich education in becoming active citizens; many of the students had never been involved politically or attended a demonstration before. Some had not been outside the Atlantic provinces. The energy and enthusiasm evident during the 8 weeks of preparation meant that by the time we arrived at Quebec, we were well on our way to becoming 'a group'.

Living and acting in Quebec

Four days of popular events, called the People's Summit, preceded the official Summit of the Americas and days of action. The People's Summit constituted a massive teach-in organised by non-governmental organisations. We attended workshops non-stop with an amazing array of people from Latin America, Africa and Europe who spoke directly of the impacts that neo-liberal policies were having on the environment and on their communities, as women, as workers and as indigenous peoples.

While it received no media attention, the People's Summit was a key part of the experience for all of us. The students still talk about the direct exposure to the people and the issues as critical for their learning and for deepening their understanding of why they were there. The face-to-face contact with people from other countries helped them to connect the issues in a way that they could relate to and respond. The sheer accessibility to so many people and worlds in one small space was a very powerful contrast to the exclusionary, closed dynamics which govern globalisation by the elites. It also provided an opportunity to feel part of the larger anti-globalisation movement and to meet key leaders, such as Canada's Maude

Barlow, who is Executive Director of the Council of Canadians, an organisation of over 100 000 citizens committed to social and global justice.

The Carnival against Capitalism, convened by groups from Quebec, constituted another important dimension of the current movement—the spirit of resistance expressed in multiple art forms. Alternative films, live music, workshops to produce banners or puppets, drumming, chanting and dancing kept motivations high and allowed for a lot of physical energy to be channelled in creative ways throughout the week. Social action could be fun! The festive atmosphere and the bonds of solidarity created through these popular events before the days of action contradicted the dominant notions of protest constructed by the mainstream media, leaving them, in their words, with no story to report.

Our group had managed to rent a big house outside Quebec City which was able to accommodate everyone, thereby giving us a rare opportunity to live under one roof as a community for that week. Living together became an extremely important dimension of the whole experience because it enabled us to participate in the larger, sometimes chaotic, events from a smaller, more manageable and grounded space. We evolved a practice of having a long evening or morning round together to 'check-in' personally and politically, so that we could reflect on what was happening and determine our next steps.

As a way of connecting with the larger movement, members of our affinity group also attended daily gatherings of a Spokesperson Council, an exercise in participatory democracy among the hundreds of affinity groups present, where information and strategies were shared. Referring to the Quebec Summit, Dinner and Levkoe (2001) reflect on the process and significance of affinity groups for movement building:

> All resistance movements whether they are large or small must be deeply rooted in community and likewise be accountable to those communities. As well, they must be inclusive through processes such as democratically based consensus decision-making. The 'affinity group model' used in recent large scale actions is one way that participants attempt to reach this balance. Through the use of local organization based on needs, issues and trust, the goal is to preserve the grassroots nature of resistance in large scale gatherings. Ideally there is leadership but no leaders. There is strength in diversity. It is an attempt to bring together individuals and groups who share something in common and build something larger: in this case, protest of the Free Trade Area of the Americas and resistance against prioritizing profits and power over people and the environment.
>
> (Dinner and Levkoe 2001, p. 17)

Following the People's Summit, the Canadian state provided another major learning experience during the days of action by means of its overwhelming military presence and its relentless inundation of tear gas. The days of action coincided with the official Summit meeting and began with a torchlight march and vigil 'against the darkness of exploitation'. Other demonstrations and actions occurred in relation to ideological zones that respected a diversity of tactics. Green zones involved more festive activities such as street theatre that were not under any threat of arrest. Yellow zones encompassed defensive, non-violent actions like blocking streets while red zones involved very direct actions such as cutting through the fence, likely to result in injury or arrest by police forces. Blue represented a mobile zone of people who opted to move throughout the crowd providing water, information and other forms of support. However, the security forces, which numbered over 6000 and represented the largest security operation ever assembled in Canada, had little intention of respecting peaceful, democratic protest as they systematically moved into the crowds in yellow and green, as well as red zones with tear gas, water cannons and rubber bullets. The 'excessive and unjustified force' used by police forces was recently condemned in the interim report of the Commission for Public Complaints Against the RCMP (*Daily Gleaner*, 14 November 2003).

At our daily check-in, a sense of profound disillusionment accompanied revolving emotions of fear, anger, guilt, shock and insight. The students questioned what their country was about and simultaneously became citizens in the process since they now had a stake in the outcomes and understood the impacts for themselves and others around the world.

In these moments of discovery, they also encountered a form and forum from which to act. They still speak of the Saturday march, surrounded by military, helicopters overhead, as the 'solidarity of strangers', the odd experience of being with over 60 000 people and feeling utterly 'safe', as one young woman put it recently. Another member of our group recounted her experience in this way:

> ... During this chaos, I noticed something amazing. Unable to see at first, I stumbled away from the group, choking and retching, and I felt someone grab my arm and guide me slowly but steadily to clearer air. I assumed it was one of my group. They had me kneel down so they could flush my eyes with water. They soaked my bandanna in lemon juice, which helps counteract the gas. When I could see, I looked into the eyes of a concerned stranger. He spoke French and asked if I was ok. I nodded and he moved on to help someone else. I grabbed water, lemon juice, and wipes from my backpack and began helping people who stumbled by. Everywhere I looked people were helping people—urging them not to panic, flushing out their eyes, taking them to safe places, and then returning, despite the burning fumes, to help someone else. It didn't matter whether you were white, brown, yellow, black or red. It didn't matter whether you were female, male, heterosexual, homosexual, young, old, transgendered, anglophone or francophone. We were the people for the people and the feeling of belonging and solidarity and justice permeated the crowd ...

Like the term 'oppression', 'solidarity' is now more than a concept; it has become a significant and personally meaningful part of the vocabulary through which they express their lives.

Returning home

Quebec was not the end of the experience though. On returning home, many members of our group felt a deep sense of alienation that they were unprepared for. In anticipation of going home we had talked about 're-entry into the ordinary' from the extraordinary, about moving from the big world back into our small worlds, and about leaving the group and being on our own again. What we didn't anticipate was the void so many would experience when friends, parents or significant others refused to listen to their stories or be there for them in a supportive way as they tried to make sense of the whole experience. However each experienced it, the distance seemed too great to bridge. In my view, this is a dangerous moment when initial enthusiasm and insight can give way to becoming cynical and thus, giving up. As a result, we continued to meet and to debrief as a group which proved to be a turning point. In the safety of the group, people were able to process their feelings, finding ways to straddle both worlds until they could integrate their experience into everyday life.

From the global to the local

In the aftermath of Quebec, we remained loosely connected as a group. Most of the students engaged in some form of public speaking. A number of articles were published in student newspapers. Some of us presented together at academic conferences, including a national social work conference. Others came together with some concerned parents to meet local politicians to demand further investigation and information. A number of students became politically active in new groups which formed as a result of the Quebec Summit.

As the question of creating meaningful, local action continued to circulate around the group, some of the social work students engaged in some serious research about fair trade practices over the summer and during the following semester, they decided to initiate a fair trade coffee shop on campus. Instead of viewing social action as an extracurricular activity, we were able to integrate their initiative as part of a learning process through an independent study course. Honing their political and organisational skills, they gathered support from faculty and student groups and successfully negotiated with the administration and the company controlling food services on campus to provide choice by establishing a fair trade alternative that supports local producers in Mexico, Guatemala, Nova Scotia and Fredericton. The café is a modest but enduring effort that acts as a catalyst for ongoing education and action by students on globalisation and positive, viable alternatives. For example, members of the Fair Trade Society are currently preparing to hold a 'No Sweat' fashion show on campus.

Challenges and openings

These students were fortunate. They took the risk to discover what they had taken for granted. And in the process they discovered what it meant to be a citizen and something of how precious and fragile democracy is. Ironically and perhaps most instructively, they did so at the very moment when their rights were being most threatened and violated. By their actions since then, they continue to demonstrate how important it to exercise democracy, to participate actively or to lose that space to forces which do not act in the interests of the people we are most concerned with as social workers. On discovering their voices, many of them have gained a new confidence, a sense of their responsibility as young adults and 'social' workers and an ability to connect their learning now to experiences in the workplace. As an instructor and a practitioner, this experience of acting/learning together raises a series of questions which I wish to pose as challenges and from which I also see openings that have transformative potential for a more engaged praxis as a profession.

Citizen social worker

The first question that arises for me out of this experience is: can we have an identity as professional social workers without a deep understanding of ourselves as citizens? We work hard to shape a professional identity, we encourage self-reflexivity and reflection along with critical analysis, but why do we stop short of that sphere that belongs to the political? If our mandate is social justice, then the polis or the 'political' in all its myriad meanings is already present. Yet as a profession not only do we not embrace the polis, we seem to work very hard to avoid it. Much social work in Canada seems to work out of an imagined and idealised space of 'neutrality'. It is as if we think it is possible to bring about social change without action on its behalf. Such action is necessarily political. Yet it seems we prefer to disassociate the social from the political, if that is possible.

Smith (1996) states that 'politics is the act of generating a public realm through which the world appears' (p. 256). Only by acting in the world can a public space exist. In this light, Quebec afforded us a tremendous opportunity to become a public. And I learned from the students that the political, the act of generating a public realm, became possible in the first instance through the social, that is, through the connections they made with speakers at the people's summit. However, unlike most consciousness-raising endeavours inside or outside the classroom, we were then offered a second moment to give voice to that learning through expressive action in the political realm. A bridge was created between the social and the political that enabled us to continue learning and acting in a way that felt natural and consistent, as well as new, different and challenging for many in our group.

Healy K (2001) points out that much critical theory in the form of social structural analysis remains disconnected from the institutional and interpersonal dimensions of critical practice. The Quebec experience is insightful on both counts. In moving from the social to the political, students were willing to enter that disjuncture both physically and emotionally in order to act on their moral and intellectual convictions. In doing so, they were willing to face conflict in all its social manifestations—political, personal and interpersonal—before, during and since Quebec. It is my view that a major stumbling block to living out a critical praxis lies precisely in a fear of conflict that manifests itself interpersonally among classmates or colleagues, in the workplace and other spaces of the everyday. The social construction of 'critical' as 'negative', which is seen to lead inevitably to 'conflict' in practice, serves to reinforce a dominant self-image in the profession as 'positive' and 'caring' helpers, peacemakers and problem-solvers. An acceptance and understanding of conflict, on the other hand, as a complex human dynamic and part of the reality of an unjust world can open avenues for constructing new social relations. While none of us from the Quebec experience would profess to feel comfortable with conflict, I believe most of us could say that our continuous processing of it has made us less afraid of it and thus, more able to act in the everyday, on behalf of clients, challenging institutional practices. Some are currently engaged in strike action. Similarly, associations of 'confrontation' and 'anger' with ' negative' or 'harmful' also need to be deconstructed, contextualised and processed in relation to both critical theory and practice if we are to move more freely from the social to the political.

Another learning from Quebec concerns the relationship between power and knowledge. Dynamics of knowing are deeply implicated in our willingness to engage in the political or public realm. In terms of globalisation, while we all felt a need to become more informed and enthusiastically engaged in learning more, none of us felt the need 'to know it all' before we were able to act. This challenges conventional discourses about 'professional' and 'the expert'. From a post-modern viewpoint, partial knowing that is grounded in clearly articulated values can and should be a sufficient basis from which to act our way into further knowing. This is the basis upon which democracy was legitimated in the first place: a well-informed public of ordinary citizens able to make decisions for the collective well-being. In this light, social workers have immense formal as well as experiential knowledge from the front lines on which to ground claims to justice in terms of healthcare, services, our jobs, our neighbourhoods, the environment, etc. Yet rarely will social workers see themselves as powerful and useful participants in civil society if notions of citizenship are not incorporated into the very fabric of what it means to be a professional social worker. The issue of the professional as citizen receives little attention in most social work textbooks, beyond exhortations to vote in elections. Some critical social work theorists, however, have begun to conceptualise what citizenship might mean in the current context (Drover 2000; McGrath et al. 1999a; Mullaly 1997).

Social work at a crossroads

A second and related challenge concerns both our past origins as a profession and the question of our future existence. In my view, globalisation calls that future into question in a very stark way. Social work was born as a discipline in the wake of the industrial revolution and the subsequent development of welfare states, as a compromise between unbridled capitalism and democracy. It is important to recall the insight of C.B. Macpherson (1962) that liberalism predated democracy in the West and that as an ideology, liberalism as 'possessive individualism' has sustained, complemented and legitimated the interests of capital in uneasy relation to the public good. As the welfare state is dismantled in the interests of capital in a new stage of technological development and expansionism globally, I think it is becoming increasingly clear that the compromise has come to an end. Thus, the dominant model of social work practice built on state-funded social services in the last half of the twentieth century has been called into jeopardy in a fundamental way. Our dependency as a profession on the welfare state raises serious questions about our future as a profession; I ask myself that question in the classroom as I teach the welfare state as 'a phase of history' that no longer guarantees any form of collective social well-being. It forces me to question what I am preparing students for. The recent past is not the world that future social workers will be practising in.

So what are the alternatives? Where are the openings? My responses are not new but perhaps take on new meaning in the context of globalisation. For responses, I have learned to look to the margins. I look to places like Nicaragua, for example, where capitalist regimes were too greedy to allow the development of a welfare state in the first place and where the state has been content to repress any attempt to change that condition. There, in the midst of sweatshops and free trade zones, people survive by necessity on what de Tocqueville in the nineteenth century called 'the art of associating': strong, complex, familial, neighbourhood and community-based social networks, some of which are becoming more formalised as organisations of civil society (de Tocqueville 2001). Although not reliant on the state, these networks both resist and challenge the state to address basic needs of its citizens. They also challenge the power of the institutions of globalisation like the IMF or the WTO to control their destiny.

Reconstituting the polis through grassroot participation at a community and public level is the role of civil society. In his analysis of globalisation, Nicanor Perlas (2000), a leading activist and thinker in the Philippines, writes convincingly of the distinct role that global civil society can play in 'securing the cultural spaces of the world' in order to preserve or restore (my addition) 'the delicate balance between the cultural, political and economic needs of countries' (p. 239).

Creating community

In advanced capitalist contexts, Smith (1996) proposes that 'social work itself must go through a major shift' from what he calls a 'social welfare to a community building mode' (p. 262). From a slightly different perspective than Perlas, Smith states:

> I would argue that social work institutions have often forgotten their community origins and have taken on the rational, bureaucratic ways of second wave institutions. The schools mimic the medical and legal professions. The agencies, whether public or private, are clones of bureaucratic government or corporation. It is far from clear whether existing social work institutions

can shift their paradigm and practice, or whether new institutions will need to be invented to meet the challenges of the information age.

(Smith 1996, p. 263)

Yet similar to Perlas, Smith directs our attention to the importance of 'relationships and culture over programs and organizations' adding that 'without culture, there is no community' and 'no democracy' (pp 263–4). He offers this way forward:

> I believe it is extremely important for the schools of social work to rediscover their local community base, recognizing themselves as institutional players in a specific social order and rediscovering that learning takes place through experience. Let the schools acknowledge that to become a social worker is to take part in community building efforts, first as an apprentice, then as a master . . ..The challenge is to be part of the action – locally and internationally.

(Smith 1996, p. 264)

This is precisely the opening that the Quebec Summit afforded our school and why it has become such an enduring experience for the students and myself. It continues to provide a living environment where we can all apprentice inside and outside the classroom. The creation of community is central to this project. In our case, the social relations of teacher/student were transformed in the process of becoming an affinity group where we came to know each other differently in an encounter with our physical, emotional and intellectual interdependence. That interdependence was reiterated in our encounter with other affinity groups and with presenters from around the globe at the People's Summit and yet again, in our acting together as adult learners and citizens and thus, 'social' workers. Community building and group development thus play a pivotal mediating role that can facilitate micro–macro connections across difference and solidarity (Leonard 1997). I believe that if we shifted our thinking, we could see many such possibilities in the different contexts in which we are located, precisely because the effects of economic globalisation are everywhere.

Connecting communities globally

A third and related challenge is to recognise that our interdependence is not simply confined to the local. In this sense, the often-constructed ideal of totally self-reliant communities is deeply flawed (Labonte 1997). Such notions of 'community' have been propagated in neo-liberal discourse to justify the dismantling of the welfare state. Operating in binary fashion, the state's responsibility for social welfare is reframed as creating dependency which then justifies notions of self-reliance in the form of unpaid, voluntary, community care independent of the state. Interdependence, as an alternative to the dependent/independent dichotomy, highlights the importance of community in its ongoing relatedness to the state and civil society. McGrath et al. (1999b) observe:

It is important not to embrace 'community' as a solution to counter the state's failure to meet its social obligations adequately. It is the function of the state to provide equitable access to health, education, and employment programs, protection in times of economic hardship, and the maintenance and enforcement of human rights. The third sector or civil society is not a replacement for the state but a mechanism to influence the form of the state and the market . . . (Community) is thus an important political arena where needs are identified and claims articulated, in short where citizenship can be exercised and developed.

(McGrath et al. 1999b, pp 17–18, 19)

Such an understanding of community as mediating between personal life and state activity takes on new meaning in the context of economic globalisation (McGrath et al. 1999b, p. 19). Anti-globalisation activists recognise that interdependence has a material as well as a socio-cultural foundation. They make the connection that there is hardly anything we eat or wear or do these days that does not reflect the reality that our survival and well-being depends on global interdependence. It is my experience with students that this concern is taken to heart in terms of a personal ethics which then connects to a sense of political responsibility and the need to act in order to be congruent with one's values. This ethical motivation is what prompted most of our students to go to Quebec in the first place and what seems to motivate their ongoing commitments to doing social justice work.

While large-scale events like Quebec provide a forum for connecting globally, ongoing solidarity at local levels provides a third challenge and opening. At first glimpse, transforming global relations is sometimes perceived as a daunting, overwhelming prospect. The sheer complexity of the issues suggests that no one strategy will suffice. Viewed from this perspective, work at the community level can be seen as a viable option. At this historical moment, however, I believe that such efforts will only be successful if they are linked to other community efforts in relations of mutual solidarity. Conceived of as particular communities connected to other particular communities, the global can become meaningful on a human and just scale. Concretely, schools of social work can develop and facilitate relationships between their local communities and communities across the globe, sharing experiences and strategies across schools and continents. Through pursuing this specific idea or other 'polis-making' experiments (Smith 1996), I believe a very different conception and practice of social work could emerge.

Conclusion

As I continue to reflect on the meaning of the Quebec experience for myself as a teacher and a practitioner, challenges and openings continue to reveal themselves. In this chapter I have discussed three such emergent issues. The first concerns the need to reconnect notions of the political with the social; to this end I have suggested the importance of integrating citizenship into our notions of professionalism as social workers. Secondly, in the context of economic globalisation and the question of our future existence as a profession, I have identified the centrality of creating community as a vehicle for mediating, resisting and transforming micro–macro relations. Lastly, in challenging the myth of self-reliance, I have posed the possibility of a situated praxis that links communities in solidarity as one strategy for attending to both the global and the local. At this crossroads, perhaps what is required most is a shift in consciousness. Smith (1996) issues this call:

> Let social workers, supported by schools of social work, attend to the civil society without which the economy will be neither just nor inclusive and without which democracy will be shallow and monotonous. There is a future to politics. There is a future to social work. These futures converge in efforts to support the civil sector locally and internationally.
>
> (Smith 1996, p. 265)

In my view, the challenge for social work in this era of globalisation will be about seeing and anticipating the global in the local and connecting to the local ever present in the global.

Part 3

Mapping a way forward?

11 American exceptionalism and critical social work: a retrospective and prospective analysis

Michael Reisch

Introduction

Recent statements by the leading professional social work organisations in the United States—the National Association of Social Workers (NASW) and the Council on Social Work Education (CSWE)—emphasising an ethical imperative to work for social justice, create the false impression that social work in the US has taken a distinctly radical turn at the start of the twenty-first century. Yet, critical or radical social work in the United States has less influence today than it did a generation ago.[1] Those who emphasise its failures blame multiple factors. These include the lack of class consciousness in US society; persistent cultural myths about economic opportunity, political pluralism, individualism, and materialism; the backlash against immigration from developing countries; fears surrounding the increasingly multicultural nature of US society; and the conservative impact of professionalism. Nevertheless, critical social work can still serve as a conceptual framework or vehicle that will contribute to efforts to resist contemporary political–economic developments such as globalisation.

This can occur in two ways. Critical social work challenges conventional assumptions about poverty, race, and gender, and the basic functions of a market-driven political–economic system. In addition, critical social work heightens awareness of the historical and contemporary relationship between social justice and social struggle. Yet, several important issues about critical social work in the US remain to be resolved. One is the ongoing tension among its proponents as to the societal contradictions (class, race, gender, sexual orientation) that should be its primary focus. A second issue involves the future viability of critical social work in a world dominated by market mechanisms and market-driven ideologies. A related theme is the suppression of critical social work ideas by mainstream institutions, including the social work profession, which involves the relationship between critical social work and the demands of professionalisation within a globalised capitalist political–economic system.

---

1 In this chapter 'radical' and 'critical' social work will be used interchangeably, despite their somewhat different connotations.

The neglect of the radical tradition in American social work

Differences between the social welfare systems of the United States and other industrialised nations are usually explained by 'American exceptionalism' (Gilbert 1983; Jansson 2003). Yet, many principles that US society now takes for granted, such as legal entitlements to social benefits, client self-determination and empowerment, the role of the environment in creating personal problems, and the essential dignity of all human beings, were introduced by proponents of critical social work. This forgotten history is, in part, the result of persistent confusion over the meaning of critical or radical social work in the United States (Reisch and Andrews 2001).

Longres (1996) argues, however, that the underlying principles of critical social work have remained constant: (1) an emphasis on the institutional structure of society as the primary source of clients' personal problems; (2) a focus on economic inequality; (3) a view of social service agencies as instruments of social control, co-optation, or stigmatisation; (4) a focus on both structural and internalised oppression; and (5) a linkage of private troubles and public issues. In recent years, US social workers have largely avoided issues of social class in favour of analyses that highlight the roles of gender, race, ethnicity, sexual orientation and, to a lesser extent, age and physical disability (Abramovitz 1999; Carlton-Laney and Burwell 1996; Iglehart and Becerra 1995; van den Bergh, 1995).

The emergence of radical social work in the United States

Ironically, radical or critical social work in the US did not emerge as an explicit framework for practice until the 1930s, after social work had become established as an organised occupation (Fisher 1936, 1990; Reisch 1998; Wenocur and Reisch, 1989). Prior to that period, radicals in the social work field reflected the influence of a variety of religious and secular utopian philosophies of the nineteenth century such as transcendentalism, Marxism, and Christian Socialism. They were closely involved with the diverse social movements of the period, including radical trade unionism, 'first wave' feminism, and religiously based pacifism (Addams 1910; Harkavy and Puckett 1994; Sklar 1995; Wald, 1915). Their ideas shaped the evolution of social work research, perspectives on women's role in society and, by substituting the concept of mutuality for charity, on the helping process itself (Dewey 1935; Harkavy and Puckett 1994; Konopka 1958, p. 90; Lovejoy 1912, p. 394; Lowe and Reisch 1998). The appearance of an explicitly radical social work in the 1930s coincided with the emergence of the first radical social work organisation, the Rank and File Movement, the creation of left-wing social work unions in the public and non-profit sectors and the involvement of social workers in the Socialist and Communist parties.

The influence of socialism on radical social work

While some radical social workers, like Florence Kelley and Lillian Wald, were Socialists, few were influenced by Marxism. Yet, the intellectual forces behind both reformist and radical progressivism and the radical ideology of the Social Gospel movement—Dewey, Marx, Henry George, Lester Ward and, later, Sigmund Freud—shared aspects of the socialist utopian vision. They acknowledged the existence of classes but did not embrace the idea of class conflict, preferring a combination of evolutionary socialism and early maternalist-oriented feminism. The imprecision of their vocabulary led both the general public and other professionals to confuse 'social work, sociology, and socialism', a confusion that frequently persists today (Brackett 1909; Shoemaker 1998; Sklar 1995; Woloch 1984).

By the mid-1890s, these tensions shaped the development of the ideology and goals of the nascent social work profession (Gettleman 1963; Kusmer 1973). As early as 1896, Mary Richmond, one of the leaders of the Charities Organization Societies (COS), argued that professionalisation could deflect the appeal of socialism and transform social service work without dramatically restructuring society and its institutions. Professionalisation, in her words, was the route 'between the . . . Scylla of an old fogy conservatism, and the . . . Charybdis of . . . socialism.' (1896, p. 59).

In response, critical social work took several forms in the US at the turn of the twentieth century. For the first time, radical social workers applied social science to the analysis of social conditions *with the specific intention* of ameliorating the plight of economically disadvantaged populations. They became directly involved in the political arena, a particularly treacherous field for women and radicals in the late nineteenth century (Chambers 1963, 1986; Davis 1964). Through their work with unions and feminist organisations, they linked radical ideas and social action. In effect, they provided an alternative solution to the violent class warfare that was sweeping the country and much of the industrialised world (Sklar 1991).

Prior to World War I, urban settlement houses served as the primary organisational vehicle for such activities. Although more often reformist than radical in their orientation, their values, goals, and accomplishments represented a threat to traditional charitable institutions (Addams 1902, pp 19–20). A 1901 editorial in the mainstream COS organ, *Charities*, pondered: 'Is there any stopping place in following out [such] principle[s], short of socialism?' (*Charities Organization Society* 1901, pp 420–1). Proponents of early forms of critical social work promoted feminist causes, such as suffrage, and demanded new roles for women in the occupational and political spheres. Through collaborative efforts on issues like suffrage, child labour, and industrial working conditions, they helped women develop a common political vocabulary and 'encouraged new ways of thinking and acting' (Evans 1989, p. 149). They joined with well-known radicals like Crystal Eastman and Emma Goldman on a variety of causes, including prostitution and white slavery.

Spurred by the efforts of African American women, white radical social workers of the period worked through such organisations as the YWCA's Committee on Inter-Racial Cooperation, the Methodist Women's Missionary Societies, and the Association of Southern Women for the Prevention of Lynching to combat lynching in the South, helped create the NAACP (1909) and the National Urban League (1911), and served as delegates to the 1921 Pan-African Congress held in London, Brussels, and Paris under the leadership of W.E.B. DuBois (Chafe 1977). Perhaps of greatest significance, they actively opposed American militarism and jingoism, particularly US entry into World War I. Their anti-war views emerged from two different sources, Quaker religious values and socialist ideals, and widened the gap between them and their liberal colleagues inside and outside the new and insecure profession (Addams 1907; Sklar 1995; Wald 1915). Yet, these class, gender, and race-bridging efforts provided the foundation for the future emergence of the US welfare state by 'serv[ing] as a surrogate for working class social-welfare activism' and 'an entering wedge for the extension of state responsibility to wage-earning men and to other aspects of women's lives' (Sklar 1993, pp 44, 50).

At this time, the introduction of Freudian and Rankian psychology reflected a different form of radical challenge to prevailing theories of human behaviour. These ideas were particularly attractive to radical social workers from the early 1920s through to at least the 1950s. For example, Bertha Reynolds tried to synthesise Marxism and Freudian and Rankian psychology into a revolutionary model of social work practice. Like many other intellectuals and activists of her generation, Reynolds found in Marxism an explanation of social conditions that complemented the 'philosophy of growth' she had expounded as the basis for social work practice since the 1920s (Reynolds 1938, 1963, p. 184). Decades before most of her colleagues, she recognised the mutuality of worker and client interests in the support of social reforms. In her words, social service work could 'free men from the crippling accumulations of fear and hate so that they may have energy to use what intelligence they possess . . . [to work for] . . . a better social order' (Reynolds 1934, p. 27). In this way, the foundation of critical social work theory and practice in the 1970s and 1980s began to emerge nearly a half century earlier.

The Rank and File Movement

During the Great Depression of the 1930s a radical 'Rank and File Movement' created an organised, collective voice for these ideas (Fisher 1936; Spano 1982; Wenocur and Reisch 1989). The movement's strength, however, came from the power of its members' personal experiences, rather than its theoretical analysis. As did many other urban intellectuals and professionals at the time, Rank and Filers embraced Marxism because it appeared to offer the most cogent and comprehensive explanation of the conditions they observed in their daily practice (Reynolds 1963). Their analysis challenged the concept of social work as a profession and undermined prevailing frameworks of social work practice. Unlike their mainstream colleagues, the Rank and File Movement identified with clients, used tactics such as strikes and boycotts, and displayed open sympathy for allied left-wing causes (Karger 1988). Its leaders played key roles in organised labour and in Popular Front organisations that were affiliated with the Communist Party.

During this period, the Functional School of Social Work, developed at the University of Pennsylvania, provided radical social workers, especially those in the public social services, with a practice paradigm that justified social action and the recognition of the mutuality of the worker–client relationship (Lewis 1966). Although its chief proponents, Jessie Taft and Virginia Robinson, were not radicals, they made several important contributions to critical social work practice theory. They rejected Freudian determinism and emphasised the centrality of the human will and process. They articulated a dynamic view of the human condition, society, and the worker–client relationship that reflected the world-view of many radical social workers (Dore 1990; Lewis 1966; Robinson 1937; Taft 1939).

McCarthyism and critical social work

After World War II, the sharp rightward swing in the US, often labelled McCarthyism, 'silenced those voices that might have raised the issues of poverty and unemployment without blaming the victim' (Schrecker 1998, p. 386). US social workers largely retreated into professionalism, which simultaneously denied the existence of class divisions within society while rewarding a particular occupation for its specific expertise. By reducing clients' control over services, professionalisation directly contradicted the democratic ideal that had guided the field for decades and obscured the effects of the political climate.

Critical social work flourished again briefly during the 1960s largely through the more experimental aspects of the federal 'War on Poverty,' such as Mobilization for Youth in New York City and other urban community action programmes, groups like the National Welfare Rights Organization, and a few social work-focused collectives, often based in schools of social work. The influence of these developments went beyond the numbers of individuals involved. By the late 1960s, all of the major social work organisations had embraced the concept of social action, particularly on behalf of poor and disadvantaged populations, as 'the business of social work.' NASW's bylaws changed to reflect social workers' obligation to use 'both social work methods . . . and social action.' (Note, however, how social action was still considered an ancillary function rather than integral to social work practice.) Long-standing social service agencies, such as the Community Service Society in New York, temporarily discontinued casework to focus on the 'pathology of the ghetto' rather than the individual problems of its inhabitants. Yet, most social workers continued to reject both radical goals and tactics, preferring roles and strategies that operated well within mainstream guidelines and that could be controlled by professionals such as legislative advocacy, community-based social planning, advocacy, and coalition-building (Brody 1969; Cohen 1966; Kurzman and Solomon 1970; Sanders 1964).

The social change orientation of the 1960s also influenced the development of social work practice methods. Spurred by criticism from organisers outside the profession like Saul Alinsky (1969), client groups, and radicals within the profession itself (Franklin 1990), the field of community organising, recognised as a social work method since the 1930s, began to acquire a renewed focus on social action. Some intellectual leaders of the profession found precedents for this development in the values of radical social workers from the 1930s and 1940s.

As the political climate became increasingly conservative during the 1970s and 1980s, radical social workers linked the rise and fall of social spending to broader political–economic motives and argued that social action, not government benevolence, had produced the modest reforms of the recent past (Abramovitz 1992; Danziger 1991; Lemann 1989; Katz 1989; Keisling 1984; Murray 1984; Piven and Cloward 1995; Quadagno 1994). The evolution of critical social work in the US at the end of the twentieth century must be seen in light of these analyses.

The emergence of social movements within the profession based on race, gender, and sexual orientation altered the nature of radical social work during the post-1960s period. These changes simultaneously broadened the scope of radicalism within the field and divided the radical wing of the profession. Ironically, so-called 'identity politics' ultimately moved critical social workers into new and important arenas of social and ideological debate while limiting the possibility of lasting radical change within the profession and the political environment.

At the outset, 'second wave feminist' social workers did not directly formulate radical feminist social work theory. Operating from assumptions that challenged prevailing conceptual frameworks, they soon challenged the unequal distribution of power, status, and income within the profession and pointed out sexist gaps in the presentation of social work history (Hooyman and Bricker-Jenkins 1984; Nes and Iadicola 1989; van den Bergh and Cooper 1986; Weick and Vandiver 1982). Much of their early work, however, was not specifically radical in its orientation. It focused instead on analysing and responding to the special problems of women and resulted in the creation of much-needed community-based services such as battered women's shelters, women's health centres, programmes for displaced homemakers, and alternatives to traditional counselling. These were often services primarily for white, middle-class women, rather than low-income clients or women of colour (Abramovitz 1999). One positive consequence of this activism, however, was that formerly radical issues became incorporated into the liberal agendas of mainstream social work organisations.

By the 1980s, feminist social workers had introduced and popularised such influential themes as empowerment, the importance of identifying and overcoming oppression, the role of group process, an emphasis on consciousness-raising and self-help, an attack on patriarchy, and increased attention to non-rational ways of knowing and depicting the world (Morell 1987; Withorn 1984). The latter helped make social workers increasingly receptive to post-modern theory in the 1990s (Sands and Nuccio 1992).

At the same time, other radical intellectuals in the social work field made concerted efforts to define critical social work theory and practice. It is largely through their contributions that radical social workers in the US continue to have some influence abroad. Many of their ideas, however, were derived from international sources, such as the UK, Canada, France, The Netherlands, and Latin America (Bailey and Brake 1975; Corrigan and Leonard 1978; Freire 1970). Much of the literature that emerged was also influenced by Marxist or neo-Marxist ideas, often under new labels like structural social work (Moreau 1978).[2] Ideas that prefigured the post-modern approaches of the 1980s and 1990s also began to appear at this time.

Martin Rein (1970) was one of the first social workers to attempt a synthesis of radical social work concepts. He defined radical social work in terms of four basic components: resistance to practice norms and standards; a commitment to the redistribution of societal resources and power; the reduction or elimination of economic and social inequalities; and the altering of social/structural conditions. Yet, Rein did not equate radicalism with any particular ideology. Instead, he conceived of radicalism as a sustained commitment to a set of critical policy and practice principles that linked social work practice with political action.

In a similar vein, Philip Lichtenberg did not connect radical social work with a specific, that is, class-bound, analysis of socio-economic conditions (1976, 1980, 1990). Instead, he linked the issue of social struggle with the identification and overcoming of *all forms* of societal oppression. He argued that 'the radical thrust or potential in casework appears to stem from the very nature of the tasks to which the field addresses itself,' that is through its focus on systemic or structural change. This became a central tenet of social work radicals during the next three decades, particularly among women, persons of colour, and gays and lesbians. While broadening the potential scope of radical social work, however, it fragmented the previously unified, largely class-based conception of radicalism in the field and made the formation of radical coalitions more difficult to develop and sustain.

Other US social workers during this period, whom Daphne Statham (1978) called 'liberal radicals,' challenged existing institutional arrangements through legitimate means (Blau 1992; personal communication). Among their tactics was a form of institutional insurgency to humanise social policies and bureaucratic procedures (Needleman and Needleman 1974). Some of them were influenced by the liberal philosopher John Rawls (1971) and regarded the principles of justice that he articulated as counterweights to the ideological status quo (Lewis 1972). Paradoxically, they also adopted social action strategies, including social conflict approaches, that operated outside conventional political channels but not usually outside the law while directing their efforts at systemic or structural transformation (Epstein 1970). According to Gil (1976), they sought the peaceful replacement of both the existing political–economic system and the values upon which it was founded.

Other critical social workers, whom Wagner (1989) termed 'militant radicals,' defined their ideology in more clearly anti-capitalist terms. For example, Norman

---

2 In fact, the term 'critical social work' first entered the US social work vocabulary during their period.

Goroff (n.d.), a leader in the group work field, described the ultimate aim of radical practice as 'a radical transformation . . . to replace a competitive, alienating and alienated society, which because it is capitalist, exploitive, individualistic and hierarchically structured developes [sic] grossly unequal life chances for its citizens, with a society based on cooperation, egalitarianism and non-exploitive relationships, where production of goods and services are for use and not intended solely for profit' (p. 1). Jeffry Galper (1975, 1980) was even more explicit. He defined radical social work as practice 'that contributes to building a movement for the transformation to socialism by its efforts in and through the social services.' In Galper's words, '*Radical social work . . . is socialist social work*' (1980, p. 10, emphasis added).

Robert Knickmeyer (1972) and John Longres (1977, 1986) also adopted an explicitly Marxist analysis. Knickmeyer identified three primary distinctions of Marxist-oriented social service. First, it regarded social welfare as an expression of the hegemonic forces in society. Second, it involved face-to-face contact between workers and clients without the mediation of official channels of communication and contact. Third, it considered the agency and not the legislature as a primary focus of political struggle (Knickmeyer 1972).

Longres asserted that radical social casework 'encourage[s] social, political and economic change . . . consonant with a Marxist social vision. [It] promotes the ideals of socialism as an alternative and works toward the alleviation of the conditions of alienation' (1977). He deduced four practice principles from Marxist theory. These focused on the centrality of the concept of alienation, the importance of analysing practice from a working class perspective, the use of social work intervention to eliminate alienation, and the importance of 'promot[ing] class consciousness and the pursuit of collective interests' (1982, p. 27).

The debate over professionalism

Leading critical social workers of the 1970s, such as Frances Piven and Richard Cloward (1975) and Ann Withorn (1976, 1984), regarded deprofessionalisation as a precondition for a truly radical social work practice. Withorn asserted that the concept of professionalism itself was based on capitalist premises about work and social status. Their work stimulated a debate among radical social workers between those who regarded social workers as mere agents of control and those who viewed social workers as advocates who could potentially help clients develop their own power (Wagner 1990). This debate enabled some radicals to rationalise working within the system through their efforts to radicalise social service organisations and thereby improve services to low income and oppressed groups (Needleman and Needleman 1974). The inherent contradictions in this perspective spurred frequent debates among US social workers. Many of those who adopted the latter perspective embraced an empowerment approach to practice that continues to influence the profession to this day (Gutierrez et al. 1998). The ongoing struggle over these different conceptions of the social work role resembled the intra-professional conflicts of the 1930s and occurred within educational institutions as well as the practice arena.

In sum, two contrasting analyses appeared among critical social workers in the late twentieth century. Some US radicals regarded, albeit to different degrees, the organisational and theoretical structure of professional social work itself as an impediment to the creation of a truly radical practice. Other self-described radical social workers in the US did not see a direct contradiction between professionalism and so-called transformative practice (Knickmeyer 1972; Longres 1986; Lewis 1982; Needleman and Needleman 1974). For the former group, critical or radical social work involved several critical elements: a decentralised, non-hierarchical, collective practice based on worker–client mutuality and power sharing; unionisation rather than professionalisation; a focus on community-based practice and politics; and the decentralisation and democratisation of social service work (Brake and Bailey 1980).

Goroff's model of critical social work contained four central components—care; responsibility; respect; and knowledge—which reflected the writings of Bertha Reynolds two generations earlier. Thomas Keefe's work on alienation adopted a similar line of analysis from an explicitly materialist perspective (1984). Arline Prigoff (1987), a long-time radical who was active in the 1980s around issues of peace and US intervention in Central America, focused on broadening the widely used framework of systems analysis to include class structure as a major feature. By incorporating Third World perspectives, such as those of Franz Fanon, into practice models, she argued that social workers could 'intervene in behalf of empowerment and liberation at a variety of levels' (p. 9). For critical social workers like Prigoff, the mode of intervention mattered less than the theories and values that guided it. This was a significant departure from the radical thought of the 1960s and 1970s, which often promoted a rigid dichotomy between conservative individually oriented practice and radical community organising or other forms of social action.

Influenced by writers like Freire (1970), these critical social workers also began to distinguish between education and indoctrination, and to promote greater equality and dialogue in the educational experience (Burghardt 1982; Lewis 1973; Piven and Cloward 1975; Reisch et al. 1981). Echoing Freire, they asserted that social work must be understood in the context of social structure and theory and action must be linked through praxis. This vision of critical social work shaped the mission of the Bertha Capen Reynolds Society, founded in the early 1980s and now called the Social Welfare Action Alliance, and encouraged the acceptance of structural social work in the 1990s (Mullaly 1997; Mullaly and Keating 1991). It introduced the theme of distributive justice as a guiding principle for social work, even though, like their professional ancestors, its proponents asserted that problems of distribution could best be solved through philosophical and institutional transformation and political action, rather than the introduction of new professional techniques. (Gil 1976; Lewis 1972; Silverstein 1975). Schools of social work, they argued, could play a critical role in the reorientation of practice along these lines.

Ironically, by the mid-1980s, the term 'radical' had virtually disappeared from the social work lexicon. Soon, it was replaced by the more inclusive, less threatening, and more ambiguous label 'progressive'. On the positive side, 'progressive' social workers, freed from a strictly class-based analysis, now addressed issues and articulated perspectives that radicals of the past had not often made a central concern. Their emphases on feminist, empowerment, and ethnic-sensitive (later ethno-conscious) models of practice, however, were often tempered by a conservative focus on clinical issues instead of broader themes of justice and equity. They frequently integrated this heightened awareness of identity issues into 'adjustment-oriented' therapies rather than a critique of the political–economic system (Specht and Courtney 1994).

A sizeable and influential group of social work radicals in the US explained this contradiction as the result of professionalism, which they viewed as the major obstacle to truly progressive or critical social work practice. They maintained that participation in existing social welfare institutions perpetuated status differentials and contributed to society's failure to respond adequately to human needs. In their view, the only way to resolve the contradiction between progressive politics and professionalism was through deprofessionalisation: specifically, the restructuring of social work programmes and practice along more egalitarian lines in which clients and community groups possessed a leading role in defining their problems and identifying potential solutions. The creation of alternative, non-hierarchical agencies—including self-help or mutual aid groups—and the strengthening of alliances with client-organised groups, such as the Kensington Welfare Rights Union in Philadelphia, were central components of this vision (Newdom 1996, 1997; Withorn 1996).

A variant of this perspective among critical social workers in the US also attempted to strengthen linkages between workers and clients. They did so, however, by arguing that social workers were, above all, members of the new working class, who shared certain experiences of oppression with other workers and their clients. Fabricant and Burghardt (1987), for example, stressed the importance of unionisation, the formation of alliances with other labour groups, and the possibility of working for change within existing organisations. The peak of such union-focused activism appears to have been between 1975 and 1980 in the aftermath of fiscal cutbacks and the severe recession of 1973–1974 (Wagner 1989).

Critical social work theory in the 1990s

By the early 1990s, the concept of critical social work was somewhat muddled. Radical ideas like empowerment, multiculturalism, and the 'strengths perspective' (Saleeby 1992) appeared to be widely accepted in the profession, yet upon closer examination much of their original meaning had been corrupted. For example, most of the literature on empowerment had abandoned its materialist core. Even its strongest proponents like Barbara Levy Simon (1994) felt that it had become 'a term that confuses even as it inspires' (Simon 1990, p. 27).

In a similar fashion, the concept of multiculturalism had lost much of its original anti-racist emphasis and had largely become a vehicle to promote racial diversity or advocate for various forms of separatist practice (Gross 1995). While much of the literature developed by social workers of colour had potentially radical implications, only a relatively small percentage of such authors self-identified as radical (Iglehart and Becerra 1995; Rivera and Erlich 1998). The literature of multiculturalism often reflected the language and goals of radical social work, yet it rarely made this connection explicit (Gutierrez 1997; Van Soest 1995). In fact, some social work radicals of colour argued that the identity politics spawned by multiculturalism weakened the overall influence of social work radicals by fragmenting their energies (Longres 1997). In their view, competing visions of multiculturalism threatened to obscure and hinder the attainment of worthy social and professional goals. The confluence of the terms multiculturalism with social justice and oppression further obfuscated serious discussions of these issues (Council on Social Work Education Conference 1998; Garcia and Van Soest 1997; Rosenthal 1993; Van Soest 1995, 1996). Others, however, applauded how a multicultural perspective broadened the horizons of radicalism in social work beyond class politics to encompass issues of race, gender, sexual orientation, and disability (Lum 1999, Van Soest 1995).

In an effort to break this ideological logjam, some radical social workers in the 1990s attempted to integrate 'new social movement theory' into a model of critical social work practice (Fisher and Kling 1994a). They focused on 'the historical dialectic between domination and resistance' and emphasised 'the interplay between class, community, and the search for new cultural orientations' (p. 16). Proponents of this perspective advocated for the construction and mobilisation of broad-based coalitions that moved beyond single-community and single-constituency efforts. To hold power, rather than merely contest it, they also argued that local and global efforts needed to be balanced and, perhaps of greatest significance, they sought to relegitimatise the state as an arena of political struggle. Many critical social workers in the US decried these trends. Longres asserted:

> . . . the search for ways to alter the structural sources of inequality and discrimination have been replaced with a search to recognize and appreciate cultural and gender differences in values, beliefs, and worldviews. Disempowerment, once thought of primarily as a political and economic issue, is increasingly thought of as a personal difficulty . . . The strengths approach . . . cautions us against problematizing the social environment. [Yet] the intellectual distance of these progressive alternatives from mainstream practice seems extremely narrow.
>
> (Longres 1996, p. 234).

Similarly, DeMaria (1992) argued that radical social work could be revived only by blending a radical analysis of society with radical action, as earlier generations of radical social workers demonstrated. By the end of the century, critical social workers in the US were attempting to do this through means as diverse as feminism, Marxism, queer theory, and post-structuralism.

The influence of critical social work at the beginning of the twenty-first century

Despite these theoretical differences, many of today's critical social workers express similar views on economic globalisation, the nature of capitalism as a socio-economic system, the role of organised labour, the relationship of individual problems to exploitation by elites, the need for a redistribution of wealth and income, and the dominance of the social work profession by clinical or psychotherapeutic perspectives. Meanwhile, in an era dominated by identity politics, at least in rhetoric, mainstream social work has abandoned any discussions of social class.

Throughout its history, a critical feature of radical social work in the US has been a willingness to challenge the status quo—inside and outside the profession—in ways that most social workers do not, out of fear of undermining their occupational goals. For some radicals, challenges to the status quo emerged from a feminist perspective. For others, the concept of social work radicalism has periodically been connected, sometimes tenuously, with Marxism, socialism, and communism (Andrews and Reisch 1997; Wagner 1990; Wenocur and Reisch 1989). While opposition to oppression in all of its forms is a consistent theme among critical social workers today, a racial gap exists between the ideas, goals, and emphases of white social workers and social workers of colour (Reisch and Andrews 2001).

In retrospect, radical ideas have had limited impact in the US on social work practice and theory, or the development of social policies. At best, critical social work helps define the centre of the political spectrum and provides an alternative vision in a world in which champions of neo-liberalism trumpet 'the end of history'. According to radical social workers interviewed by the author, the mainstream of the social work profession relies on radical ideas for inspiration and makes radical thought more palatable to the general public. Radical perspectives, even if often a minority and subversive view, have served as the moral conscience and redeeming element of the profession. Radical social workers comprise 'one of the forces that work to block the ascendancy of conservatives' (J. Blau, personal communication).

Although the remnants of a class-based or structural analysis of US society still exists within critical social work in the US, radical social workers have largely incorporated the perspectives of 1990s 'identity politics' into their thinking. They believe issues such as multiculturalism, feminism, and gay/lesbian rights should be at the centre of a radical agenda. They struggle, however, with how to fuse these identity concerns with a class perspective. The concept of social justice, particularly through its application to current attacks on the poor, women, and children, could serve as a unifying theme. An important question for radical social workers in the years ahead, therefore, will be how to balance a more universalistic perspective that could have broad political appeal with a focus on the particular and more pressing needs of oppressed populations.

Some painful questions persist for critical social workers in the US. Were radical ideas, based to a large extent on socialism or other now discredited ideologies, simply wrong for the US, politically and culturally? Were they constructed on faulty premises about the causes of social problems, human nature, and the possibility of individual or social change? Were radical ideas in US social work largely confined to selected regions, populations, or cultures (e.g. large cities, Jewish social workers) and, therefore, marginalised from the outset? Or, were radical ideas once right but are now consigned to the dustbin of history by sweeping economic, political, and technological changes?

A more optimistic analysis holds that at critical junctures in modern US history, a radical vision of society and of practice played a key role in shaping social work's development and the direction of US society. Radical social work in the United States was one of the few vehicles through which abstract socialist ideas were translated into practical policies, programmes, and means of intervention. Social work radicalism, therefore, has never been a fixed phenomenon. It exhibited both expansive and adaptive qualities and has incorporated new ideas, such as feminism and multiculturalism, into its critique of society and social welfare with varying degrees of success.

Now that socialism is no longer a global counterweight to free market ideologies, can radical social work survive, particularly in the centre of global capitalism? Recent events provide only a partial answer. On the one hand, for the past generation, social workers in the US have struggled to justify their existence in the face of a concerted political and ideological attack. Despite its rhetoric of social justice and empowerment, the mainstream profession has largely failed to present a viable alternative to the individualistically oriented philosophy that prevails throughout much of the country, especially in the increasingly corporate-dominated media. In response, many social workers have succumbed to the allure of the marketplace or have resigned themselves to its permanence (Specht and Courtney 1994; Strom-Gottfried 1997). This has limited the profession's ability to translate its rhetoric into reality around such issues as welfare reform, managed care, and the privatisation of social services.

A central issue in crafting a viable response to these structural developments is the role of professionalism. Opponents and critics of professionalism, from Bertha Reynolds to Ann Withorn, regard its salient negative features as the perpetuation of status and salary hierarchies, elitism, patronising views of clients, and top-down conceptions of individual and social change. In this view, professionalism is a by-product of capitalism as an economic and cultural system, and a means of maintaining structural and status inequalities. Professional social workers must, by this definition, be conscious or unconscious agents of social control, who adapt their own behaviour and those of their clients to the demands of dominant cultural institutions (Gordon 1998; Mullaly 1997; Newdom 1997; Reynolds 1963; Withorn 1996).

Other critical social workers, however, believe that radical ideology can be reconciled with the requirements of professional practice. For them, the key components of professionalism are competence, integrity, and fairness. While mindful of the perils of capitalism, they argue that a revised form of social work practice could synthesise the best features of radicalism and professionalism.

Often drawing on models outside the United States, these radicals emphasise the linkage between economic and social development and the importance of identifying common ground between workers and clients (Lewis 1982; Midgley 1997; J. Blau, personal communication; A. Prigoff, personal communication).

If the former group is correct, that is, if radicalism and professionalism are fundamentally incompatible, then critical social work ideas and practice can only survive outside mainstream organisations and institutions. Few critical social workers, however, have seriously examined the implications of this argument for contemporary US society. What viable alternative structures, comparable to settlement houses or the radical trade unions of the 1930s and 1940s, exist or could be created in which radical ideas could be translated into practice? Where would the funds for such institutions be found? Who would establish and maintain standards of practice and professional integrity? Since radical social work has traditionally regarded the state as a means to implement its vision, what alternatives to state intervention exist in an era of increasing privatisation (Fisher and Karger 1997; Johnson 1999)?

Both sides see a partial solution to these dilemmas for critical social work in a major reorientation of the nature of the social work profession, its policy and programme goals, and its educational institutions. This approach harks back to the models of social work proposed by radicals of earlier generations. It also borrows from more recent developments abroad, particularly from the lessons of social work activists in Latin America and South Africa (Friere 1990; Midgley 1997). The philosophical foundation for this change already exists in US social work: the primacy of social justice, the celebration of human diversity; the synthesis of political action and social service throughout the profession's history; and the appreciation of the inevitability and desirability of individual and social change.

One essential component of this change is the development of critical practice frameworks that are truly multicultural. Despite a demographic transformation unprecedented in human history, the concept of multiculturalism is still largely muddled rhetoric. Most of the literature of multiculturalism focuses on differences rather than common characteristics and—purposefully or not—reinforces separatist and, ultimately, self-defeating positions (Council on Social Work Education 1998; Gitlin 1995; Longres 1997). The absence of a viable multicultural framework to guide policy, practice, and education compels social workers to accept narrow, racially and class-biased formulations of complex individual and social problems.

A second component of critical social work in the twenty-first century would involve the reintegration of politics into practice. Radical social workers have long promoted a conception of practice as more than the aggregation and application of sophisticated techniques. Critical social work practice involves an awareness of issues of power and partisanship in which politics and social work are inextricably linked, not incompatible. This reflects a broader view of politics itself. The role of radical social workers, however limited, has been to contain the anti-egalitarian tendencies of the market economy, raise the level of political awareness among clients, colleagues, and constituents, and develop new methods to fight the abuses of the socio-economic system.

A third component of a revised view of critical social work would involve efforts to translate the principle of social justice into specific policies and modes of intervention. Radical social workers need to construct a theoretical framework that simultaneously acknowledges the inherent dynamism of the social environment and the holistic nature of the human condition. The challenge, as framed by Titmuss (1958), of creating social policies that address selective needs within a universalist framework is even more viable today.

12 Working in a different space: linking social work and social development

Ingrid Burkett and Catherine McDonald

Introduction

Our space of practice, the Australasian and South Pacific region, offers unique challenges to social work. This is particularly the case if, as we would expect, social work continues to declare that it is a vehicle for continuous promotion of human well-being within a theoretically informed critical framework and socially just and sustainable moral vision. In this region human experience is of diversity, presenting challenges to the practices of social work. So called First and Third World or North–South economies, for example, are not only regionally juxtaposed; they also coexist within national boundaries of countries such as Australia. The traditional indigenous cultures of the Pacific islands, of Papua New Guinea, and of the Australian and New Zealand mainlands struggle for existence along side the dominant contemporary and global cosmopolitanism of twenty-first-century white Australia and New Zealand. Urban conglomerations such as Sydney, Melbourne and Auckland, orientated towards a global culture and economy, coexist regionally with other radically different forms of inhabited space. These range from the tribal villages of Papua New Guinea, the rural and remote indigenous communities in Australia, depressed rural communities in Australia, and the sprawling and decaying urban fringes of Australia's big cities, all shaped by the ravaging effects of economic globalisation.

This diversity challenges social work to think about alternative ways of engaging that also have the potential to reinvigorate the political and moral agendas of radical social work in an era increasingly dominated by the rationalities of neoliberalism. While not necessarily completely new, when contrasted with 'traditional' or professional social work, they are sufficiently different to be considered unusual. Specifically, we argue that it allows us to see a new space—conceptually and materially—in which we can practice social work. To further these claims, we begin by discussing contemporary social work and the challenges it faces. We then identify the four dominant modes of response to these challenges articulated in the social work literature. We conclude this discussion by suggesting that forms of community-based practice possess considerable capacity to promote well-being, particularly in the types of diverse settings present in this region of the world.

Before posing our ideas, we bear in mind the grave dangers we see of cooption of community practice in the current environment, particularly from the assertion of notions of 'community' within neo-liberal-inspired political projects, policies and programmes. We do this to remind our readers and ourselves that the threat of cooption is ubiquitous, mutating over time and in such ways as to demand unremitting and critically reflexive vigilance. These caveats in place, we are able to sketch our vision for an alternative form of practice, one that draws on current and emerging practices of social development. Social work, we believe, both reflects and represents the optimism of the twentieth century welfare state. The ideas and aspirations fuelling that optimism are not misplaced in the twenty-first century and we offer this chapter in that spirit.

The winds of change

It is almost passé these days to note that the circumstances in which social work is practised have changed considerably and that the seeming certainties of the past have vanished. We do so here, not so much as to educate our readers about tendencies of which they are no doubt already aware, but rather to underscore the profundity of change, and consequently, the futility of relying exclusively on past ways of practising. From the 1960s to the second half of the 1980s, almost every Western democracy developed the modernist infrastructure of an advanced welfare state. The spread and degree of consensus about social responsibility for the well-being of all citizens and the acceptance and development of the welfare state led Daniel Bell (1960) to declare that capitalist societies had arrived at the 'end of ideology'.

Those halcyon circumstances have faded into memory. Instead, as Gilbert (2002) suggests, there has been from Stockholm to Sydney, in Great Britain, Western Europe, North America and the 'Anglo' countries of the South Pacific, a silent surrender of public responsibility. The dominance of neo-classical economics with its horror of budget deficits and associated need for fiscal conservatism, the ascendancy of new public management and the hollowing out of the state, the introduction of market mechanisms in the delivery of welfare, the transformation from the workfare to the welfare state (Harris 2002) are processes which have fundamentally reshaped the institutional arrangements of modern welfare states.

As a consequence, modes of social organisation such as social work are subject to processes of reconstruction, translating into developments such as the whittling away of professional privilege and autonomy, the tightening of professional accountability to managers, and the relaxation of professional boundaries. Linking this explicitly with the prevailing ideology of neo-liberalism and to sets of practices such as new public management, authors such as Lymberly (2000) suggest that the benign conditions of the high point of the social work professional project (Friedson 1970; Larson 1977) are gone. Instead, the regime surrounding the welfare state, service delivery and professional practice has experienced significant change and perhaps, complete restructuring (Clarke 1996; Leonard

1997). It is claimed, for example, that social work is experiencing a period of discontinuity, prompting some observers to adopt an apocalyptic tone (e.g. Kreuger 1997; Meinert et al. 2000), suggesting that the forces of discontinuity are so great that its demise is inevitable. Others are more sanguine, suggesting instead that the manner in which social work is practised is changing (Harris 2003; May and Buck 2000).

In Gilbert's analysis (2002, p. 61), these developments are neatly represented in three tightly connected rhetorical themes in the public discourses of change: a shift from passive to active policies towards dependent people, an emphasis on the responsibilities of these people over their rights, and a redefinition of objectives from support to social inclusion. All, he suggests, indicate that collective responsibility has given way to increased private responsibility for life contingencies. Adopted across the political spectrum and across the globe, by neo-liberals, liberal democrats and communitarians alike, these themes represent not the end of ideology, but its reassertion. As a direct result of the triumph of the new rhetoric of welfare and of the refabrication of the institutional framework of social services, the operational domains in which social workers plied their craft have been reshaped, dismantled, and relocated.

Does social work have a place in this new moral landscape? Zigmund Bauman (cited in Powell 2001, p. 23) remarks that social work is currently haunted by uncertainty. But it is, we suggest, ultimately a welcome uncertainty endemic to an undiminished moral responsibility. Even if that responsibility is publicly repudiated, as increasingly seems to be the case, the need for social work has not gone away nor has its moral legitimacy. In view of that, it is incumbent upon us to find ways of not only surviving the frosty conditions but of working out how to foster the moral agendas to which social work remains committed. In the next section we review what we suggest are the primary strategies or options for the future found in the social work literature. We do this to locate and ground the option we canvass here.

Four options for the future

There are, we suggest, four types of proposals found within the social work literature that may be read as responding to current circumstances. Not all of these strategies are new, but represent contemporary reworkings of pre-existing themes in social work. The four responses are:

- Evidence-based practice
- Enterprising professionalism
- Critical/post-modern/post-structural social work
- Global/international social work (including human rights based practice).

Evidence-based practice clearly sits as the natural heir to the professional social work project developed in the heyday of the twentieth century. It draws on a variety of sources: behavioural social work, medical and healthcare research, positivist and empirical research, evaluative research of practice effectiveness. Some claim that its popularity resides in its apparent capacity to respond to the managerialist agendas of contemporary governments concerned with such issues as effectiveness and accountability (Harris 1998; Webb 2001). While strategically dominant in the professional literature, questions remain about whether evidence-based practice can respond critically and justly to the diversity of human experience found, for example, in this region of the world. Our conclusion is: probably not. While it might be usefully deployed in some forms of clinical interventions, it will not achieve what it claims across the broad domain and in the multiple contexts we identify. In other words, the conceptual space it promotes is far too constrained. Evidence-based practice aggressively places boundaries around what can be known and how knowing is done in ways that we consider counterproductive. Rather, if social workers are to be in any way successful in promoting the goals of sustainable, responsive and authentic justice, then all forms of knowledge and ways of knowing need to be available and, as far as is humanly possible, taken up.

Enterprising professionalism is a frank call for strategic opportunism by social workers in response to contemporary conditions (Jones 2000). It argues, for example, that professional associations should create different categories of membership, thereby retaining a commitment to forms of exclusivity and expertise we consider unhelpful. Further (and more importantly), social workers should actively embrace change in twenty-first century welfare regimes, most notably developments such as welfare reform in the US (Linhorst 2002). Enterprising professionalism hopes to reposition social work as the lead profession in an increasingly diverse and dispersed human services labour market. The enterprising profession is one that should nurture a 'new' set of attributes compatible with current conditions, thereby allowing social work to adapt to the contemporary environment in a manner that will rearticulate social work's linkages and position with the emerging institutional arrangements. The enterprising profession does not reject or challenge the twentieth century professional project or its attendant epistemological and ontological assumptions. Rather, it seeks to promote an almost 'natural' evolution of social work into a 'newer', better-adapted form. From our point of view this, along with its exclusivity, its undeniable Western and urban bias and its relatively uncritical stance, limits the capacity of the enterprising profession idea thus defined to sustain the agenda we set, in that the space it creates is both materially and conceptually inadequate.

Critical post-modern social work is one of the more recent developments that, as yet, has limited expression in social work practice (Healy 2000; Pease and Fook 1999). Conceptually it represents a clear break with the twentieth century professional project. It attempts to engage with social work as discursive practice and social work 'knowledge' as discourse. It proposes that social workers can engage with people in ways significantly different from those promoted by the professional social work interventions developed within the professional project. Specifically, these developments suggest that social workers should develop a more sophisticated analysis of power operating in social work interactions. Critical social work theorists encourage social workers to understand the implications of their privileged position in relationships, and develop ways of working that are more democratic and participatory. For all of these reasons, we consider that it has significant potential to respond to the dimensions of diversity we observe, primarily in that it also opens up conceptual space for other non-dominant voices to be heard, but also because of its explicit focus on power relations. This latter focus is particularly relevant in working with and through the pervasive and damaging North–South/indigenous–non-indigenous relations of the region.

Finally, global or international social work (here incorporating human-rights based practice) has been around as a mode of practice for some time (Healy LM 2001; Ife 2001; Nagy and Falk 2000). In many of its manifestations it represents a variation of, or more accurately, an application of the mode of practice associated with the twentieth century Western professional project, but in different contexts. Recently, interest in international social work as a distinct area of field of practice has escalated, emerging in part as a result of economic, social and cultural globalisation. It is an omnibus term for diverse practices incorporating such activities as cross-cultural social work within advanced welfare regimes, international adoptions, work with legal and illegal refugees, and other forms of migration-related work such as settlement services, health promotion, policy development and advocacy in international arenas. International social work also reflects the long-standing professional interest in social development worldwide. For the most part, this transnational professional project was and is a modernist enterprise (Leonard 1997). Importantly, more recent versions represent, like critical post-modern social work, a distinct break with the twentieth century professional project, particularly those which draw on post-colonial and post-modern thinking and on different domains of thought such critical geography (Harvey 2001). These developments reconceptualise social work within frameworks of social development, working in a conceptual and material space known as the 'global–local nexus'; that is, working developmentally via non-state organisations with local communities in First and Third World countries struggling with the impact of economic globalisation (Burkett 2001).

It is in the third and fourth options for the future of social work that we find elements of the basis for the mode of practice congruent with the imperatives our region poses and with the spaces we confront. As we will demonstrate in the next section, it is a mode of practice that is irredeemably a function of community, but not the community of the neo-liberal project. That community is a key site of the peculiar morality of advanced liberalism (Rose 1999). It is a seductive community that binds people to particular identities and commitments seemingly beyond the sphere of the state, and ostensibly 'free'. It is the community invoked by governments engaged in the silent and insidious surrender of public responsibility for human well-being. It is the abandoned community of the urban fringes and the decimated community of neo-colonialism drawn into a politics of self-regulation and discipline. That community is the community of the New Right and the World Bank, one which does little to address the real effects of economic globalisation, and which offers little hope for just and sustainable futures.

Rather, the community that we propose attempts to reclaim a range of conceptual and material spaces for a mode of social work practice so often and so readily coopted in contemporary modes of governance. Similarly, the mode of practice we propose is also entrepreneurial, but it is not the empty entrepreneurialism of a reworked professional project hopping on board the neo-liberal agendas of welfare reform. Nor is it the enterprise of the 'third way' (Gray et al. 2003). Rather, the enterprise we promote is, as we will demonstrate, that of social development. The neo-liberal community and neo-liberal social enterprise are both clear sources of the contemporary moral uncertainty facing social work. Promoted as the ideal site and process for the management of risky spaces and risky people, it presents a minefield of dangers, particularly in the attractiveness of the visions promoted and in the seeming virtue of the alliances forged. The multitude of state-inspired programmes and processes operating at the community level present the contemporary version of a long-standing dilemma for social work.

How should social work pursue its moral agenda? Within the neo-liberal community via entrepreneurial means? Beside it? Or in spite of it? We suggest that there is no clear-cut answer to this dilemma, and that there never was. We propose that one of the effects of so-called post-modern analytics of government (Dean 1999) as applied to social work practice is to call into question irrevocably the notion that purity of will and strength of purpose can act as a sufficiently strong talisman to ward off danger. Adopting an analogy developed within organisational theory (Meyer and Zucker 1989), we are, in every sense, a 'permanently failing' profession in that we are constantly implicated in the production of the very power relations we so wish to dismantle. Furthermore, we walk and always will walk a fine line between negotiating and resisting different agendas promoted in the political domain. Accordingly, notions of continuous critical reflexivity, undertaken with a constant and routine yet deliberate awareness of our ever-present foibles and continuous failures, takes on a new and heightened sense of urgency. It is with this realisation at the forefront of our minds that we can, haltingly, talk about the emerging spaces for a 'new' mode of social work practice.

Spaces of practice: social development and difference

Our naming of this part of the chapter '*spaces* of practice' is quite deliberate, for we believe that social work has, to a large extent, explored the *sociality* of the human condition in relative isolation from the '*spatiality* of human life' (Soja 1996, p. 2, italics in original). In speaking of 'new' spaces of practice we are referring not only to the physical or material spaces but also include in these spaces mental and conceptual spaces, or states of mind, arenas where we unsettle totalising ideologies of social change. The spaces of practice which we propose are physical, mental, real, imagined, political and ideological spaces in which and from which social workers can engage in social struggles. These spaces are filled with 'perils as well as possibilities' (Soja 1996, p. 68) for struggle, liberation and emancipation (Lefebvre in Soja 1996, p. 68).

But what do we mean by 'social development'? Defining social development would require a chapter in its own right. In social terms, 'development' has also been used in various ways: to refer to processes of societal evolution, economic growth, and modernisation, in addition to aspirational and self-determined transformation; and in relation to different levels of society, from the development of local communities, regions, states, nations, international groups, and, more recently, of global society. In very simple terms, what we mean when we refer to 'social development' relates to the theoretical terrain (both positive and normative), and the practice and policy domains which have sought to address questions of sustenance, justice, self-determination, freedom and quality of life in the face of poverty, injustice and oppression.

Whilst the goals of social work have also been directed at these questions, the points of intervention have been directed predominantly at individual and state mechanisms (within a conceptual framework of welfare responses). Social development, however, has sought to define these questions within different frameworks, using broader economic and political frames of reference, linking the policies of the nation-state into a wider 'international' and/or global system, and considering to a much greater extent than social work traditionally has, the role of communities, non-government players (such as NGOs and corporations), and global bodies such as the World Bank, the United Nations and the World Trade Organization. In the past 50 years it is the case that the terminology of social development has been applied predominantly to economically poorer countries, regions and communities (who have disparagingly been referred to as 'developing' or 'underdeveloped'). It is the case now, however, that this terminology and the associated theories and practices, are also becoming increasingly relevant in relation to the social, economic, political and cultural conditions of people in so-called 'developed' areas, who are still experiencing poverty, social exclusion and injustice despite (or perhaps because of) high levels of economic growth.

Finding spaces for social development and difference in social work is not a totally new endeavour: as we suggest above there have been various expressions of each of these in literature related to international and global social work (see for example Gil 1999; Meinert 1991; Midgely 1995, 1996; Mohan 1992, 1995). Social development has been cited as a space for social workers to further explore *difference*. We would suggest that there is another space which has the potential to more radically influence social work practice in this Australasian and Pacific region than has previously been realised. It is a 'third space', created between the intersections of 'social development' and 'difference' which we suggest opens 'new' spaces of practice in social work. We are not proposing any kind of clean new space for social work free of ideological and conceptual tensions. The spaces that we promote here are, by their very nature, spaces of tension. They neither shut down possibilities, nor present themselves as representing the answer to complex issues. They are spaces in which practitioners engage reflexively, are able to situate themselves socially, spatially, historically and politically can recognise the fallible and unfinished nature of themselves and thus of their practices.

The need for engaging with this third space will be made clearer if we outline the dangers of merely adopting social development and some of the reasons why the particularities of social work practice in this region demand a more critical approach. This third space recognises that engagement is much more complex than merely adopting a new conceptual or practice arena. Social work cannot merely 'add social development and stir' in order to create a space for revisioning social work.

The notion of social development has been in a constant state of revision since it gained international currency as representing a means of defining progress—US style (Rist 2002). It is conceptually much older than this, and some critics suggest that it is 'the last and failed attempt to complete the Enlightenment in Asia, Africa and Latin America' (Escobar 1995, p. 221). It has been subjected to fierce criticism on conceptual, ideological and practical grounds. Just like Daniel Bell declared the 'end of ideology' in relation to capitalist society, many voices have over the past three decades suggested that notions of development are 'doomed to extinction' (Esteva 1993), have called for the 'end of development', or at the very least, an examination of what notions of 'post-development' could offer in terms of revisioning the development project (see for example Escobar 1995; Rahnema 1997; Rist 2002).

Others have called for alternative visions of development rooted in groups building projects of emancipation based on principles of participation and 'least violence' (Parfitt 2002). Within this environment, development practitioners have had to face a paradoxical tension: that their spaces of practice have simultaneously been defined as representing the greatest challenge for a global society, as well as one of the most 'contested and contentious' of practice arenas (Kaplan 1996, p. ix). Despite the fact that the concept of development has been undressed ideologically and practically, the global emperor of the 'development industry' continues to push forward and parade the naked dominant 'growth-centred' visions of progress.

Meanwhile, gaps between the richest and the poorest widen, economic growth has not eradicated poverty, and the litany of disastrous environmental and social consequences of so-called 'modernisation' grow daily. Just as neo-classical economics and neo-liberal political ideologies have fundamentally altered the shape of institutions of 'welfare' in the North, these same forces have reshaped the institutional arrangements of 'development' in the South (Chossudovsky 1998). Indeed, some authors have argued that globalisation is actually a replacement for what are characterised as two parallel symbiotic mechanisms: 'the Welfare State in the North, and "development" strategies in the South' (Rist 2002, p. 212). Social work has traditionally been associated with the *management of poverty* under conditions of industrialisation within capitalism in Europe and then in the 'colonies' (particularly America and Australia). 'Development' has equally defined people in particular nations (in fact, the majority of the world's people) as 'poor', and therefore as 'objects of knowledge and management' (Escobar 1995, p. 23).

Uncritical adoption of 'social development' as another sphere for social work to engage is problematic, for both of these projects are built on modernist foundations that have (at the very least) been seriously disturbed. (We note that there is a great deal more critical discussion of this disturbance in the social develop-ment literature than is the case for social work.) The third space we suggest is not one that stands securely on the solid ground of modernity. It lies in uncertain ter-rain that situates development on contested ground (Parfitt 2002, p. 7), where def-initions remain unstable, unfinished, emergent and manifold. Central to such understandings of development is an understanding of *difference*.

We believe that the geographical and historical context in which social work is practiced in the Australasian and Pacific region demands an engagement with the notion of difference, particularly when we are speaking in cultural and linguistic terms (see particularly Harrison 2003). Social work here is still very much influ-enced by frameworks developed in British and American contexts, and these have a tendency to blind practitioners to the particularities of, for example, Australia's colonial past in which racism and intolerance of difference figure highly, both within the Australian mainland context and in terms of Australia's growing role in social work education in the region. While political rhetoric celebrates Australian multiculturalism, the reality has been the containment of diversity that continues to exoticise the Other and promote erroneous ideas of the existence of fixed, separate cultures (Bhabha in Harrison 2003) rather than encourage open and ongoing engagement with difference.

We practise in a context in which 'the surface acceptance of multiculturalism has . . . required no major reconfiguration of existing social arrangements that primarily benefit the white Australian population' (Harrison 2003, p. 261; Stratton and Ang 1994). Further, there is an increasing recognition of the mani-fest failures of social work to engage in the realm of cultural difference charac-teristic of this context. Western models of welfare have actually contributed to the entrenchment of disadvantage, marginalisation and dependence of Australia's indigenous people, and yet there has been relatively little active consideration of this in mainstream social work education. Further, cultural difference has contin-ued to receive relatively marginal emphasis in Australian social work educa-tion and research, despite the fact that we are increasingly exporting social work education to the region.

Merely embracing the potentials offered by linking social work and social development without using difference as a critical reference point leaves us in danger of extending exploitative colonial relations. Further, there is a particu-larly treacherous potential dimension of an uncritical linking of social work and social development. The global development industry has historically encour-aged a predatory approach to intervention. As such there is a danger that uncrit-ical linkages between social work and the arena of social development could engage this predatory potential, particularly as it represents a fiscal goldmine for social work to ensure its own survival. If, as we suggested previously, social work is to explore a continued moral vision based on social justice, any link with the field of social development **will require** an engagement with notions of difference and a fundamental reappraisal of many of the core concepts on which the professional project of social work is built, as well as a commitment to ongoing critical reflexivity. This third space we identify opens up three possible arenas/fields of questioning which could lead to 'new' spaces of practice for social work. We discuss these next.

A critical revisioning of community and locality as spaces for practice in the context of the 'local–global nexus'

Social work has traditionally concentrated on the nexus between the individual and the nation-state as the arena of practice and policy, and on the state as the central vehicle of structural change. We believe that this nexus needs critical questioning in our geo-cultural context. Such questioning could open up possibilities for a re-engagement in community practice in social work. We suggest two points of reference for this.

In the context of globalisation, there is a sense in which the nation-state is now 'becoming too small for the big problems of life, and too big for the small problems of life' (Bell, in Waters 1995, p. 96). Social development has had to move above and beyond the nation-state and state-based responses to poverty. Though the state has always played a role in social development processes, much greater emphasis has been put on the role of non-state players and on transnational or international organizations and bodies. Given that globalisation has heightened the influence of such players in the welfare and well-being of individuals, communities and societies, we suggest that much could be learnt from the experiences of social development practitioners. The advent of the 'Global Age' (Albrow 1996) suggests that the spaces of practice move down (towards the local) and out (towards the global) and away from the traditional interpretation of the state as the centre of action. Albrow (1996, p. 64) argues that 'it is now possible to think of the state as a worldwide web of practices with no one centre.' This opens up the 'local–global nexus' as a space of practice.

Within this space, an engagement with 'community' (interpreted as an ongoing processual creation rather than as a fixed site or object; see Burkett 2001) could move beyond the imaginary nostalgic, whitewashed site it has predominantly occupied in social work, towards a position which interprets it more as an 'orientation which emphasises the relationality and contextuality of human practice, in all its messiness' (Burkett 2001, p. 239). Such a space of practice needs to traverse the fine line between a neo-liberal politics of fragmentation, and universalising construction of the local as merely a handmaiden of the global. Rather than bemoaning the 'death of community', this third space opens up the possibilities inherent in realising that 'there is no unspatialised social reality' (Soja 1996, p. 46). This reimagines space (and with it community) not as fixed, homogeneous and innocent, as was the case in many modernist political action theories, but as a contested, shifting, uncertain site of struggle; a site full of possibilities for resistance and 'radical openness' (Hooks 1990, p. 149). It is crucial that any reopening of community as a space for social work practice sees it as part of broader social, economic, political processes, and links practice methodologies to social policy processes, advocacy and campaigning strategies which can engage in structural change, and particularly with social movements.

In this region there is a sense that the individual–society nexus with which social work has traditionally aligned itself is often inadequate and indeed inappropriate in engaging with communally oriented cultural groups. Social interventions have often failed to appreciate the intricate familial and communal interrelationships central to many cultural groups, and the differences between intra-cultural groupings. They have frequently served to divide and alienate people rather than promote their well-being. As non-governmental development organisations revise their moral agendas so that their focus is not merely on the 'overseas' Other but also on addressing poverty and social exclusion 'in their own backyards' (for example the huge gulf between the social and economic well-being of indigenous and non-indigenous people in Australia), more attention is being paid to the possibilities which development practice[1] offers. Clearly such practices need to be grounded in the cultural contexts in which they are used rather than using practices developed in very different cultural, social and economic contexts. The indigenisation of development practice is occurring, informed by notions of difference, which is very much community-based and culturally grounded. In Australia this exploration has largely occurred outside spaces engaged with social work.

We suggest that this points to two possible spaces of practice for social work. First, there is a reflexive space in which social work could explore its own cultural discourses, its alignment with racist policies in this context, and, in particular, its continued failures to address the multiple marginalisations of indigenous people. Second, there is the space that disrupts both development practice and social work practice in exploring social development in contexts which defy the North/South, Developed/Underdeveloped binaries, and position notions of development and welfare in relationship to one another and to their joint cultural failures. The space thus exists for charting 'new' visions of culturally based and community-based social interventions.

A critical exploration of the 'shadow' of welfare as creating spaces for examining participation and enterprise in social work practice

Social workers can also radically explore the underside or shadow of welfare-based interventions, something that we have been politically reluctant to do, but which is necessary. In this country, it is clear that welfare, particularly passive income support payments, have limitations both as a means of breaking the cycle of disadvantage and in terms of its universal social and cultural appropriateness

---

1   We refer to development practice rather than social development practice as this incorporates a broader range of practice fields and methodologies, which integrate relief, locality work/community development, policy and campaigning work and practice associated with social movements (for an analysis of this see Korten, 1990).

(see Midgely 1996). This obviously opens up a Pandora's box of ideological questions and tensions, but the underside or shadow of welfare needs critical exposure. Social development, on the other hand, has a long history of engaging in such questioning; with aid, technical assistance, relief payments and top-down welfare having long been criticised in both academic and practice circles.

The new spaces for practice which could emerge are situated in relation to two major points of reference: first, it could open up spaces for more critical explorations of participation in social work; and second, it could create spaces in which social work could more fully explore and engage with concepts and practices related to enterprise and particularly social enterprise. Social work has had an ongoing commitment to methodologies such as community development. However, there has always been a tension between community development and the professional project of social work. The latter focus defined social work's territory of expertise and systems of knowledge with scant attention to definitions of 'clients' own knowledge and expertise. The first point of reference for this new space for practice entails a much more radical exploration of professionalism, power relations and notions of service than has been seen in social work in recent years.

In such approaches people are engaged as co-producers of endeavours to enhance their welfare, as opposed to recipients of welfare 'solutions' designed by professionals. Strategies such as co-production (see Cahn 2000), some of the new forms of mutual aid, particularly those addressing financial exclusion (see Burkett 2003), co-management in social development and endogenous development processes (see Pretty 1995, 1998) provide a base for beginning. Notions of power and power relations have been closely examined in the field of social development with much attention being paid to opening up real spaces for participatory ways of working and in examination of colonising agendas in practice.

We claimed early in this chapter that there are as yet relatively limited expressions of critical post-modern social work. We suggest that there is much to be gained from an examination of ways in which social development practices have explored this territory. However, it is clear that any such developments will need to address key issues dear to the heart of the professional project of social work. Some of these are more ideologically fraught than others, such as how professional principles of confidentiality and privacy support individualised approaches while denying approaches that seek to open community-based relational approaches to practice. As discussed earlier, in the neo-liberal environment social workers need to walk a very fine line between 'using' participation as a tool to be applied to people, and engaging with participation as a principle of practice that informs but does not dictate the nature of the methodologies used in practice.

Social enterprise is a framework that has received much attention both in Northern contexts in relation to the futures of the welfare state, and for addressing issues of social development in the global South. Such approaches seek to enact social purposes using entrepreneurial approaches which harness initiative within organisations and groups of constituents, increasing the access of individuals and communities to material and social resources, and working on the common good whilst building financial sustainability and maximising efficiency (see Gray et al. 2003; Rogaly et al. 1999). Examples include building microenterprises, initiatives aimed at building the assets and independence of community organisations, building partnerships between business and community, and strengthening local economies by exploring ways to maximise efficiency of resource sharing in communities.

The field of social development, however, has engaged much more readily with notions of enterprise than is the case for social work, and much learning could be gained from explorations of this experience and its relationship with the current policy focus on social enterprise in Australia and New Zealand (see for example Gray et al. 2003). In particular, explorations of microenterprise and microfinance as tools in the social development approach to poverty alleviation offer an entry point into a range of economic development tools that could open up 'new' practice spaces for social work (see for example Burkett 2003). This 'new' space for social work is, like that of participation, fraught with both possibilities and perils: on the one hand, it offers the promise of reframing traditional welfare in such a way that people and communities can play an active role in applying their particular local knowledges and skills to addressing their needs and issues. On the other hand, great care must be taken to ensure that principles of social justice and structural analyses of poverty and social exclusion are not lost amidst the race to reframe individuals as 'self-maximising entrepreneurs' (Rankin 2001). We should not forget to 'look forward to the past' (Lane 1997, p. 337) to spaces within and outside social work which have long been engaged in critiques of professionalism and passive forms of welfare, and in which enterprise has long been a concept around which to organise responses to poverty and social exclusion.

A critical examination of culture and cultural process and of social workers as cultural workers

This is one of the most culturally diverse regions in the world, and within this region Australia has, for the last three decades, politically celebrated its multicultural nature. Here social work education is increasingly internationalised, and programmes are now enrolling students from many parts of the region who will not practise social work under the conditions of a welfare state, nor in cultural spaces where the social work's traditional focus on the individual–society interface will be particularly helpful. In this context it is interesting to note that culture continues to remain somewhat marginalised in much mainstream Australian social work education, despite the condition of globalisation heightening the need to understand and engage with the political, social and economic implications of cultural flows, and despite the fact that 'culture has become a very conspicuous concern of sociologists and social theorists' over recent years (Robertson 1992, p. 32). In this last section we suggest that examining broader notions of culture and difference opens up new spaces for social work in two ways. First we consider what spaces could open if social work was to engage further with post-colonial theories attending to the signposts of post-colonial politics; and second we suggest that there could be new practice spaces in understanding social workers as cultural workers.

Cultural difference has been explored more deeply in the field of social development than has been the case in social work. In many ways this has resulted from the influence in social development of post-colonial writers, and challenges to notions of development based in understanding cultural difference. In social work, post-colonial theory has been relatively unexplored and explorations of culture are often limited to examinations of models of cultural sensitivity. Though there have been some attempts in social work internationally to move beyond a multi-cultural model of culture which 'translates cultural difference into merely learning styles' and treats 'difference as a technical rather than a political category' (Giroux 1991, p. 226), these have tended to represent culture and power in fairly simplistic, universalised terms.

Further, though explorations of racism have been helpful in terms of social work politicising race and culture, often the practice strategies which are linked to anti-racist approaches to social work are universalised, centred on what individual social workers can do in relation to their use of self. Race and culture are actually depoliticised, and are instead personalised. We suggest that in the Australian context where colonialism has been intimately imprinted on national cultural identity, superficial, individualised 'technical' approaches for addressing cultural difference are grossly inadequate. New spaces for social work could be opened through the exploration of possibilities inherent in post-colonial theories and politics which could address the specific intersections between culture, oppression and emancipation.

There are three core reasons why we suggest that social work engages with a post-colonial stance. First, social work is a product of modernity and could be seen to intersect with colonial relations in two major senses: in the sense of relations with those defined as the poor whom social work was to 'treat', and in the sense that it is historically a Western project that has been, and continues to be, exported to the rest of the world through colonial or neo-colonial political, economic and cultural relations (Hugman 1996). Acknowledging the colonial nature and histories of social work is a crucial dimension of any attempt to conceive of an international or global social work project. Second, colonialism has had a major influence on the ways in which cultural difference is responded to. Colonialism continues to impact on fundamentals of cultural interpretation in social work practice. Third, rapid changes in the global social and cultural landscape mean that questions about race, racism, ethnicity and culture are becoming more central to understanding what is happening in Australia and the geopolitical region of Asia and the Pacific. In order to ensure that social work, and in particular, social work education, avoids the pitfalls of professional colonialism, social work needs to engage with bodies of theory which will assist them to become more culturally reflexive in nature.

One way in which social work could explore new spaces for practice is to explore the notion of social workers as 'cultural workers', a term originally coined by Freire, but more recently used by educators exploring the links between post-modernism and critical pedagogy. Such writers suggest that any engagement with notions of difference must move beyond mere theorising and explore possibilities for 'progressive visions' (Giroux 1991, p. 226). Exploring social workers as cultural workers places them in a position of creating possibilities for social justice in the uncertain and ideologically fraught spaces where radical Marxist traditions of social work confront challenges from post-colonial writers questioning the very basis of ideas such as 'rationality', 'emancipation' and 'human nature', ideas upon which these radical traditions have been built. If social work is to explore any progressive visions of itself as a vehicle for promoting human well-being and social justice, it is this murky, shifting and infinitely contextualised terrain in which it must situate itself.

Conclusion

The notion of social development has been subject to sustained but ultimately invigorating critique, and as such has emerged in a much more reflexive, culturally sensitive form. Paradoxically, it makes it simultaneously more fragile and more robust as a concept, particularly in the Australian and Pacific context. It is a concept not used lightly, and one that is recognised as necessarily balanced on shifting sands. Social development is no longer considered to represent a unified concept associated with universalisable practices, as the terrain in which it continues to exist has been well and truly unsettled. We suggest that for these reasons there is much that social work can learn. We have advanced the notion that linking contemporary visions of social development grounded within appreciation of difference, and informed by the theories and politics of post-colonialism and cultural theory, can promote a version of social work more appropriate to the realities of this region. While it presents unique cultural experiences, its experience of difference, of oppression and of resistance is hardly unique. Increasingly, it represents one version of the global, post Cold War experience of humanity found across the world: in Africa, in the Americas and in Europe. We hope that our ideas about new spaces for practice speak to, and, hopefully, find some purchase beyond our shores.

13 Popular resistance to global corporate rule: the role of social work (with a little help from Gramsci and Freire)

Elizabeth Whitmore and Maureen G. Wilson

Introduction

In the context of the declining ability of governments to protect their citizens from the negative impacts of the neo-liberal global agenda, civil society organisations worldwide have been moving into the breach. Working at social and political levels, as well as on the terrain of economic survival, a wide range of groups and organisations are now engaged in confronting the threats of corporate globalisation to democracy, economic justice, the environment, and protection of the commons. Social workers, with their long history of activism, are active in many of these organisations and movements.

Yet these developments have not been adequately theorised in terms that can guide social workers in playing out their professional obligation to work for social justice. In this chapter, after reviewing some of the debates around 'social capital' and the 'new social movements', we will argue that these currently influential schools of thought, while having generated some lively debate, fall short in helping us to understand and relate to what has been called 'the potential other superpower' (Barlow 2003, p. 1). We will suggest instead that the contributions of Antonio Gramsci and Paulo Freire are more useful in understanding these movements, and in guiding social workers in whatever roles they might play in relation to these civil society movements and organisations.

Based on this analysis, we will discuss a range of roles and skills that social workers can bring to these movements. This will include an identification of specific conceptual and practical skills that social workers can offer to these movements, as well as a discussion of *acompañamiento,* or 'accompanying the process' as a potential model for relationships between social workers and these movements. Again guided by the thinking of Gramsci and Freire, we will argue for ongoing collaborative research into the effectiveness of these efforts. Recommendations will be made regarding research approaches that might be useful to these groups and organisations in monitoring their process and outcome effectiveness, while offering those directly involved a way to reflect systematically on their work.

The context

> Economically, politically and technologically, the world has never seemed more free—or more unjust.
>
> (United Nations Development Program 2002, p. 1)

Globally, we are confronted with critical challenges in the areas of economic justice and democracy. While some advances have been made, especially in improvement in some nations in the universality of primary education and in gender equity in access to education, the realities we face are stark. More than a billion people struggle to survive on less than a dollar a day, most also lacking access to basic health services and safe drinking water. Globally, one child out of five does not complete primary school. Nearly 800 million people, or 15% of the world's population, suffer from chronic hunger. A sub-Saharan African child has only a 1 in 3 chance of completing primary school, and half a million women die in pregnancy or childbirth each year—or one every minute of every day (United Nations Development Program 2003). At the same time, the gap between rich and poor continues to increase, including within the richest countries. Globally, 'the richest 1% of the world's people receive as much income as the poorest 57%' (United Nations Development Program 2002, p. 2).

While the world is more *democratic* than ever before, in the sense that 140 countries now hold multiparty elections, only about half (55%) of the world's population live in these countries.

> Even where democratic institutions are firmly established, citizens often feel powerless to influence national policies. They and their governments also feel more subject to international forces that they have little capacity to control.
>
> (United Nations Development Program 2002, p. 1)

In Gallup's International Millennium Survey, when more than 50 000 people in 60 countries were asked if their government was governed by the will of the people, less than a third said yes. Asked if their government responded to the people's will, only 1 in 10 said yes (United Nations Development Program 2002, p. 1).

Democracy is important in its own right: participation in decisions that shape one's life is a basic human right. But democratic governance can also trigger what has been called a 'virtuous cycle of development—as political freedom empowers people to press for policies that expand social and economic opportunities, and as open debates[1] help communities shape their priorities' (United Nations Development Program 2002, p. 3).[2]

---

1   E.g. participatory budgeting, gender-responsive budgeting.
2   But this requires recognition that the link between democracy and human development is not automatic; that democracy that empowers people must be built—it cannot be imported. While

Globalised free trade, in the words of philosopher John McMurtry, 'has brought us to the age of disposable humanity' (McMurtry 1997, p. 12). We have previously suggested (Wilson and Whitmore 2000) that effective responses to the disastrous human and environmental consequences of globalisation are most likely to come from those rooted in the struggles of this 'disposable humanity' itself. And in fact, popular movements are now organising themselves transnationally in a variety of ways, to seek means of resisting or reversing the devastating human and environmental impacts of globalisation in its current form.

Social policy is subject to profound transnational influences, predominantly those of the neo-liberal agenda. There is clearly a need for transnationalised efforts to counteract these developments enforced through international financial institutions (IFIs) and 'free' trade agreements. However this can be effective only in the context of a realistic understanding of the power contests which produce such policies. Prescriptions and proposals for internationalising social protections have little value in the absence of a realistic assessment of how the political power to make these things happen can be mobilised. What this means is that efforts to internationalise social policy in a positive direction must be rooted in solid work at the local and national levels, in popular sectors from which new leadership is emerging, and in the mobilisation of political forces to make accountable the politicians and bureaucrats who coordinate their actions at the international level.

In the face of the apparent weakness of traditional sources of opposition leadership, such as organised labour and political parties, there are hopeful signs in the emergence of transnational alliances and strategic networks among popular groups and their allies. This self-organised, amorphous 'cloud of mosquitoes' which 'stays together, but has no chief,' Max-Neef (1997) suggests, may represent a formidable adversary to the existing order. This, as social movements emerge linking people in the global South 'in a dialectical relationship with the globalization movements of the world's power elites' (Huizer 1996, p. 300), is 'globalization from below.'

Social capital

One approach taken to explaining the above-noted disaffection of populations with governments and with traditional forms of social and political engagement is through the concept of 'social capital.'

membership has declined in political parties, trade unions and other traditional vehicles for collective action, there has been an explosion in support for NGOs and other new civil society groups, and so there is a growing view that democratic politics must be promoted by expanding education, and by fostering the development of civil society groups.

It is possible to see the growing tide of protest, and the difficulties faced by national governments and international organisations trying to respond to it, as evidence of a lack of international social capital.

(Helliwell 2002, p. 79)[3]

Social capital refers to 'the norms and networks that facilitate collective action' (Woolcock 2001, pp 12–13). It signifies connections among individuals, and the 'social networks and the norms of reciprocity and trustworthiness that arise from them' (Putnam 2001a, p. 19).[4] This is distinguished from human capital, which refers to properties of individuals, such as tools and training that enhance individual productivity.[5]

The concept of social capital, a term in use since at least 1916 (Putnam 2001a, p.19) has been given new currency in recent years by the work of a number of social scientists, prominent among these being US political scientist Robert Putnam.[6] Using a variety of indicators, Putnam (2001a) documents the dramatic decline of social capital in the US over the past several decades; he and others argue compellingly for the centrality of social capital to a range of economic and social outcomes. They demonstrate, for example, strong positive correlations between measures of social capital and health status, tolerance, economic and civil equality, and negative correlations with time spent watching TV, violent behaviour, child welfare issues, and even tax evasion (Putnam 2001b; LeBlanc 2001). According to Putnam, an examination of social capital allows us to see '[how] our lives are made more productive by social ties' (Putnam 2001a, p. 19).

3   'In the absence of networks and norms that are shared across borders, it is easy to assume that what comes from afar comes with evil intent. This is too simple a story since, as has often been noted, what commonly makes a protest movement so tactically efficient is its use of transnational electronic networks. The presence of shared values, or at least a pool of shared suspicions, among the protesters combines with easy communication to build and exploit globe-spanning social capital of a bonding type' (Helliwell 2002, p. 79).

4   'Social capital is a key concept in the growing recognition of the interconnections between social and economic structures . . . .Social capital is generally defined as the relationships, networks and norms that facilitate collective action. Some include trust in the definition . . .' (LeBlanc 2001, p. 6). For the majority of writers, [social capital] is defined in terms of networks, norms and trust, and the way these allow agents and institutions to be more effective in achieving common objectives (Schuller 2001, p. 19).

5   'Human capital focuses on the economic behaviour of individuals, especially on the way their accumulation of knowledge and skills enables them to increase their productivity and their earnings—and in so doing, to increase the productivity and wealth of the societies they live in' (Schuller 2001, p. 19).
Human capital is defined by the OECD as 'the knowledge, skills, competences and other attributes embodied in individuals that are relevant to economic activity' (OECD 1998).

6   '[Social capital] owes its prominence mainly to the work of Robert Putnam in political science, James Coleman in educational psychology, and Francis Fukuyama in economic history and sociology, as well as to the active patronage of the World Bank.' (Schuller 2001, p. 19).

In other words, human and social capital, along with physical capital, are tools that enhance productivity.

Social capital is said to take various forms (e.g. formally organised versus informal, public versus private purpose), but perhaps the most important distinction is seen to be that between *bonding* and *bridging* forms of social capital. Bonding is a form of social capital that tends to develop among members of a group that is homogeneous in some way. Thus it is more inward looking, reinforcing exclusive identities (e.g. ethnicity, religion) and is *exclusive* in nature. In Putnam's view, '. . . we might expect negative external effects to be more common with this form of social capital' (Putnam 2001a, p. 23). Bridging social capital, on the other hand, is *inclusive*. It is outward looking, and brings together people across diverse social cleavages. (Examples given are the US civil rights movement, ecumenical groups, and healthcare coalitions.) Thus '. . . bridging social capital can generate broader identities and reciprocity, whereas bonding social capital bolsters our narrower selves' (Putnam 2001a, p. 23).

In addition to these there is seen to be a 'vertical' dimension: *linking*. Thus poverty, for example, is viewed as '. . . largely a function of powerlessness and exclusion' (Woolcock 2001, p. 13). Development, then, requires upscaling and mainstreaming of the participation of the poor, with a forging of alliances with 'sympathetic persons in positions of power . . . The capacity to leverage resources, ideas and information from formal institutions beyond the community is a key function of linking social capital' (Woolcock 2001, p. 13).[7]

One is tempted to point out that what is being talked about here, while perhaps new to some economists, is really just well-known textbook sociology. However the currency of these ideas, their influence and incorporation into programmes of important institutions such as the World Bank make it important to note the underlying focus in these discussions. The central concern seems to be with *productivity* outcomes, with the contribution social capital can make to individual and collective *economic growth*. While acknowledging this bias, Canadian economist John Helliwell asserts that there are also linkages between social capital and subjective well-being (2002, pp 43–4):

> . . . many of the same features of society that are needed to support a successful economic transition are of even greater importance to broader measures of well-being . . . measures of trust and social capital, which have been previously studied mainly in relation to their impacts on economic growth

---

7 Development economist Michael Woolcock argues that any definition of social capital should 'focus on its sources rather than consequences, i.e. on what social capital *is* rather than what it *does*' (Woolcock 2001, p. 13). Thus trust, for instance, is seen as an *outcome* (e.g. of repeated interactions, reputations). Social capital, he declares, 'makes most sense when it is understood as a relational (sociological) rather than psychological (individual) or political (institutional/national) variable' (Woolcock 2001, pp 12–13). He also notes that communities can be highly engaged because they are ignored or mistreated by public institutions, or because they are positively engaged with them.

and human mortality, have strong effects on well-being in addition to those effects operating indirectly through incomes and health.

(Helliwell 2002, p. 12)

Anti-globalisation mobilisations are misguided, according to Helliwell, as '. . . globalization seems as much hype as reality—a slow-moving process that has increased international interdependence but has left nation-states and local communities with their basic capacities intact' (Helliwell 2002, p. 77). His research on trade flows demonstrates, he says, that '. . . there is much more scope and need for national policies than one would think from wide-spread media and other commentaries about the irrelevance of the nation-state . . . are not just more global but also more local than is commonly assumed' (Helliwell 2002, p. 11). Regarding anti-corporate globalisation protest, 'the presence of shared values, or at least a pool of shared suspicions, among the protesters combines with easy communication to build and exploit globe-spanning social capital of a bonding type' (Helliwell 2002, p. 79). However, he warns:

> The internet offers the ability to gather tiny minorities from vast populations, giving them an unprecedented collective weight . . . In this sense, the ability of advanced communications to broaden the scope of rapid organisation helps to build social capital, but it is of a type that may serve the narrower interests of the group while threatening the legitimate aspirations of the unrepresented and increasing the possibilities of escalated conflict. The need is for more international social capital, especially of the bridging and linking types. Bridges are needed between those with diverging views, and they must be matched by trust and information flows linking those at different levels in various hierarchies.
>
> (Helliwell 2002, p. 79)

Thus in this view, corporate globalisation is not the real issue. It is 'as much hype as reality,' and so the rising tide of protest is evidence not of a need for fundamental change in the way in which global economic integration is occurring, but of *a lack of international social capital*, not only to maintain and increase levels of productivity but also to improve the subjective well-being of the protesters and the people they represent.

There is undeniably much of value in recent work that has been done on social capital. It has been used as a way to integrate 'non-economic' factors into economic analysis, something that has long been called for by activists, scholars and commentators on both domestic and international scenes. However it has been pointed out that its popularity 'reflects the growing influence of neo-classical economics over the social sciences' (Spronk 2002, p. 2). From that perspective, social capital is seen as important in terms of its potential to contribute to economic growth. Thus Woolcock reasons:

If it is true that meager stocks of bridging social capital make it more difficult for ideas, information and resources to circulate among groups, then it
follows that larger economic, social and political forces that divide societies
will be harmful for growth. Economic inequality, and overt discrimination
along gender and ethnic lines, for example, should be harmful for growth.

(Woolcock 2001, p. 15)[8]

Further, with the preference in the social capital literature for bridging over
bonding forms of social capital, there is an evident devaluation of 'political' civil
society.

Since the concern is for regime maintenance rather than social change,
Putnam is reluctant to count among his 'civil associations' any that advance
a cause, pursue policy changes as their central vocation, or provoke conflict—
only those that 'rise above' these sources of divisiveness.

(Spronk 2002, pp 5–6)

Thus '. . . only those associations which bridge social and political divisions are to
be positively associated with good government'(Spronk 2002, p. 5). Implicit in this
is 'the classical liberal fear that if such associations follow the pattern of divisive
political solidarities too closely, they may sharpen social cleavages and actually
undermine the capacity for effective governance' (Spronk 2002, p. 5).

Putnam thus de-emphasizes the role civil associations can play as counterweights to potentially oppressive states. There is no acknowledgement that, as
Foley and Edwards (1996) point out, oppositional activity in civil society can help
democratise repressive states. Critics have suggested that 'this restricted view of
democracy is what has made Putnam's work so popular in development policy
circles, especially in the World Bank' (Spronk 2002, p. 5). 'Democratization *as a
value in itself ceases* to be of much interest, because what matters in the governance
agenda is to get the politics of development policy right' (Schmitz 1994, p. 43).
'This narrow view of democracy owes some debt to the plural-elitist literature in
its concerns with policy performance and outcomes rather than deepening and
extending the democratic process' (Spronk 2002, p. 5).

Social movements and social movement organisations

The debates around social movements go back many years and the literature
(mostly North American and European) is extensive. Scholars come primarily
from sociology, political science, anthropology and international relations, though
there is a need for more activity across these disciplinary boundaries (Alger 1997;
Edelman 2001, McAdam 1994; Moyer 2001). These researchers focus on theory,

8   In fact, he is able to cite econometric evidence that 'countries with divided societies (along ethnic
    and economic lines) and weak, hostile or corrupt governments are especially prone to a growth
    collapse' (Woolcock 2001, p. 16).

understanding and explaining the what, why and how of social movements, though some ground their work in their own involvement in movements (Ruggerio 2000). Social work has a role to play in this discussion, in that it is more inclined to begin with practice and move inductively to theory (Moyer 2001). Our conceptual and practical skills and our training and experience equip us to assist in building the capacity of ordinary people to conceptualise, to take action and to link the two. Social work also transcends disciplinary boundaries, in that it draws from a variety of theoretical traditions, including sociology, psychology, political science, economics and more recently, international social development.

Here we will briefly summarise some of the major discussions and debates. There are as many definitions as writers, but most would agree that social movements 'result when networks of actors relatively excluded from routine decision-making processes engage in collective attempts to change "some elements of the social structure and/or reward distribution of society"' (Smith et al. 1997, p. 59, citing McCarthy and Zald 1977). Social movement organisations (SMOs) are 'those formal groups explicitly designed to promote specific social changes' (Smith et al. 1997, p. 60). There have been a number of paradigms involved in the study of social movements: mass behaviour, resource mobilisation, new social movements, political process models, and, more recently, transnational social movements.[9]

Mass behaviour

Since the 1920s and into the 1970s, mainly through the functionalist school of thought (the 'Chicago school'), social movements were seen as symptoms of social imbalance, or tensions in otherwise 'normal' patterns of behaviour. Collective behaviour (crowds, sects, mass movements) were regarded as deviant or as outcomes of social. Drawing on psychology and economics, the focus of study was on who becomes involved, and what motivates people to engage in such behaviour. Marxist scholars, on the other hand, were more likely to see this as based in class conflict and the fundamental contradictions of capitalism. Thus, social movements were put in the context of wider historic meaning, and success was viewed in terms of the radical transformation of society. These 'old social movements' were critiqued as increasingly parochial and self-serving and later, as ignoring the voices of minorities and especially silencing women (Fisher and Kling 1994b, cited in Mullaly 2002, p. 197). Neither of these explained the activism of the 1960s, which was largely based in the middle classes and represented far more than 'tensions' in conventional patterns of everyday life. The social upheavals of this decade renewed the study of social movements in both North America and Europe.

---

9   These are not as discrete as this set of categories implies, of course, for theorists and researchers don't develop their ideas in such a segmented or linear fashion. Rather, the debates go back and forth and new ideas are generated in the process.

Resource mobilisation theory

In the US, scholars focused on individual attitudes, social movement organisations, mass violence, and conditions that make social movements able to take action (McCarthy and Zald 1977). The emphasis was on *how* people mobilise (versus *why*) and focused on an 'analysis of resources—material, human, cognitive, technical and organizational—that movements deployed in order to expand, reward participants, and gain a stake in the political system' (Edelman 2001, p. 289). Strategies were characterised as instrumental-economic, as rational, normal, institutionally rooted political challenges by aggrieved groups (Ruggerio 2000, p. 168, quoting Bluechler 1993). Movements were seen as structured and patterned so that their organisational dynamics could be analysed, like any other form of political action. This perspective stresses the normality of conflict and the rationality of actors and centres on the effectiveness with which social movements and organisations use resources to achieve their goals; it tries to determine why some movements are more successful than others (Ruggerio 2000, p. 169). Theorists focused on SMOs, as centres of movement activity, and regarded collective action as mainly representing interest groups (Edelman 2001, p. 289).

Later, the concept of 'political opportunity structures' (POS) was incorporated into this model, looking at internal dynamics of organisations and the balance of opportunities/threats for challengers and facilitation/repression for authorities (Tarrow 1998, cited in Edelman 2001, p. 290). Later, in response to critiques of POS as far too broad and ignoring issues of identity, gender and how the concept itself was socially constructed, proponents included a greater emphasis on cultural–historical sources of discontent (Edelman 2001, p. 290).

Critics argued that resource mobilisation (RM) theory ignored poor people's movements that emerged with few resources or organisation that were often hidden but none the less existed, even if they did not always result in overt collective action (Edelman 2001, p. 290). Some of the important theorists later recognised that the centrality of deliberate strategic decisions was exaggerated and that contingencies, emotions, flexibility and the interactive character of movement politics were downplayed (McAdam et al. 2001, p. 15). Many also recognised that the debates about the distinctions between some of the major concepts masked the common agenda among them (Carroll and Ratner 1996).

More recently, some of the major theorists have moved beyond disciplinary boundaries and classic social movement agendas to look at similar roots, causal mechanisms and processes in a wide variety of struggles in what they call 'forms of contention' (Carroll and Ratner 1996, p. 6). They do this by looking at various forms (revolutions, social movements, industrial conflict, war, interest group politics, nationalism, democratisation), arguing that, while different in some respects, they have similar roots, dynamics, patterns, connections and variations that can be analysed and compared. This broadens the perspective, allowing for an analysis of a 'wide variety of forms of contentious politics outside the world of democratic western polities' (Carroll and Ratner 1996, p. 18). One result has been their recognition of interpersonal networks, communication and various forms of continuous negotiation as central features of the dynamics of contention (Carroll and Ratner 1996, p. 22). They do not seek to build general models of all contention, but rather 'search for robust, widely applicable causal mechanisms that explain crucial, but not all, features of contention' (Carroll and Ratner 1996, p. 32). Their hope is 'to inspire new ways of studying contentious politics' (Carroll and Ratner 1996, p. 34).

New social movements or 'contemporary movements'

These theories, emerging initially in Europe, are premised on the notion of a central conflict but, rather than being class focused, they centre on the increasing differentiation of 'life world' and 'system,' with a concomitant colonisation of the former by the latter (Tarrow 1991). Habermas (1981) has been highly influential in this approach in his thinking about the resistance of people to the increasing rationalisation of modern life. His notion of the 'life world' (or individual and communal civil society 'space') as being colonised by state structures and the market economy articulated what many people were experiencing in their daily lives (Melucci 1994). New social movements (NSMs) are characterised as expressive-cultural and occur at the 'seam' between the public and the private, expressing the tension between them (Foweraker 1995, p. 10). In a time when those in power use information systems to maintain and extend their control, NSMs hold up a mirror to the system and reveal the 'dominant codes' used to manipulate the meanings of what we see and experience. They shift the emphasis from structure to social actor and the search for identity, individual self-realisation, participation and human rights.

NSMs tend to be fragmented, disorganised and often ephemeral. This is seen as both a strength and a weakness. The practical problem of building alliances is the struggle to move beyond the differences and build genuine solidarity among participants. Leonard (1997) points to the focus of NSMs on the local and the particular needs of a social group, which limits the ability to develop universal claims around social injustice. There is little opportunity, he argues, to establish solidarity among NSMs; whatever the faults, traditional trade union conflict with capital and its owners did provide a basis for collective action.

There is much discussion around moving beyond the dichotomy between these strategies (RM and NSMs, which are no longer 'new') and integrating them in some way. Critics argue that neither examines the larger political, social and economic context, and there have been various attempts to fill this gap: the political process model, the micromobilisation context, intermediate levels between individuals and structures (Foweraker 1995). While there are differing definitions of social movements, most do now agree that it is a process (Edelman 2001; Foweraker 1995).

Transnational social movements

'Social movements may be said to be transnational when they involve conscious efforts to build transnational cooperation around shared goals that include social change' (Smith et al. 1997, pp 59–60). 'In contrast to social movement organizations within nation-states, transnational social movement organizations (TSMOs) incorporate members from more than two countries, have some formal structure, and coordinate strategy through an international secretariat' (Smith et al. 1997, p. 61). In general, they 'contribute various forms of political leverage needed to overcome systemic barriers to global problem solving' (Smith et al. 1997, p. 60). Many respond to broad global issues, such as the environment, free trade, corporate power and human rights or common experiences (such as the women's movement), all of which grew as activists participated in international fora, summits, etc.

While these theoretical approaches and debates provide important background for social work, none offer a comprehensive view of social movements or offer much guidance for practice (Moyer 2001). What, then, can or should social workers add, as professionals whose daily work brings them into intimate contact with the human consequences of oppression? Our grounding in both theory and practice can contribute (and has) valuable insights and strategies for action, though this work is often unnoticed by mainstream theorists. New social welfare movements, such as the disabled people's movement and the psychiatric survivors' organisations, however, are challenging social work academics and practitioners to involve service users in developing theory and practice (Wilson and Beresford 2000). This is a good example of the dynamism inherent in social work as both theory and practice are confronted by those we work with. If we do not listen, and act, we risk alienating the very people we claim as allies, or becoming irrelevant.

What do Gramsci and Freire add?

For many years, social workers have struggled with the failure of the profession to confront the structural conditions that lay at the root of the problems they met in their daily practice: poverty; unemployment; child neglect and abuse; violence against women, etc. (McLaren and Leonard 1993, p. 157). How do we work with marginalised people to overcome the feelings of powerlessness in the face of the seemingly endless encounters with overwhelming human problems and suffering?

McLaren and Leonard (1993) write of their efforts to move beyond classical Marxism and the deterministic and pessimistic accounts of social work and state welfare he was encountering among workers in the field and in the literature:

> Given the historical emphasis within social work on the importance of subjectivity, the connection made between individual consciousness and subordination to dominant ideology by both Freire and Gramsci was used to show that the struggle against fatalism, including amongst social workers, was likely to be a significant part of a critical social work practice.
>
> (McLaren and Leonard 1993, p. 161)

Gramsci

Antonio Gramsci made several important advances over classical Marxist theory, developing a body of work which has been widely influential and, importantly for our purposes, having a significant influence on the work of Paulo Freire. Gramsci, born in 1891 to a southern Italian peasant family, worked organising workers' groups as bases for revolution and was imprisoned for these efforts in 1926 by Mussolini. During the 11 years between his imprisonment and his death in jail in 1937, Gramsci developed some advances in Marxist thought that have had wide impact in social scientific thought. For us, the following are some of Gramsci's most important contributions:

The concept of the organic intellectual

Gramsci (1976) disagreed with early Marxist theorists of social democracy over the role of intellectuals. He rejected the mechanistic view that intellectuals, some of whom would turn traitor to their class, were needed to provide theory and ideology (and often leadership) to the masses. Lenin (1963) had written about the need for socialist consciousness to be brought to the working class from outside, by the revolutionary party itself, through the fusing together of former workers and former intellectuals of bourgeois origin. Advancing beyond Lenin's view that in the revolutionary party all distinctions should be erased between workers and intellectuals, Gramsci argued that the working class, like the bourgeoisie before it, is capable of developing from within its own ranks its own 'organic intellectuals.' For Gramsci, the role of the political party is to channel the activity of these organic intellectuals and to provide a link between these and certain sections of the traditional intelligentsia. Organic intellectuals are at once ordinary workers and leaders. Gramsci argued that through their assumption of conscious responsibility, and with assistance from 'the more advanced bourgeois intellectual strata,' the proletariat can advance toward hegemony.

The distinction between structural and conjunctural analysis

Gramsci noted that some aspects of the social structure are more fundamental and comparatively permanent (structural), while others are more temporary (conjunctural). While structural analysis helps us to look at what broad-based changes we would like to see in the society, conjunctural analysis is needed to help us to assess opportunities for action at a given point in time, thus making our strategies and tactics most effective.

The importance of ideological hegemony

Gramsci affirmed that economic, ideological and political forces must *all* be taken into account in advancing a social democratic agenda. That is to say, the way in which people's thinking and ideology are formed must be addressed and understood. This means that actions must start from where people are, so that they can move to greater levels of awareness and political organisation.

Freire

Brazilian educator Paulo Freire's advocacy of 'popular education' as an option for the poor emerged out of his work in literacy training in the 1960s, and from Gramsci's concept of the organic intellectual. Freire (1973) argued that education systems are not neutral: they usually serve the interests of those in power. Popular education, or 'education for critical consciousness,' involves 'a participatory process that helps develop people's critical thought, creative expression, and collective action'. Freire's ideas and methods quickly attracted attention among Latin American social workers, many of whom began to talk of 'the social worker as popular educator.' The influence of this thought quickly spread from there to social workers in other poor countries, and finally to some parts of the 'developed world'. Three main ideas of Paulo Freire have contributed important concepts to social work theory and practice

The banking and dialogic approaches to teaching and learning

The conventional way of teaching is to assume that students come as 'empty vessels' to the classroom and the teacher's job is to fill them with content. This content is detached from reality, disconnected from the world of everyday living beyond the walls. The banking model assumes that 'knowledge is a gift bestowed by those who consider themselves knowledgeable upon those whom they consider to know nothing' (Freire 1973, p. 58). The assumption of a dichotomy between the individual and the world is implicit: the person is merely *in* the world, not *with* it; a spectator not a recreator (Freire 1973, p. 62).

Freire contrasts this with a problem-posing approach, in which learners are viewed as conscious beings, capable of critical reflection. The result is critical co-investigators in dialogue with one another, exploring an issue and drawing on their own experience to understand and take a critical stance towards what they have always assumed to be true. Both are assumed to be actors ('subjects') in the world, capable of intervening actively and creatively to change it. A part of this process is what Freire calls *'conscientizacao'* (education for critical consciousness), the development, through dialogue, of awareness of one's reality and engaging in critical thinking about it as process, as transformation, rather than as something static and unchangeable (Freire 1973, p. 81). Implicit in all this is the assumption that every human being is capable of understanding complex phenomena, engaging in an interactive process with others to develop a critical analysis of their reality, and individually and collectively taking action to change their world.

This certainly has direct application to our teaching/learning process in schools of social work. How we approach the classroom, how we understand the work that we do with students reflects one, or some combination of these approaches. In the same way, this applies to practitioners in their assumptions about the people they work with.

Praxis

Action and reflection are a continuous process, thinking clearly and thoroughly about one's reality, and then acting to change it. Reflection without action, however, is 'verbalism,' idle chatter; action without reflection is 'activism,' action for action's sake without thought. It is the back and forth between the two that is crucial to dialogue and transformation. (Freire 1973). Social workers, often caught up in a crisis, must focus on solving the immediate problem and have little time to reflect. The challenge is how to build in time to reflect in a job that has built in pressures to act.

Participatory research

Freire's work has been pivotal in establishing the philosophical foundations of participatory research (PR) (also called PAR, participatory action research, or AR, action research). His assumption that ordinary people are capable of generating valid knowledge challenged the view that only 'experts' can create 'real' knowledge. This was in part a reaction to positivist models of inquiry that were seen as exploitive and detached from the urgent social and economic problems that people were facing. The work of these researchers was framed explicitly within a context of power and transformation (Hall 1977, 1992).

McLaren and Leonard (1993) noted that the feelings of powerlessness of social workers paralleled the fatalism of peasants described by Freire. Freire's focus on cultural action showed that human intention, organised collectively, could count (McLaren and Leonard 1993, p. 161). The authors recognised, from Freire's analysis of structures of domination in Latin American countries, how a conditioning of fatalistic passivity is incorporated into these structures. They become part of 'common sense,' the taken-for-granted. Thus people consent to their own oppression by internalising the dominant ideology (McLaren and Leonard 1993, p. 161).

The work of Freire and Gramsci enables social worker educators to:

> move from a determinist and monolithic view of state welfare to one that emphasized struggle and contradiction . . . The role of the critical social worker was to be committed to conscientization, to enable service users and others . . . to develop their consciousness of the structural forces which shaped their lives and their deprivations. No longer would the social worker reinforce the official state definitions of social problems which focused on individual, family or community pathology, but would resist them and help others to do the same, individually and collectively.
>
> (McLaren and Leonard 1993, p. 162)

The next step is to examine social work theory and practice, as informed by Gramsci and Freire, looking specifically at how these can contribute some useful conceptual ideas and practical skills to the discussion.

Social work theory and practice

As noted earlier, social work theory draws upon a wide range of traditions. Which theoretical perspective dominates varies depending on the region and, within these, schools will differ in their approach to teaching and practice. While clinical approaches focusing on individual change within a social systems framework is probably the most broadly disseminated approach in North America, European and South American theorists and practitioners are more likely to focus on collective issues and action (Ramon 1999). Within this broad generalisation, of course, there is much variation. All social work practice, however, supports individual and collective well-being and recognises the interaction between the personal and the political, the person and her/his environment.

Throughout the history of social work, there has been a long-standing tension between those who see social work as focusing on individual and family problems, and those who regard advocacy and social change as a key part of their work. (It is the latter that are most attracted to the work of Gramsci and Freire). In North America, these tensions have shifted over time, as social and historical conditions have changed (Lundy 2003). In other parts of the world, there is extensive debate around these issues, given that the US model, with its primary emphasis on individual work, has been 'exported' to many other regions of the world (Asamoah et al. 1997; Gray 2002; Haug 2001; Healy LM 2001; Midgley 2001). Yet, in many cases, social workers in the 'South' have developed their own variations of social work in response to differing social, historical and cultural contexts (Gray 1998).

One key factor is the fact that the social work Code of Ethics obliges social workers to act, as an ethical imperative (Gil 1998). The Code outlines a set of principles, including a commitment to social justice, and a set of standards for practice. In other words, social work is about putting principles into action.[10] It is in linking theory, values and practice that makes the contribution of social work particularly useful.

There are three recent theoretical frameworks used widely in Canada—empowerment, structural social work and anti-oppressive practice—that incorporate the insights of Freire and Gramsci. Though differing in history and emphasis, all three share a common understanding of the role of larger systemic issues and practices in people's everyday lives. We will briefly summarise them here before outlining some important practice skills that are consistent with these approaches.

At the core of the three is an analysis of the links between broad systemic issues and individual struggles, and the focus on transforming the larger social, political

10 IFSW Code of Ethics: **www.IFSW.org**; CASW **www.casw-acts.ca**; IASSW **www. iassw-aiets.org**

and economic structures that oppress people. Oppression, rather than individual pathology or moral weakness, is seen as the main explanation for social problems. This does not mean that work with individuals is irrelevant or that the individual is totally powerless in the face of these forces. Rather, direct intervention work is understood in this context. Social workers concern themselves with individual change and broader group, organisational, social policies and administrative practices and institutional change. An analysis of oppression includes examining how race, class, gender, ability, sexual orientation, etc., play out in relations of domination and subordination. These 'isms' are seen as intersecting rather than parallel or competing. The insights of feminism, anti-racist theory, political economy, Marxism, critical social theory, along with post-modernism, post-structuralism and post-colonialism all contribute to deepening the analysis and linking it to practice (Campbell 2003; Dominelli 2002; Fook 1993; Lundy 2003; Moreau and Frosst 1989, 1993; Mullaly 1997, 2002; Shera 2002; Shera and Wells 1999). Over time, researchers, practitioners and scholars have articulated a range of practice skills consistent with these frameworks (Fook 1993; Goldberg Wood and Middleman 1989; Lundy 2003; Moreau and Frosst 1993).

Conceptually, the above approaches help bring a clarity, and a breadth in perspective, to the discussions and actions of global movements and organisations. They stimulate vibrant, ongoing debate and are thus continually 'in process' as new challenges and critiques emerge (Tester 2003). The fact that social work theory is always developed with an eye to 'what does this mean for practice' grounds it in reality and in action. We will now highlight a number of conceptual and practical skills social workers can bring to these movements.

Social work practice skills and their potential contribution

Structural and conjunctural analysis

This forms the basis for thorough understanding and for effective action. 'Structural analysis involves examination of the wider economic, social and political structures which oppress people (everywhere) and which are pervasive in relationships between partners. Conjunctural analysis relates to the immediate situation and involves examining the balance of political forces at a given moment in time and the opportunities for action. Effective development work rests on a foundation on ongoing analysis of both types' (Wilson and Whitmore 2000, p. 131).

Accompaniment (accompanying the process)

This is an expression (acompañamiento) often used in Latin America to refer to the relationship of social workers to the people (communities, groups, individuals) with whom they work. There is an inherent clarity in this about who owns and controls the process: our partners do. It is *we* who accompany *their* process. Wilson and Whitmore (2000) outline a set of principles for accompaniment, including non-intrusive collaboration, mutual trust and respect, the importance of a common analysis of what the 'problem' is: Northerners must understand that we have a stake in what happens in other parts of the globe; mutuality and equality in the relationship; a focus on process and a sensitivity to issues of language (the process needs to occur in various languages, not only English). This has direct applicability to the relationship between social work academics and practitioners advocated by service user group organisations and movements.

Social workers as allies

Bishop (2002) elaborates on the importance of, and difficulties in, building alliances among people. However well intentioned, people who wish to contribute to making a better, less oppressive world must be willing to confront their own power and privilege, in order to engage in the complex and emotionally charged process of becoming allies. She outlines six steps, including understanding oppressions, consciousness and healing, liberating oneself, allying with others and maintaining hope (Bishop 2002, p. 22). Skills include listening to others without personalising the issues, developing a capacity for critical analysis (of one's own privileges as well as social and political institutions), conflict resolution, the ability to 'read a situation' and respond appropriately and with flexibility and sensitivity, coalition building and group building skills.

Organising

Social workers have well-honed organising skills: how to bring people together to identify common grievances, getting them to communicate with each other across differing and even conflicting agendas; enabling them to run effective meetings; empowering them to recognise suitable strategies in a given context; assisting people in identifying points in a political regime that are vulnerable to pressure by collective action (Fisher and Kling 1994b, p. 19). One of an organiser's most valuable skills is 'the ability to challenge the accepted vision of things and develop ideological congruence with other oppositional efforts' (Fisher and Kling 1994a).

Relationship and trust building skills

These are some of our most traditional and finely honed skills. We know how to *listen*, really listen, not only for content but for feelings. We know how to build relationships based on mutuality and trust. Social workers also have a well-developed understanding of group dynamics and how to work with groups in a variety of circumstances.

Advocacy

Skills include many of the above, plus good tactical knowledge of where best to assert pressure and how, to maximise desired change. Effective advocates leave room for grassroots people to speak at the microphone (Shillington 2004).

Conclusion

We began this journey by looking at the current global political and economic context and the effects of the neo-liberal project on governments, and on civil society groups and organisations. We then reviewed the literature on social capital and social movements, concluding that, while offering many important insights, these are incomplete in helping social workers to understand or practice effectively in the current context. We considered the work of Gramsci and Freire and what they might usefully add in guiding our thinking and practice. The Gramscian concepts of the organic intellectual, ideology and hegemony, and structural and conjunctural analysis, and the problem-posing approach, praxis, and conscientisation of Freire not only deepen our analysis but also offer some clear guidance in how do our work. Finally, we talked about what social work, both theory and practice, bring to the discussion. It is clear that we have something quite unique and important to contribute to these debates, and more importantly, to taking action as active partners in the global movements for social justice.

One piece that is still missing is understanding the degree to which all the activity, by so many groups and organisations, is making any difference. Are they effective in what they do, and how do we know? Though many researchers have reflected on this, and activists certainly engage, in a variety of ways, in examining their own successes (or lack thereof), there are fewer instances of combining these two; that is, that researchers (or evaluators) have engaged with activists in exploring these questions. We propose to initiate a collaborative research process with a number of groups, using a participatory approach (e.g. PAR, appreciative inquiry, etc.). This would actively involve members of these groups and organisations in the 'how' and the 'what' of their work. We would work together to probe the ways they work together that are successful and the conditions that support or hinder this, and critically examine what they hope to achieve and whether or not they are effective. Have they made a difference? If so, how? How do they know?

There are many 'spaces' for progressive work. We, as social workers, activists and researchers, do bring a valuable combination of understanding and skills. Let's recognise this and put it to work.

14 'Another world is possible': social work and the struggle for social justice

Iain Ferguson and Michael Lavalette

The social work profession promotes social change, problem solving in human relationships and the empowerment and liberation of people to enhance well-being. Utilising theories of human behaviour and social systems, social work intervenes at the points where people interact with their environments. Principles of human rights and social justice are fundamental to social work (**www.ifsw.org.com**)

Introduction

Social work has lost its way. The loss of direction may have gone furthest in the UK but Butler and Drakeford's description of a social work profession that has become 'the unwitting but not unwilling partner of political and ideological processes that have robbed social work of its essential radicalism and transformatory potential' (2002, p. 7) is likely also to be recognisable to social work academics and practitioners in many other countries. Far from principles of human rights and social justice being at its heart, social work practice is increasingly dominated by managerialism, by the fragmentation of services, by financial restrictions and lack of resources, by increased bureaucracy and work-loads, by the domination of care-management approaches with their associated performance indicators, and by the increased use of the private sector.

A growing number of writers have begun the essential task of making sense of these changes and charting the ways in which the introduction of market forces has transformed all aspects of social work (e.g. Ferguson et al. 2002; Harris 2003; Jones 2000; Jones and Novak 1999;). This chapter will draw on these analyses but will also seek to move beyond description and analysis to locate some of the directions from which change may come; to identify, in other words, the 'green shoots' of a new, engaged social work practice. It is crucial that we know how social work got into this mess but if we are to avoid falling into pessimism and despair, it is no less crucial that we begin to locate the forces that will help us move out of our current predicament.

Elsewhere we have explored the ways in which popular struggles from below, from the Glasgow rent strikes in 1915 to the disability movement today, have played an important role in shaping welfare provision (Lavalette and Mooney 2001). In respect of social work, the great movements of the 1960s and early

1970s—the women's' movement, the civil rights movement, the gay movement (as well as the struggles of organised workers)—were crucial in informing the development of a radical social work practice in the 1970s (Thompson 2002). In this chapter, we want to explore the ways in which the most significant social movement of our own time can play a similar role in the rediscovery of a new, engaged social work practice. We refer of course to the movement that was born on the streets of Seattle in November 1999 where it brought the proceedings of the World Trade Organization (WTO) to a halt and which, following similar huge mobilisations in almost every corner of the globe, has become known as the anti-capitalist movement, or the global justice movement, or (misleadingly) the anti-globalisation movement. The first part of the chapter will outline the main features of that movement, and its relationship with the worldwide movement that developed in opposition to war in Iraq in 2003. The second part of the chapter will explore debates within the movement, including the extent to which change will come from above or from below and also debates around the concept of 'civil society'. Finally, we will consider some of the implications of this new movement for the future of social work.

Cracks in the neo-liberal consensus

For most of the 1990s, the idea that there was 'no alternative' to the market as a basis for organising social and economic life was the common sense not only of the political Right but also of the main Western social democratic parties (albeit wrapped up in Third Way clothing). The implications for welfare provision were profound. As Hall comments:

> The passing-off of market fundamentalism as the new common sense has helped to drive home the critical lesson which underpins the 'reform' of the welfare state: the role of the state 'nowadays' is not to support the less fortunate or powerful but to help individuals themselves to provide for all their social needs. Those who can must. The rest must be targeted, means-tested and kept to a minimum of provision lest the burden threaten 'wealth creation'.
>
> (Hall 2003)

As the twentieth century drew to a close, however, the claim that neo-liberal globalisation could provide a fairer, more equitable world system began to look increasingly empty. The collapse of the so-called 'Asian Tiger economies' in 1997, the devastation wrought by unbridled free-market policies in the former USSR and the social impact of structural adjustment programmes across the Third World left a number of 'official' critics uneasy about the effects of the 'Washington Consensus' (Hertz 2001; Stiglitz 2002). Over the same period, the scandal of Third World debt and increasing inequality across the globe produced the global *Jubilee 2000* campaign, organised originally through various Christian groups and NGOs, which was able to mobilise large numbers of people (particularly young people) against poverty and indebtedness (Pettifor 1998). The late

1990s also witnessed an increasing number of 'IMF riots' against the social consequences of Structural Adjustment Programmes (SAPs) across the second and third worlds (Bond 2001), which even spread to engulf some G7 countries themselves (notably in the public sector strikes in France in late 1995). Together, these various events meant that by the end of the century 'neo-liberal globalisation' had become a highly contested concept.

The level of contestation, however, was to reach a qualitatively new level in Seattle in November 1999. The disruption of the WTO Third Ministerial has been described, by US environmentalist Ralph Nader, as representing a 'fork in the road' (cited in Harman 2000). The 60 000–80 000 people who marched and demonstrated in Seattle not only forced the WTO to close early but they represented, according to two of its organisers, 'a turning-point in history' (Danaher and Burbach 2000, pp 7–8). Seattle's significance was that previous specific concerns (for example with the impact of free trade, or with environmental destruction) became merged. What became clear was the interconnectedness of a variety of injustices and dangers to our world. What was created was an anti-systemic movement. In the words of Joseph Stiglitz, Nobel Prize winner and former Chief Economist at the World Bank:

> Until the protestors came along, there was little hope for change and no outlets for complaint. *Some* of the protestors went to excesses; *some* of the protestors were arguing for higher protectionist barriers against the developing countries which would have made their plight even worse. But despite these problems, it is the trade unionists, students, environmentalists—ordinary citizens—who have put the need for reform on the agenda of the developed world.
>
> (Stiglitz 2002, p. 9)

Seattle was a turning point in more ways than one. A mere decade earlier, the collapse of the Berlin Wall, the Soviet Union and the Communist regimes of Eastern Europe were hailed by many commentators and politicians as signifying the 'end of history'; not least in the sense that ideological debates over the form which 'the good society' should take were now obsolete: the market and liberal democracy had definitively triumphed. Seattle challenged that assertion and led to the revival of social critique.

Second, Seattle had a profound impact on the nature of protest politics. After a decade in which radical politics had been dominated by notions of identity and difference (Fraser 2000), Seattle saw the birth of a new 'unity in diversity'. Alongside core sections of American organised labour (including Teamsters, longshoremen and machinists) was a plethora of non-governmental organisations and activist groupings around issues such as the environment, fair trade and Third World debt (Charlton 2000). As Naomi Klein, one of the early leaders of the movement has noted, unity was based not on the suppression of identity, on some homogenising of difference, but rather on the incorporation of identities within a radical critique of neo-liberalism which recognised the threat posed by the neo-liberal agenda to various aspects of social life, the environment and to the peoples of the world (Viner 2000). The nature of that unity is perfectly captured in the comments of the Zapatista leader *comandante* Marcos when he writes: 'It is necessary to build another world. A world in which there is room for many worlds. A world capable of containing all the worlds' (cited in Callinicos 2003a, p. 112).

Third, Seattle was no flash in the pan. In the 2 years that followed, even bigger mobilisations against the G8, the WTO and the World Bank took place in locations as diverse as Washington, Melbourne, Seoul, Prague, Quebec City, Genoa and Barcelona. But the movement wasn't restricted to protests in 'first world' cities. Strikes and demonstrations against neo-liberal policies erupted across the globe; in Palestine it gave birth to the second *Intifada* and in Argentina the movement presented a significant challenge to state power.

Moreover, it is a movement that has had to overcome profound political and ideological challenges. It was widely predicted (in Britain by the *Financial Times* among others) that the movement would not survive the post-9/11 fallout and, certainly, in the confusion and disorientation that followed the horror of that event, the movement did come to a temporary halt, particularly in the US. The rapid awareness, however, that Bush and Blair's 'war on terrorism' had much less to do with justice for the victims of the Twin Towers and much more to do with securing the geo-political interests of the US state and guaranteeing the interests of the US oil companies—what Ahmed Rashid (2000) has called 'the new Great Game'—led to the growth of the movement on a massive scale. Activists quickly made the links between the economic and environmental destruction being wrought on the planet by unbridled capitalism and the wars now being unleashed in Afghanistan and Iraq: what Claude Serfati (in Callinicos 2003a) calls 'armed globalization'. That new understanding was reflected in slogans such as *'No MacDonalds without McDonnell Douglas'* and the internationally popular *'No blood for oil'*, and also in the widespread use of the term 'imperialist' to describe the policies of the US and Britain. As the British MP George Galloway, expelled in 2003 from the Labour Party for his anti-war activities, has commented:

> I used not to use the word imperialism. I thought young people wouldn't even know what it meant. Then Robert Cooper [former policy adviser to Blair] writes a pamphlet in which he openly calls for what he describes as a new imperialism. Suddenly I find that everyone is using the words imperialism and anti-imperialism and I think that is a jolly good thing. If something looks like a duck and walks like a duck, the chances are it is a duck. That's exactly what we've got going now—a new imperialism. All sides are using its real name.
>
> (Galloway 2003, p. 117)

The fusion of the anti-capitalist movement and the anti-war movement meant that some 18 months after the bombing of the Twin Towers, the biggest worldwide demonstrations ever against war took place on 15 February 2003. Millions marched across the globe against the impending war on Iraq (including 2 million in London, the largest demonstration in British history).

Unsurprisingly, the movement is clearer about what it is against—neo-liberal globalisation, environmental destruction, Third World debt and imperialist war—than what it is for. As an example, a British television programme attempted to introduce a 'spoof' banner on the Mayday demonstration 2001, with the slogan 'Overthrow capitalism and replace it with something nicer', only to find the slogan was taken up by sections of the movement as an expression of both their critique of capitalism and their openness to the shape of future possibilities (Bircham and Charlton 2001, p. 377).

Nevertheless, the point should not be exaggerated; this is not a movement that lacks either goals or direction. From its earliest days, the movement on the streets has found ideological articulation in a body of engaged, critical writing by a variety of movement intellectuals; writers like Pierre Bourdieu, Noam Chomsky, Walden Bello, Michael Albert, Naomi Klein, Susan George and Alex Callinicos have explored the concerns of the movement and the necessity of finding 'something nicer'. Further, there has always been debate within the movement over what should replace capitalism, or even whether it is the system as a whole that needs replacing or just specific policies and institutions (see Bircham and Charlton 2001; Harman 2000). These issues have been debated at the various World, European, Asian and African Social Forums that have been held over the last few years. As the movement has progressed, activists have moved from asserting that 'another world is possible' (itself a necessary corrective to pessimistic notions that 'there is no alternative to the market') to addressing what that better world will be like.

Anti-capitalist debates

Debate has been central to the anti-capitalist movement. From the beginning serious consideration has been given to analysing and understanding the problems of the modern world and what links the various aspects of anti-capitalist concerns (environmental destruction, oppression, inequality, war, debt, etc.) together. These issues have been considered at meetings and conferences across the world over the recent period, but are at their most remarkable at the various World and sectoral Social Forums. The Forums have been organised by various NGOs, movement organisations and trade unions and have produced significant social space for debate and engagement. The first World Social Forum took place in Porto Alegre, Brazil in January 2001, in opposition to the Economic Forum being held in Davos. As Sader (2002) notes:

> The Social Forum is a unique meeting place for anti-systemic forces to gather. . . . It is unprecedented both in its diversity—bringing together not only political parties and political currents but social movements, NGOs, civil-rights groups, unions—and in its own non-state, non-partisan character. It proposes to formulate global alternatives to current capitalist practices, and strategies for their implementation.
>
> (Sader 2002)

Strategic debate has always been central to the movement and at the Forums there are important (though friendly) arguments and debates between various individuals and currents inside the anti-capitalist movement. Some of the most important of these are considered below.

Change from above or change from below?

Perhaps the most useful distinction to make is between those who want to initiate some form of change in the regimes of global governance (who want to initiate 'change from above') and those who, broadly, want change to be brought via the democratic involvement and 'empowerment' of various grassroots networks and communities in opposition to local and global state building projects (those who want to initiate 'change from below').

In relation to the first group, Held and McGrew (2003, pp 116–17) have identified groups of writers they label 'liberal internationalists', 'institutional transformers' and 'global transformers'; what unites these various groups is their commitment to some form of reform of the global economic and political institutions that impact on the modern world.

Our second group are the 'radicals' who see the problem as lying not in this policy or that institution but rather in the very dynamic of capitalism itself, the dynamic of 'accumulation for accumulation's sake'. Held and McGrew sum up their position as follows:

> The radical project is concerned to establish the conditions necessary to empower people to take control of their own lives and to create communities based on ideas of equality, the common good and harmony with the natural environment. For many radicals of this kind, the agents of change are to be found in existing (critical) social movements, such as the environmental, women's and anti-globalisation movements . . . which challenge the authority of states and international agencies as well as orthodox definitions of the 'political'.
>
> (Held and McGrew 2003, pp 112–13)

As Held and McGrew note, within this radical wing of the movement, there is a reluctance to prescribe blueprints or lay down plans, as this would be seen as a 'top-down' approach which would conflict with the spirit of 'change from below' which characterises the politics of this section of the movement.

For those within the 'change from above' camp, developments brought about by globalisation have left the nation-state weak and relatively impotent in contrast to the power of multinational capital. The conclusion drawn by some theorists is that there is a need for a global social policy that includes a commitment to global social redistribution and global social regulation. Such a position can be found in the work of George and Wilding (2002) and Deacon et al. (1997).

For these writers, the modern era of neo-liberal globalisation brings the very real danger that social and labour rights will be eroded by the power of multinational capital. Trans- and multinational capital has become so powerful, their ability to move and relocate around the world so easy, that individual states are increasingly forced to compete against each other to provide the most attractive conditions for companies in the hope that they will locate within their borders. This means (as critical welfare writer Peter Leonard puts it) states become either 'reluctant' or 'enthusiastic' welfare dismantlers (1997, p. 114). To stop the 'race to the bottom' in labour and social standards, it is necessary for a new regulatory regime of governance to be established, one that is suitable to the global era within which we now operate.

For Deacon et al. (1997, p. 203) for example, it is necessary, in order to protect the poor and vulnerable, and establish internationally agreed standards, to undertake the following measures:

1   regulating global competition;
2   making the Bretton Woods institutions more accountable; and
3   reforming the United Nations.

Control of multinational capital is, of course, vital. But will these measures succeed in the task Deacon et al. set them? Underpinning their argument is an assumption that the UN and the international financial institutions (IFIs) are capable of being brought under the 'democratic' control of the world's nations, with each nation having an equivalent voice. Now ignoring the fact that many members of the World Trade Organization and the UN are not themselves democratic countries, neither of these institutions (nor indeed the World Bank or the IMF) are built on any notion of democracy. They reflect the power of the most powerful states in the world, in particular the political, economic and military interests of the US.

If we take the WTO, for example, decisions (which are binding on all members) are theoretically arrived at by 'consensus'. In reality the consensus is established by a group of states called the 'quad', the representatives of the US, Canada, Japan and Europe, who meet on a daily basis and establish how various issues should be addressed. When they come to a conclusion they then announce 'consensus' has been achieved. Further, as Bakan notes:

> The WTO . . . differs from any other global institution by having the ability to both legislate against particular practices and to act as judge to determine if those rules are being broken. This makes it an incredibly powerful tool for corporate interests. The rules of the WTO essentially define what areas of economic activity may be challenged as being a barrier to the development of the free movement of trade or investment by foreign corporations. The decisions regarding disputes are reached in secret by a panel of three unaccountable bureaucrats.
>
> (Bakan 2000, p. 23)

If any country flouts the 'consensus' or the rules they can expect sanctions and/or retaliation against them, unless, that is, they happen to be amongst the most powerful states when rules are ignored if they do not suit domestic policy, as was the case when the US government erected protective barriers against steel imports in 2002–2003. As Aziz Choudry notes when discussing Vietnam's application to join the WTO, the country will need to get used to US 'double standards and protectionism which exist . . . [because the WTO is based upon] a deeply unequal relationship.' (2002, p. 7)

This case is accepted by Iris Young who argues for closure of the IMF and World Bank because these 'do not even pretend to be inclusive and democratic' institutions. But she continues, 'the best existing starting point for building global democratic institutions [is the UN] . . . As members of the General Assembly, nearly all the world's peoples today are represented at the UN' (2000, pp 272–274).

Now of course this is technically true in the sense that all governments, no matter the validity of their democratic credentials, send an unelected representative to the UN assembly. But Young's prognosis ignores the extent to which the UN is built upon protecting the power of the most powerful imperial states. The real power at the UN rests not in the assembly but in the Security Council, and within this body the 'permanent members' comprising the most powerful military regimes from the Cold War era (USA, Britain, France, USSR (now Russia), and China). Even here however, the reliance of China and Russia on Western aid and economic agreements in the post-Cold War era has left real decision-making power with what is known as the 'permanent three' (US, France, Britain) and it is this group which have been able to provide UN cover for the various imperialist interventions in the Middle-East and the Balkans in the 1990s and early twenty-first century. And, of course, when the UN Security Council takes a (limited) stand against the interests of the most powerful imperialist countries, it is easily side-stepped, as the example of the most recent Iraqi war emphasises. Recent evidence indicates that the US has altered direction from 'coalition building' (in its interests) under Clinton to a more aggressive unilateralism under Bush the younger, a change which further marginalises the power and authority of the UN (Callinicos 2003b). The prospects of a rejuvenated UN representing a real extension of democracy, able to control the activities of the most powerful imperial states and multinational corporations seem, to us at any rate, slim at best.

In contrast, writers advocating 'change from below' express the hope that the new movement can provide the resources to harness the power of both multinational capital and the dominant imperialist states. In *The Age of Consent* (2003), for example, the British journalist and activist George Monbiot, while rejecting both Marxism and anarchism, calls for 'a global democratic revolution' based on four main measures: the democratisation of the United Nations; the establishment of a global parliament; the scrapping of the World Bank, the IMF and the WTO and their replacement by a International Clearing Union; and the establishment of a new International Trade Organisation. In calling for the scrapping of the major institutions of neo-liberalism (as opposed to their reform) Monbiot is clearly locating himself within the radical wing of the movement. His proposals to reform the UN, however, are open to the same criticisms that were made above, as would be his proposed World Parliament, which as Monbiot himself admits, could do no more than monitor the activities of rich nations and corporations. His third and fourth proposals (based on ideas originally put forward by Keynes) have the merit of recognising that any solutions need to be global in nature and that neither 'localisation' nor protectionism can adequately address the problems caused by globalisation. They have been criticised, however, for placing unwarranted faith in the progressive nature of Third World governments (whose withdrawal from the WTO, the IMF and the World Bank Monbiot sees as precipitating the collapse of these bodies; Ashman 2003). As the experience of the PT government in Brazil demonstrates, even the most radical of these governments can quickly succumb to the pressures of these global institutions (Gonzalez 2003). Only where they are under pressure from a mass movement from below (as during the WTO talks at Cancun in 2003) can representatives of these governments be forced to act in ways which really do challenge the interests of the major economic powers.

A different kind of anti-capitalist manifesto is suggested by Callinicos (2003a). Unlike Monbiot, he places his hopes not in the creation of new global institutions or in the progressive potential of Third World governments but rather in change from below, in the growth of the movement itself, a movement which, he argues:

> bears the real promise of modernity by promoting a genuinely universal emancipation that would make the fate of the planet and those on it a collective and democratic project.
>
> (Callinicos 2003a, p. 149)

Writing from a classical Marxist perspective (Anderson 1976), Callinicos sees the roots of the problems thrown up by globalisation as lying not in unfair trade but rather in the inequitable distribution of the means of production. Consequently he argues for a democratically organised socialist planned economy as the best means of realising the values of the anti-capitalist movement, which he identifies as justice, efficiency, democracy and sustainability. As his reference to modernity implies, he also sees the anti-capitalist movement as offering a new synthesis to the tension between universalist values and the protection of diversity (what he has called elsewhere 'the radicalised Enlightenment'; Callinicos 1995, p. 194). Finally, in contrast to most other movement theorists, he sees a global working class as having a key role to play within the anti-capitalist movement which, he argues, can only achieve its goals through a revolutionary strategy (Callinicos 2003a, p. 143).

Civil society

'Civil society' is a key concept within the anti-capitalist movement, and one that has been taken up enthusiastically by social work theorists (with the 2004 IFSW Conference in Adelaide, for example, entitled 'Reclaiming Civil Society'). It originates in the work of Hegel, Marx and particularly Gramsci. Gramsci (1971) was concerned (among other things) with the nature of bourgeois rule. One of his central arguments was that, in the established democratic capitalist states of the West (he was writing in the early 1930s), the continuation of bourgeois rule occurred less through the use of naked violence or the coercive rule of the state than through:

> the acceptance by the ruled of 'a conception of the world' which belongs to the rulers. The philosophy of the ruling class passes through a whole tissue of complex vulgarisations to emerge as 'commonsense': that is, the philosophy of the masses, who accept the morality, the customs, the institutionalised rules of behaviour of the society they live in.
>
> (Fiori 1965/1990, p. 238)

A strengthened civil society could be understood as one of the mechanisms through which bourgeois rule legitimated itself. The separation of the state, the economy and various non-state institutions, such as the mass media, the churches, etc., hid the true, exploitative nature of society and helped the process of establishing bourgeois hegemony. For Gramsci, therefore, a strengthened civil society also represented a more secure state and a more stable form of bourgeois rule.

As more commonly used today, 'civil society' has been transformed into a short-hand term to refer to an arena where discrete, self-organised interest groups, separate from the state, promote a variety of interests and, hence, ensure the maintenance of a democratic and peaceful society (Keane 1998; Touraine 2001).

In these more recent formulations the concept can be traced to a body of work by a number of dissident intellectuals in Eastern Europe, South Africa and Latin America in the 1980s (see Keane 1989). Here it was suggested that an overbearing or 'totalitarian' state had invaded social life so that the vast majority of the population was effectively excluded from political life and economic power. In this context there was the growth of a 'civil society' of organised resistance. In other words, in those societies where there was a merger of state and economic power (the more overt forms of state capitalism or state-directed capitalism) combined with a level of political exclusion—one-party rule, military regime, corrupt dictatorship of some form, racial exclusion, or other barrier to democratic participation—then the notion of civil society offered a concept that could mobilise 'the people' against a corrupt, unjust and unequal form of society. Here we have civil society against the state, a conception of civil society that has little connection with Gramsci's work (despite some authors claiming roots in his theoretical framework). Indeed, rather than having its origins in the classical Marxist tradition represented by Gramsci, this perspective on civil society is closer to classical theories of pluralism (Ungpakorn 2003).

Clearly the concept of civil society has been a useful umbrella term that has brought disparate groups together to organise and participate in acts of resistance. But the difficulty starts to arise when we begin to pose political solutions to the problems of the day. How useful is the concept of civil society as an organiser of a new world?

Here we have to recognise that the concept of civil society is nebulous. It incorporates a very broad range of institutions and activities and reflects many contradictory interests, each with a different perspective of what the 'good life' would or should be like. It includes capitalist economies, households, social movements, NGOs, voluntary political institutions such as the church, professional organisations, trade unions, cultural organisations, independent media organisations, political parties, electoral associations and a range of welfare and disciplinary institutions such as schools, hospitals, asylums and prisons. This range is portrayed as a strength because these organisations provide the resources and the general focus for a more democratic, pluralist and inclusive political involvement by 'the people'.

However, there are some problems here. First, the range of institutions covered by the label 'civil society', the private capitalist enterprise, the democratic trade union and the church, etc., are all fundamentally different types of organisations, with a range of (often opposed) interests and varying capacities to shape the world. As Sader argues:

> The very concept of 'civil society' masks the class nature of its components— multinational corporations, banks and mafia, set next to social movements, trade unions, civic bodies—while collectively demonising the state.
>
> (Sader 2002, p. 5)

Second, the uncritical celebration of civil society against the state, therefore, is an immense hostage to fortune in the present political climate. Multinationals, vast corporations, and smaller local enterprises all inhabit civil society. Their goal is to make vast profits by exploiting the labour of those they employ. In this form, theories of civil society are in grave danger of being apologia for private capitalism, and in Britain, for example, the right-wing, neo-liberal think-tank the Institute for Economic Affairs has recently changed its name to Civitas, the institute for the study of civil society.

Civil society is a site of immense inequalities. And those inequalities necessarily impinge on the freedoms of the majority within civil society. Hence, strengthening civil society does not necessarily mean more democracy. In Britain, the privatisation of British Gas, British Telecom, British Rail, etc. (when these companies went from state control back into civil society in the form of a private enterprise) has not made any of them more accountable, it has made them less so. As Tariq Ali puts it: 'Capitalist democracy = privatisation + "civil society"' (2003, p. 3).

Finally, the conception of civil society has gained such pre-eminence because of the involvement of large numbers of non-governmental organisations (NGOs) in the various movement actions and Forums. The NGOs, in particular, promote the language of civil society; after all they define their very status by their 'non-governmental', non-state label. But as we will see this creates problems.

The role of the NGOs

There has been a remarkable expansion of NGOs over the last 30 years: 'Between 1975 and 1985 the amount of aid transferred from developed nations to developing nation via NGOs increased 1400% and the number of NGOs proliferated in countries as far apart as Brazil, Kenya, Philippines and Thailand' (Ungpakorn 2003, p. 1).

In his important study of NGO activity Gerald Clarke suggests a number of reasons for this expansion, and interestingly these divide into 'top down' and 'bottom up' drives. First, he suggests there was an expansion of NGO activity because governments in the developed world recognised their beneficial role in service provision in less developed regions of the world, and that in a neo-liberal climate the NGO was preferred because this coincided with a determination by these governments to role back the state as a provider of services. Second, he notes the expansion of NGOs in the West into the developing countries, either directly or as funders of local projects. But these 'top down' determinants were also matched by 'bottom up' imperatives. In particular he suggests the fragmentation and collapse of left-wing movements and the failure of the political parties of the left and the trade unions to adequately articulate the demands of the poor and dispossessed created a space into which the NGOs could expand (Clarke 1998, pp 7, 198).

This theme, the growth of popular NGOs stepping into the space vacated by a weakened left movement, is taken up by others. Ungpakorn (2003, p. 1) suggests: 'Although N.G.O.s existed well before the mid-1980s, it was the "collapse in confidence" in a Marxist alternative to capitalism, together with a generalised ruling class offensive against struggles from below from the mid-1970s, which gave the N.G.O. movement its real growth spurt'. Sader argues:

> As the old left got weaker, lost its mass base or deserted the field, the space of anti-neoliberal resistance was occupied by NGO-type groupings, deliberately distanced from the political arena and thus from any serious reflection on strategy.
>
> (Sader 2002, p. 5)

While Petras (1999) suggests that NGOs have successfully displaced, destroyed or coopted movements of the left in developing countries.

However, the contrasting drives promoting NGO growth identified by Clarke mean the movement encapsulates a major contradiction. On the one hand, often despite the moral and political position of local workers, NGOs can find themselves coming to an accommodation with global IFIs and in effect carrying through the project of global neo-liberalism. On the other hand, the small number of, what Bond terms, radical NGOs struggle for resources to fund their projects.

Many NGOs have found themselves incorporated into various state and IFI projects. As Bond notes:

Some local activities undertaken by grassroots groups too easily [fall] . . . into the trap of neo-liberal economic policies. This was a logical corollary to the rise of so-called 'civil society' discourses . . . The rise of community based organisations and associated development NGOs closely corresponds with the desire of the international agencies to shrink Third World states as part of an overall effort to lower the social wage.

(Bond 2001, pp 228–9).

Bond also notes that by the early 1990s two out of every five World Bank projects across the globe involved NGOs 'and in projects involving population, nutrition, primary healthcare and small enterprise, the ratio rose to more than four out of five' (Bond 2001, p. 229). The consequences, as Jonathan Neale argues, is that:

Instead of the government of Nepal or Afghanistan getting aid for education and using some of it to pay teachers, more and more NGOs get the money direct. This shift is driven by US government policy. The idea . . . is that . . . civil society is better than governments. Better to give the money direct to Oxfam to administer than to give it to a government, even an elected government. In practice, NGOs are part of the privatisation of the world. The business of governments is privatised, and now the NGOs are responsible to no one except the funders . . . [and] NGOs working in developing countries get most of their money from Western governments, Japan, the UN and the European Union.

(Neale 2002, p. 41)

Such financial considerations can, in turn, have an impact on the NGOs, campaigning work. At the start of the war on Iraq the NGO Save the Children (UK) put out a press release that was mildly critical of the war and raised fears about its effects on the civilian population. This led to a heated exchange with their US wing, Save the Children (US), who demanded the release be pulled and no further reports of a similar nature be put out. According to Kevin Maguire, the US organisation was concerned that any such critical stance may impact on their future funding (*Guardian*, 28 November 2003).

There is no doubt that such funding concerns are real. Tariq Ali writes about the prospects of occupied Iraq:

This is imperialism in the epoch of neo-liberal economics. Everything will be privatised, including civil society. Like aliens from another planet . . . the NGOs will descend on Iraq like a swarm of locusts . . . Intellectuals and activists of every stripe in all the major cities will be bought off and put to work producing bad pamphlets on subjects of purely academic interest. This has the effect of neutering potential opposition or, to be more precise, of confiscating dissent in order to channel it in a safe direction. The message . . . is straight forward: make some noise, by all means, but if you do anything really political that seriously affects the functioning of the neo-liberal state on any level, your funds might not be renewed . . . This is then characterised as 'civil society' or 'real grass-roots democracy', cleaner and more user-friendly than any political party.

(Ali 2003, p. 3)

NGOs, therefore, find themselves in an increasingly contradictory position. On the one hand they remain philosophically committed to substantial reform of the existing world, but on the other they are increasingly the vehicle for the extension of the privatisation agendas of the dominant neo-liberal players.

Social work and the struggle for social justice

The previous sections have focused on some of the key debates within the anti-capitalist movement. Yet as recent conferences in Cairo (Rees 2003) and Mumbai (the site of the World Social Forum in 2004) have shown, not only is the movement proving capable of containing these and other differences without splitting or fragmenting but it also continues to spread and grow, both geographically and socially (with organisations of the lowest castes in Indian society, for example, playing an important role at the Mumbai Forum; see Harman 2004). Given the need to reassert the social justice agenda within social work, in what ways then might this new movement help to inform the development of a new, engaged practice? In part, the answer to that question will depend on the extent to which individual social workers, as well as national and international social work organisations, are prepared to engage with these movements, and on what basis.

In a discussion of issues in international social work, Midgely refers to the long-standing debates between proponents of remedial, activist and developmental social work (Midgely 2001). By remedial social work, he is referring to the practice of direct work with individuals and families with a focus on their personal problems, often drawing heavily on psychological, behavioural and treatment approaches. Developmental social work is concerned with promoting the social and economic development of local populations, often through the use of community work approaches, while activist social work is primarily concerned with challenging structural oppressions and promoting liberation. He makes a plea for an end to these 'internecine disagreements which have plagued social work since its formative years' (Midgely 2001, pp 28–30). Given that these debates are often rooted in genuine differences over the role that social work should play in social and political change, they may not be so easily wished away. That said, a refreshing feature of the anti-capitalist movement is the determination of its participants to overcome old enmities and divisions and to work to ensure that sectarian attitudes and practices do not block the unity and progress of the movements, as they have done so often in the past.

In the same way, dissatisfaction with the effects of marketisation and managerialism within social work is creating the basis for potentially much broader alliances amongst workers, and service users, than was possible in the radical social movement of the 1970s (Bailey and Brake 1975). Then, the fault lines were usually drawn between 'traditional' social workers who defended a notion of social work rooted in psychosocial approaches on the one side and those who looked towards more collective approaches and emphasised the need to address the impact of structural factors on clients' lives on the other. It is clear, however, that the pressures and consequences of marketisation have created a level of dissatisfaction and a sense of alienation which extends very far beyond the small number of social workers who would identify themselves as 'radical' (Jones 2000). At the core of that dissatisfaction is the fragmentation of social work produced by the purchaser/provider split, the dominance of care management approaches and the increasing specialisation of social work. The effect of that fragmentation has been to push social workers into increasingly bureaucratic, service-rationing and controlling roles. This, in turn, undermines the worker–service user relationship, transforming it into what is essentially a commercial activity, less and less concerned with addressing the totality of people's lives. The result is a widespread feeling amongst social workers that 'I didn't come into social work for this' (the title of a series of meetings for practitioners and academics in Britain in 2003–2004 which sought to address the current impasse) and the beginnings of a search for new directions (Jones et al. 2003).

A rejection of the market, however, is not the only point of convergence between contemporary social work and the new movements. There is also considerable overlap between the values of social work and the values of anti-capitalism. The resonance between the IFSW definition of social work cited at the beginning of this chapter and some of the key values of the anti-capitalist movement are obvious: the promotion of social change; the commitment to social justice; and the emphasis on human rights, empowerment and liberation. There is a critical kernel within social work values which can inform the development of more radical approaches and which allows connections to be made with these new movements.

In the 1960s and 1970s, it was the awareness of that emancipatory potential of social work that made it an attractive career option to many young radicals (Pearson 1975). While there is less evidence of such an explicitly political motivation in today's graduates, our experience of teaching social work students for over a decade suggests that concerns for social justice and ideas of empowerment are still powerful motivating factors for at least a minority of students on social work courses. The fact that social work is still viewed this way is also reflected in the fact that social work is included as an 'ethical profession' within the Ethical Careers Service hosted by the international campaigning organisation People and Planet (**www.peopleandplanet.org.uk**).

But we must add a caveat. By their very nature, values are open to widely different interpretations (one reason, for example, why New Labour in Britain prefers to talk about 'values', rather than ideologies or beliefs; Callinicos 2000). In addition, the dominance of a market-driven agenda in social work over the past decade has meant that social work values have often lost their meaning, or in some cases, been turned into their opposite. That process has sometimes been made easier by the willingness of the leadership of the profession to see only the apparently 'progressive' side of neo-liberal reforms which use the language of 'empowerment' and 'choice' but whose primary aim is the commodification of welfare (Jones 1999). There has been, as Butler and Drakeford point out:

> a very real cost in the flexible exploitation of ambiguity which has allowed social work to retain the semblance of loyalty to its own values, while carrying out the bidding of political masters with very different ideas and purposes.
>
> (Butler and Drakeford 2002, p. 8)

Values by themselves, therefore, do not provide a sufficient basis for a renewal of an engaged social work. To avoid incorporation of the sort described by Butler and Drakeford, social work values need to be underpinned by a much more rigorous theoretical analysis of the ways in which the neo-liberal agenda has impacted on social work at the level of organisation, practice and ideology (including, here, an exploration of the ways in which social work as a profession has been influenced by the social authoritarianism which informs attacks on 'welfare dependency'; Lavalette and Mooney 1999). As mentioned, texts such as Jones and Novak (1999) and Harris (2003) have already made an important contribution in this respect.

Finally, there is the question of organisation. The triumphalism of the Right during the Thatcher–Reagan era, their insistence that 'there is no such thing as society', and their defeat of major trade unions, led many people to accept the argument that collective action to change society was futile, a view whose theoretical underpinning was often provided by a post-modernism which argued that attempts to bring about large-scale change could only end in tyranny (Ferguson and Lavalette 1999). After Seattle however, and even more so after the worldwide mobilisation against war on 15 February 2003, that argument became less and less convincing (and in fact was often parodied by placards on demonstrations bearing the message 'Resistance is fertile'). It was, in Bertinotti's (2003) words, a '20th century myth':

> The anti-globalisation movement is the first movement that represents a break with the 20th century and its truths and myths. At present it is the main source of politics for an alternative to the global right. When, on February 15, 100 million people took to the streets, the *New York Times* referred to it as a second 'world power', a power that in the name of peace opposed those who wanted war.
>
> (Bertinotti 2003)

In terms of social work, the rediscovery of the effectiveness of collective action and organisation has important implications both for social workers and for the service users with whom they work. For social workers, it means recognising that one factor that has allowed us to get into this mess (in Britain at least) has been the weakness of professional representation and organisation. The dissatisfaction with social work as currently practised, and the new mood of radicalism represented by the anti-capitalist movement, the anti-war movement and the creation of new electoral alternatives, provides both the necessity and the opportunity to create new, much stronger, and much more radical, networks of social workers and service users, both nationally and internationally.

In terms of work with service users, it means reasserting the value of collective approaches, following a decade in which community development approaches have been increasingly squeezed out of both social work practice and education, in the UK at least. Such approaches have continued to thrive both in many voluntary organisations and also in the new movements of service users, such as the disability movement and the mental health users' movement. It is time for social workers to re-engage with them.

Conclusion

The anti-capitalist and anti-war movements both reflect and contribute to a new-found mood of radicalism of a type and on a scale not seen since the great social upheavals of the 1960s and early 1970s (Harman 1988). In this chapter, we have argued that these movements offer social work and social workers a glimpse of how the ravages inflicted by neo-liberal welfare polices over the past decade might begin to be overcome. If real change is to happen, however, it means that social workers need to begin to connect with these new movements for global justice and against war and become actively involved in their activities, whether globally or locally (as social workers in the US and elsewhere have done in the past; Reisch and Andrews 2001). The splendid statement issued by the IFSW during the protests against the World Trade Talks at Cancun in Mexico in 2003 gives some sense of what such connection might mean:

> This is not the place for a reasoned argument on trade rules and economic systems. They can be found elsewhere. This is the time and the place for social workers to express our frustration with the slow pace of change in world trade rules. We have a duty to speak out about the impact of these rules on those who are poorest and most vulnerable. As a profession we daily experience how poverty translates into human misery. Poverty is an affront to human civilisation.
>
> (International Federation of Social Workers 2003)

Finally, we need to make these connections and carry out the practical, intellectual and emotional work of developing a new, engaged practice with a sense of urgency. If we are able to do that, then the pessimism and despair that has surrounded social work practice for so long can begin to be replaced by the hope that (to paraphrase the key slogan of the anti-capitalist movement) another social work is, indeed, possible.

Bibliography

Aballéa F (2002) Travail social et travailleurs sociaux: le divorce ? *Recherche Sociale* **163**: 16–30.

Abramovitz M (1992) The Reagan legacy: Undoing race, class, and gender accords, *Journal of Sociology and Social Welfare* **19**: 91–110.

Abramovitz M (1999) *Regulating the Lives of Women: American Social Policy from Colonial Times to the Present* 2nd edn. Boston: South End Press.

Addams J (1902) *Democracy and Social Ethics*. New York: MacMillan.

Addams J (1907) *Newer Ideals of Peace*. New York: MacMillan.

Addams J (1910) *Twenty Years at Hull House*. New York: Crowell and Co.

Aidara N (2003) *Aux victimes du Bateau 'le Joola': L'hommage d'un père*. Compte d'auteur.

Alayón N (1980) El asistencialismo en la política social y en el trabajo social. In: *Revista Acción Crítica* N° 7, Celats-Alaets, Lima, 1980.

Alayón N (2000) *Asistencia y asistencialismo. Pobres controlados o erradicación de la pobreza?* 3rd edn. Buenos Aires: Lumen.

Alayon N (2003) Pobreza, Derechos Humanos y Política Social. Conferencia en el III Congreso Internacional de Trabajo Social. San José, Costa Rica. Setiembre de 2003.

Albrow M (1996) *The Global Age: State and Society beyond Modernity* Cambridge, UK: Polity Press.

Alger CF (1997) Transnational social movements, world politics and global governance. In: Smith J, Chatfield C and Pagnucco R (eds) *Transnational Social Movements and Global Politics: Solidarity beyond the State*. Syracuse, NY: Syracuse University Press.

Ali T (2003) *Bush in Babylon: The Recolonisation of Iraq*. London: Verso.

Alinsky S (1969) *Reveille for Radicals*. New York: Vintage.

Anderson A (1998) *Politiques de la ville: de la zone au territoire*. Paris: Syros.

Anderson P (1976) *Considerations on Western Marxism*. London: New Left Books.

Andrews J and Reisch M (1997) Social work and anti-communism: A historical analysis of the McCarthy era. *Journal of Progressive Human Services* **8**: 29–49.

Asamoah Y, Healy LM and Mayadas N (1997) Ending the international-domestic dichotomy: new approaches to a global curriculum for the millennium. *Journal of Social Work Education* **33**: 389–401.

Ascher F (2001) *Ces événements nous dépassent, feignons d'en être les organisateurs. Essai sur la société contemporaine*. La Tour d'Aigues: Aube.

Ashman S (2003) The anti-capitalist movement and the war. *International Socialism* **2(98)**: 7–22.

Audibert A (1977) *Le service social en Afrique francophone dans une perspective de développement.* Thèse de doctorat de 3eme cycle. Paris: Sorbonne.

Audit Commission (1983) *Performance Review in Local Government: A Handbook for Auditors and Local Authorities.* London: HMSO.

Audit Commission (1988) *The Competitive Council.* London: HMSO.

Audit Commission (2002) *Recruitment and Retention: A Public Service Workforce for the Twenty First Century.* London: Audit Commission.

Austin J (2003) *From Nothing to Zero.* Melbourne: Lonely Planet.

Australian Association of Social Services (2001) *Achieving Justice for Indigenous Australians,* Joint statement by the Community Services Sector, October 14,

Australian Association of Social Workers (2002) *Submission to the National Inquiry into Children in Immigration Detention,* http://www.humanrights.gov.au/human_rights/children_detention/submissions/aasw.html

Australian Association of Social Workers (2003a) *Social Workers' Partnership Highlights Commitment to Reconciliation* (Media release) May. http://www.aasw.asn.au/adobe/news/sorry_day/SOCIAL_WORKERS_PARTNERSHIP_HIGHLIGHTS_COMMITMENT.pdf

Australian Association of Social Workers (2003b) *Submission to the House of Representatives Standing Committee on Aboriginal and Torres Strait Islander Affairs, Inquiry into Capacity Building in Indigenous Communities,* March. http://www.aasw.asn.au/adobe/advocacy/submissions/atsisub111.pdf

Autès M (1999) *Les paradoxes du travail social.* Paris: Dunod.

Azpiazu D (1997) El nuevo perfil de la elite empresaria. Concentración del poder económico y beneficios extraordinarios. *Revista Realidad Económica* **145**: 7–32.

Bachmann C and Leguennec N (1996) *Violences urbaines. Ascension des classes moyennes à travers cinquante ans de politique de la ville.* Paris: Albin Michel.

Bailey R and Brake M (1975) *Radical Social Work.* London: Edward Arnold.

Bakan A (2000) After Seattle: the politics of the World Trade Organisation. *International Socialism* **2(86)**: 19–36.

Baldock J and Evers A (1991) Citizenship and frail elderly people: changing patterns of provision in Europe. In: Manning N (ed.) *Social Policy Review, 1990–91.* Harlow: Longman.

Balloch S, McLean J and Fisher M (eds) (1999) *Social Services: Working Under Pressure.* Bristol: Policy Press.

Barlow M (2003) The other superpower: how civil society can stand up to free trade and continental integration. *Annual Meeting of the Council of Canadians,* October 2003. Vancouver, BC.

Barnado's (2003) Barnado's launches hard hitting campaign as NOP Poll shows 86% are unaware that 1 in 3 children live in poverty in the UK. Press Release, 12 November 2003. (*http://www.barnardos.org.uk/newsandevents/media/press/release.jsp?id=1295*)

Barns I, Dudley J, Harris P and Petersen A (1999) Introduction: themes, context and perspectives. In: Petersen A, Barns I, Dudley J and Harris P (eds) *Poststructuralism, Citizenship and Social Policy.* London: Routledge.

Beck U (2001) *La société du risque. Sur la voie d'une autre modernité* (1986). Paris: Alto/Aubier.

Bell D (1960) *The End of Ideology.* New York: Free Press.

Bell D (1979) *Les contradictions culturelles du capitalisme.* Paris: Puf.

Bertinotti F (2003) Reformist social democracy is no longer on the agenda. *The Guardian* 11 August 2003. http://www.guardian.co.uk/comment/story/0,3604,1016107,00.html

Beyeler M (2003) Globalization, Europeanization and domestic welfare state reforms. *Global Social Policy* **3**: 2.

Bircham E and Charlton J (eds) (2001) *Anti-Capitalism: A Guide to the Movement.* London: Bookmarks.

Bishop A (2002) *Becoming an ally: Breaking the cycle of oppression -in people.* Halifax: Fernwood, and London: Zed.

Blair T (1998) *The Third Way: New Politics for the New Century.* London: Fabian Society.

Blau J (1992) *The Visible Poor: Homelessness in the United States.* New York: Oxford University Press.

Bond P (2001) *Against Global Apartheid.* Lansdowne: UCT Press.

Boucher M (2003a) *Turbulences, contrôle et régulation sociale. Les logiques des acteurs sociaux dans les quartiers populaires.* Paris: L'Harmattan.

Boucher M (2003b) Turbulences, contrôle et régulation sociale. Les logiques des acteurs sociaux dans les quartiers impopulaires. *Déviance et Sociétés* **27**: 161–182.

Boucher R and Batime C (1992) *Le travail social, les travailleurs sociaux ou les professions sociales: une déclinaison nécessaire. Contribution aux travaux de la mission déontologie.* Canteleu/Rouen: IRTS de Haute-Normandie.

Bourdieu P. (1996) *Le Mythe de la 'mondialisation' et l'Etat social.* Bibliothèque virtuelle.

Brackett J (1909) *Social Work.* Jeffrey Brackett Papers (MS 8). Boston: Simmons College Archives.

Brake M and Bailey R (eds) (1980) *Radical Social Work and Practice.* Beverly Hills, CA: Sage Publications.

Briskman L and Fraser H (2002) Freedom first, then education. *The Age*, 7 August.

Briskman L and Noble C (1999) Social work ethics: embracing diversity. In: Pease B and Fook J (eds) *Transforming Social Work Practice: Postmodern Critical Perspectives.* Sydney: Allen & Unwin.

Brody SJ (1969) *The Coalition as a Tool for Social Action and Social Change.* New York: National Conference on Social Welfare.

Burghardt S (1982) *The Other Side of Organizing.* Cambridge, MA: Schenkman.

Burghardt S and Fabricant M (1987) *Working under the Safety: Policy and practice with the new American poor.* Newbury Park, CA: Sage Publications.

Burkett I (2001) Traversing the swampy terrain of postmodern communities: towards theoretical revisionings of community development. *European Journal of Social Work* **4**: 233–246.

Burkett I (2003) Microfinance in Australia: current realities and future possibilities. Online document: *http://www.social.uq.edu.au/research/finance/index.htm*

Burns D, Hambleton R and Hoggett P (1994) *The Politics of Decentralisation.* Basingstoke: Macmillan.

Butler I and Drakeford M (2002) Which Blair project? communitarianism, social authoritarianism and social work. *Journal of Social Work.* **1**: 7–19.

CACI (2003) *Wealth of the Nation 2003.* London: CACI.

Cahn (2000) *No More Throw Away People.* Washington: Essential Books.

Callinicos A (1995) *Theories and Narratives.* London: Polity.

Callinicos A (2000) *Equality.* London: Polity.

Callinicos A (2003a) *An Anti-Capitalist Manifesto.* London: Polity.

Callinicos A (2003b) *The New Mandarins of American Power.* London: Polity.

Campbell C (2003) Anti-oppressive theory and practice as the organizing theme for social work education: the case in favour. *Canadian Social Work Review* **20**: 121–125.

Carey M (2003) Anatomy of a care manager. *Work, Employment and Society* **17**: 1.

Carroll E (2002) The clear and present danger of the 'globaloney' industry. *Global Social Policy* **3**: 2.

Carroll WK and Ratner RS (1996) Master frames and counter-hegemony: political sensibilities in contemporary social movements. *Canadian Review of Sociology and Anthropology* **33**: 407–435.

Castel R (1981) *La gestion des risques. De l'anti-psychiatrie à l'après-psychanalyse.* Paris: Minuit.

Castel R (1995) *Les métamorphoses de la question sociale.* Paris: Fayard.

Chafe W (1977) *Women and Equality: Changing Patterns in American Culture.* New York: Oxford University Press.

Chakravarty S (1987) *Development Planning: The Indian Experience.* Oxford: Clarendon Press.

Chambers C (1963) *Seedtime of Reform: American Social Service and Social Action, 1918–193.* Minneapolis: University of Minnesota Press.

Chambers C (1986) Women in the creation of the profession of social work. *Social Service Review* **60**: 1–31.

Charities Organization Society (1901) Editorial, *Charities*, pp. 420–421. New York: Charities Organization Society.

Charlton J (2000) Talking Seattle. *International Socialism* **2**: 3–18.

Chauvière M (1980) *L'enfance inadaptée. L'héritage de Vichy.* Paris: Ouvrières.

Chauvière M (1998) Les pratiques socio-éducatives sont-elles encore adaptées aux changements de la société?. *Sauvegarde de l'enfance* **1**: 45–52.

Chopart J-N (ed.) (2000) *Les mutations du travail social.* Paris: Dunod.

Chossudovsky M (1998) *The Globalisation of Poverty.* London: Zed Books.

Choudry A (2002) Laying Uncle Ho to rest. *New Internationalist* **344**.

Clarke G (1998) *The Politics of NGOs in South-East Asia.* London: Routledge.

Clarke J (1979) Critical sociology and radical social work: problems of theory and practice. In: Parry N, Rustin M and Satyamurti C (eds) *Social Work, Welfare and the State.* London: Edward Arnold.

Clarke J (1996) After social work. In: Parton N (ed.) *Social Theory, Social Change and Social Work*, pp 36–60. London: Routledge.

Clarke J (2000) A world of difference? Globalisation and the study of social policy. In: Lewis G, Gewirtz S and Clarke J (eds) *Rethinking Social Policy.* London: Sage.

Clarke J, Cochrane A and McLaughlin E (eds) (1994) *Managing Social Policy.* London: Sage.

Clarke J, Gewirtz S and McLaughlin E (2000) Reinventing the welfare State. In: Clarke J, Gewirtz S and McLaughlin E (eds) *New Managerialism, New Welfare?* London: Sage.

Cloward RA and Ohlin L (1960) *Delinquency and Opportunity: a theory of delinquent gangs.* Glencoe, IL: Free Press.

Cm 849 (1989) *Caring for People. Community Care in the Next Decade and Beyond*, London: HMSO.

Cmnd 3703 (1968) *Report of the Committee on Local Authority and Allied Personal Social Services.* The Seebohm Report. London: HMSO.

Cochrane A (1994) Restructuring the local welfare state. In: Burrows R and Loader B (eds) *Towards a Post-Fordist Welfare State?* London: Routledge.

Cohen S (1987) *It's the same old story.* Manchester, UK: *Manchester City Council Public Relations Office.*

Cohen W (1966) What every social worker should know about political action. *Social Work* **11(3):** 3–9.

Cohen S, Humphries B and Mynott E (2001) *From Immigration Controls to Welfare Controls.* London: Routledge.

Coquery-Vidrovitch (1979) *Afrique Noir: Permanences et Ruptures.* Paris: L'Harmattan.

Corrigan P and Leonard P (1978) *Social Work Practice Under Capitalism: A Marxist Approach.* London: Macmillan.

Coulibaly AL (2003) *Wade un opposant au pouvoir: L'alternance piégée.* Orstom, Paris: Les Editions Sentinelles.

Council for Aboriginal Reconciliation (2003) Additional information from Reconciliation Australia to Senate Legal and Constitutional References Committee, Inquiry into Progress of National Reconciliation, May. *http://www.reconciliationaustralia.org/docs/ra/senate_inquiry.pdf*

Council on Social Work Education (1998) *Proceedings of Conference on Multiculturalism.* Alexandria, VA: author.

Cusson M (1983) *Le contrôle social du crime.* Paris: Puf.

Danaher K and Burbach R (2000) *Globalize This! The battle against the world trade organization and corporate rule.* Philadelphia, PA: Common Courage Press.

Danani C (2003) Condiciones y prácticas sociopolíticas en las políticas sociales: las obras sociales, más allá de la libre afiliación. In: Lindenboim J and Danani C (eds) *Entre el trabajo y la política. Las reformas de las políticas sociales argentinas en perspectiva comparada.* Buenos Aires: Editorial Biblos.

Danziger S (1991) Relearning lessons of the war on poverty. *Challenge* **September–October**: 53–54.

Davies JA (2002) Child abuse experts act on Woomera. *The Age.* 21 March.

Davis A (1964) Settlement workers in politics, 1890–1914. *Review of Politics* **26**: 505–517.

Day P and Klein N (1990) *Inspecting the Inspectorates.* Bath: University of Bath, Centre for Analysis of Social Policy.

Deacon B, Hulse M and Stubbs P (1997) *Global Social Policy: International Organizations and the Future of Welfare* London: Sage.

Dean M (1999) *Governmentality.* London: Sage.

DeMaria W (1992) On the trail of a radical pedagogy for social work education. *British Journal of Social Work* **22**: 231–252.

Department of Health (1990) *Community Care in the Next Decade and Beyond: Policy Guidance.* London: HMSO.

Department of Health (1992) *Memorandum on the Financing of Community Care.* London: Department of Health.

Department of Health (1998) *Modernising Social Services.* London: HMSO.

Department of Health (2000) *A Quality Strategy for Social Care.* London: HMSO.

Department of the Environment, Transport and the Regions (1999) *Local Government Act 1999: Part 1 Best Value, Circular 10/99.* London: DETR.

De Ridder G (ed.) (1997) *Les nouvelles frontières de l'intervention sociale.* Paris: L'Harmattan.

De Ridder G (1999) Les professions sociales: du modèle de la qualification au modèle de la compétence. *Revue Française des Affaires Sociales* **2**.

Desai M (2002) *Ideologies and Social Work: Historical and Contemporary Analyses.* Jaipur: Rawat Publications.

de Tocqueville A (2001) *Democracy in America.* Toronto: Signet Classic/Penguin Books Canada.

Dewey J (1935) *Liberalism and Social Action.* New York: G.P. Putnam & Sons.

Dia M (1988) *Le Sénégal trahi, un marché d'esclaves.* Paris: Sélio.

Dinner A and Levkoe C (2001) Building a movement from the grassroots. *Briarpatch* **30**: 16–17.

Diop M (1993) "Participation sociale et économique dans le milieu de vie, des participants du foyer Clair Logis Thies-Senegal". Unpublished PhD thesis, Ecole Service Social, Université Laval, Senegal.

Dodson M (1997) *Bringing Them Home.* Sydney: Human Rights & Equal Opportunity Commission (video).

Dodson M (1996) First fleets and citizenship. In: Davis SR (ed.) *Citizenship in Australia: Democracy, Law and Society* Melbourne: Consitutional Confederacy Foundation.

Dominelli L (2002) *Anti-oppressive Social Work Theory and Practice.* London: Macmillan.

Donzelot J (1977) *La police des familles.* Paris: Minuit.

Donzelot J (1984) *L'invention du social.* Paris: Seuil.

Donzelot J and Estèbe P (1994) *L'Etat animateur. Essai sur la politique de la ville.* Paris: Esprit.

Dore M (1990) Functional theory: its history and influence on contemporary social work practice. *Social Service Review* **64**: 358–374.

Dréano G (2002) *Guide de l'éducation spécialisée.* Paris: Dunod.

Drover G (2000) Redefining social citizenship in a global era. Social work and globalization. *Canadian Social Work.* (Special Issue) **2**: 29–49.

Drucker D (2003) Whither international social work. *International Social Work* **46**: 53–81.

Dubet F (2000) *Les inégalités multipliées.* La Tour d'Aigues: Aube.

Dubet F (2003) *Le déclin de l'institution.* Paris: Seuil.

Dubet F and Martuccelli D (1998) *Dans quelle société vivons-nous?* Paris: Seuil.

Dubet F and Wieviorka M (eds) (1995) *Penser le sujet. Autour d'Alain Touraine.* Paris: Fayard.

Du Gay P (2000) Entrepreneurial governance and public management: the anti-bureaucrats. In: Clarke J, Gewirtz S and McLaughlin E (eds) *New Managerialism, New Welfare?* London: Sage.

Durkheim E (1998) *De la division du travail social (1893).* Paris: Puf/Quadrige.

Dutrenit JM (1989) *Gestion et Évaluation des services sociaux.* Paris: Economica.

Edelman M (2001) Social movements: changing paradigms and forms of politics. *Annual Review of Anthropology* **30**: 285–317.

Epstein I (1970) Organizational careers, professionalization, and social work radicalism. *Social Service Review* **44**: 123–131.

Escobar A (1995) *Encountering Development: The Making and Unmaking of the Third World.* Princeton, NJ: Princeton University Press.

Estèbe P (1998) Les métiers de la ville. *Esprit* **3–4**.

Esteva G (1993) Development. In Sachs W (ed.) *The Development Dictionary: A Guide to Knowledge as Power.* London: Zed Books.

Evans S (1989) *Born for Liberty: A History of Women in America.* New York: Free Press.

Ewald F (1986) *Histoire de l'etat providence, les origines de la solidarité.* Paris: Grasset.

Ewald F (1996) Philosophie de la précaution. *L'Année Sociologique* **46**: 383–41.

Ewald F, Gollier C and Sadeleer N (2001) *Le principe de précaution.* Collection *Que sais-je?* Paris: Puf.

Fabricant M and Burghardt S (1987) *The Welfare State Crisis and the Transformation of Social Work.* Englewood Cliffs, NJ: Prentice Hall.

Fairclough N (1992) *Discourse and Social Change.* Cambridge, UK: Polity.

Fall N (1980) *Les services sociaux au Sénégal: pour une concertation dans les prises de décisions et une coordination des actions.* Mémoire de maîtrise en AES option développement. Université d'Aix-Marseille II, Faculté des Sciences économiques.

Fanon F (1966) *The Wretched of the Earth.* New York: Grove Press.

Ferguson I and Lavalette M (1999) Social work, postmodernism and marxism. *European Journal of Social Work* **2**: 1.

Ferguson I and Lavalette M (2004) Beyond power discourse: alienation and social work. *British Journal of Social Work* **34**: 297–312.

Ferguson I, Lavalette M and Mooney G (2002) *Rethinking Welfare: A Critical Perspective*. London: Sage.

Fiori G (1965/1990) *Antonio Gramsci: Life of a Revolutionary*. London: Verso.

Fisher J (1936) *The Rank and File Movement in Social Work, 1931–1936*. New York: New York School of Social Work.

Fisher R and Karger HJ (1997) *Social Work and Community in a Private World: Getting Out in Public*. New York: Longman.

Fisher R and Kling J (eds) (1994a) *Mobilizing the Community: Local Politics in the Era of the Global City*. Newbury Park, CA: Sage Publications.

Fisher R and Kling J (1994b) Community organization and new social movement theory. *Journal of Progressive Human Services* **5**: 5–24.

Fleming P and Spicer A (2003) Working at a distance: implications for power, subjectivity and resistance. *Organization* **10**: 1.

Flynn N (2000) Managerialism and public services: some international trends. In: Clarke J, Gewirtz S and McLaughlin E (eds) *New Managerialism, New Welfare?* London: Sage.

Foley MW and Edwards B (1996) The paradox of civil society. *Journal of Democracy* **7**: 38–52.

Fook J (1993) *Radical Casework: A Theory of Practice*. St. Leonards, NSW: Allen & Unwin.

Foucault M (1975) *Surveiller et punir. Naissance de la prison*. Paris: Gallimard.

Foweraker J (1995) *Theorizing Social Movements*. London: Pluto Press.

Franklin D (1990) The cycles of social work practice: social action vs. individual interest. *Journal of Progressive Human Services* **1**: 59–80.

Fraser N (2000) Rethinking recognition. *New Left Review* (new series) **3**: 107–201.

Freire P (1970a) *Pedagogy of the Oppressed*. New York: Continuum.

Freire P (1970b) *Cultural Action for Freedom*. Harmondsworth: Penguin.

Freire P (1973) *Pedagogy of the oppressed*. New York: Seabury.

Freire P (1990) A critical understanding of social work. *Journal of Progressive Human Services* **1**: 3–9.

Friedson E (1970) *The Profession of Medicine* New York: Dodd, Mead and Co.

Galloway G (2003) Palestine. In: Reza F (ed.) *Anti-Imperialism: A Guide for the Movement*. London: Bookmarks.

Galper J (1975) *The Politics of Social Services*. Englewood Cliffs, NJ: Prentice-Hall.

Galper J (1980) *Social Work Practice: A Radical Perspective*. Englewood Cliffs, NJ: Prentice-Hall.

Garcia B and Van Soest D (1997) Changing perceptions of diversity and oppression: MSW students discuss the effects of a required course. *Journal of Social Work Education* **33**: 119–129.

George V (1998) Political ideology, globalisation and welfare futures in Europe. *Journal of Social Policy* **27**: 17–36.

George V and Wilding P (2002) *Globalization and Human Welfare*. London: Palgrave.

Gettleman ME (1963) Charity and social classes in the U.S., 1874–1900, I. *American Journal of Economics and Society* **22**: 313–329.

Giddens A (1972) *Emile Durkheim: Selected writing*. Cambridge: Cambridge University Press.

Giddens A (1984) *The Constitution of Society: Outline of the Theory of Structuration*. Berkeley: University of California Press.

Giddens A (1994) *Les conséquences de la modernité*. Paris: L'Harmattan.

Gil D (1976) *The Challenge of Social Equality: Essays on Social Policy, Social Development, and Political Practice*. Cambridge, MA: Schenkman.

Gil D (1998) *Confronting Injustice and oppression: concepts and strategies for social workers*. New York: Colombia University Press.

Gil D (1999) Developmental social welfare services: a solution for the challenges facing social welfare globally. *New Global Development* **XV**: 1–7.

Gilbert N (1983) *Capitalism and the Welfare State: Dilemmas of Social Benevolence*. New Haven, CT: Yale University Press.

Gilbert N (2002) *Transformation of the Welfare State: The Silent Surrender of Public Responsibility*. New York: Oxford University Press.

Giroux HA (1991) Postmodernism as border pedagogy: redefining the boundaries of race and ethnicity. In: Giroux H (ed.) *Postmodernism, Feminism, and Cultural Politics*, pp 217–256. New York: SUNY.

Gitlin T (1995) *The Twilight of Common Dreams: Why America is Wracked by Culture Wars*. New York: Metropolitan Books.

Goffman E (1968) *Asiles. Etudes sur la condition sociale des malades mentaux*. Paris: Minuit.

Goldberg Wood G and Middleman RR (1989) *The Structural Approach to Direct Practice in Social Work*. New York: Columbia University Press.

Gonzalez M (2003) Brazil in the eye of the storm. *International Socialism* **98**: 57–76.

Gonzalez M and Bonofoglio N (2002) Evidencias sobre el deterioro de la calidad del empleo en la Argentina' Trabajo presentado al V Simposio Internacional 'América Latina y el Caribe: El desafío de los procesos de desarrollo e integración en el nuevo Milenio', Facultad de Ciencias Económicas de la Universidad de Buenos Aires, 23 al 25 de octubre de 2002.

Goroff N (n.d.) *A pedagogy for radical social work practice*, unpublished paper. West Hartford, CT: University of Connecticut.

Gramsci A (1971) *Selections From the Prison Notebooks*. London: Lawrence and Wishart.

Gramsci A (1976) *Selections from the Prison Notebooks* (Edited and translated by Quintin Hoare and Geoffrey Nowell Smith). New York: International Publishers.

Grassi E (2003a) Investigación y Trabajo Social: complicidades del pensamiento naturalista. Segundas Jornadas de Investigación en Trabajo Social. Universidad Nacional de Entre Ríos, Argentina. Octubre de 2003.

Grassi E (2003b) *Política y problemas sociales en la sociedad neoliberal. La otra década infame (I)*. Buenos Aires: Espacio Editorial.

Gray M (ed.) (1998) *Developmental Social Work in South Africa: Theory and Practice*. Cape Town: David Philip.

Gray M (2002) Is there a 'universal social work'? Paper presented at the 30th Bi-Annual Congress of IASSW, Montpellier, France

Gray M, Healy K and Crofts P (2003) Social enterprise: is it the business of social work? *Australian Social Work* **56**: 141–154.

Gross ER (1995) Deconstructing politically correct practice literature: the American Indian case. *Social Work* **40**: 206–213.

Gutierrez L (1997) Multicultural community organizing. In: Reisch M and Gambrill E (eds) *Social Work in the 21st Century*, pp 249–259. Thousand Oaks, CA: Pine Forge Press.

Gutierrez L, Parsons R and Cox E (eds) (1998) *Empowerment in Social Work Practice: A Sourcebook*. Pacific Grove, CA: Brooks/Cole.

Guy R (1982) Retour aux solidarités du quotidien: Les nouvelles orientations du travail social en France. *Qu'est-ce que le social?* **8**: 129–134.

Habermas J (1981) New social movements. *Telos* **49**: 33–37.

Hall B (1977) *Creating Knowledge: Breaking the Monopoly*. Toronto: Participatory Research Group, International Centre for Adult Education.

Hall S (1998) The great moving nowhere show. *Marxism Today* **November/December**: 9–14.

Hall S (2003) New Labour has picked up where Thatcherism left off. *The Guardian* 6 August 2003. (*http://www.guardian.co.uk/comment/story/0,3604,1012982,00.html*)

Harkavy I and Puckett J (1994) Lessons from Hull House for the contemporary urban university. *Social Service Review* **68**: 299–321.

Harman C (1988) *The Fire Last Time: 1968 and After*. London: Bookmarks.

Harman C (2004) *Caste and Class. http://www.istendency.net/pdf/casteandclass*

Harris J (1998) Scientific management, bureau-professionalism, new managerialism: the labour process of state social work. *British Journal of Social Work* **28**: 839–862.

Harris J (1999) State social work and social citizenship, *British Journal of Social Work* **29**: 915–937.

Harris J (2003) *The Social Work Business* London: Routledge.

Harris J and McDonald C (2000) Post-Fordism, the welfare state and the personal social services. A comparison of Australia and Britain, *British Journal of Social Work* **30**: 51–70.

Harris P (2002) Welfare rewritten: change and interplay in social and economic accounts. *Journal of Social Policy* **31**: 377–398.

Harrison G (2003) Language, diversity and difference: bilingual perspectives in social work. PhD Thesis, School of Social Work and Applied Human Sciences, University of Queensland, Australia.

Harvey D (2001) *Spaces of Capital Towards a Critical Geography*. Edinburgh: Edinburgh University Press.

Hatzfeld H (1989) *Du paupérisme à la sécurité sociale (1850–1940)*. Nancy: Pun.

Haug E (2001) Writing in the margins: critical reflections on the emerging discourse of international social work, MSW thesis, Faculty of Social Work. University of Calgary, Calgary.

Hayes D and Humphries B (2004) *Social Work, Immigration and Asylum*. London: Jessica Kingsley Publishers.

Healy K (2000) *Social Work Practices*. London: Sage.

Healy K (2001) Reinventing critical social work: challenges from practice, context and postmodernism. *Critical Social Work* **2**(1), online at **http://www.criticalsocial-work.com/ o1_1_reinventing_healy**

Healy LM (2001) *International Social Work: Professional Action in an Interdependent World*. New York: Oxford University Press.

Held D and McGrew T (2003) *Globalization/Anti-Globalization*. London: Polity.

Helliwell JF (2002) *Globalization and Well-being*. Vancouver: UBC Press.

Hertz N (2001) *The Silent Takeover*. London: Heinemann.

Hills J (ed.) (1995) *New Inequalities: The Changing Distribution of Income and Wealth in the United Kingdom*. Cambridge: Cambridge University Press.

Hills J (1998) *Income and Wealth: the latest evidence*. York: Joseph Rowntree Foundation.

Hintze S (1989) *Estrategias alimentarias de sobreviviencia*. Buenos Aires: Centro Editor de América Latina.

Hokenstad MC and Midgley J (eds) (1997) *Issues in International Social Work: Global Challenges for a New Century*. Washington, DC: NASW Press.

Hood C (1991) Contemporary public management: a new global paradigm? *Public Policy and Administration* **10**: 104–117.

Hood C, Scott C, James O, Jones G and Travers T (1999) *Regulation Inside Government: Waste-watchers, Quality-police and Sleaze-busters*. Oxford: Oxford University Press.

Hooks B (1990) *Yearning*. Boston: South End Press.

Hooyman N and Bricker-Jenkins M (eds) (1984) *Not for Women Only: Social Work Practice for a Feminist Future*. Silver Spring, MD: National Association of Social Workers.

http://www.aasw.asn.au/adobe/news/sorry_day/antar_statement.pdf

http://www.austlii.edu.au/au/special/rsjproject/rsjlibrary/hreoc/stolen/

http:/sami.is.free.fr/Œuvres/bourdieu_mythe_mondialisation.htlm.

Hugman R (1996) Professionalization in social work: the challenge of diversity. *International Social Work* **39**: 131–147.

Huizer G (1996) Social movements in the underdevelopment of development dialectic: a view from below. In: Chewand SC and Denemark RA (eds) *The Underdevelopment of Development: Essays in Honor of Andre Gunder Frank*. Thousand Oaks, CA: Sage.

Hunyadi M (2003) Pourquoi avons-nous besoin du raisonnement de précaution? *Esprit* **8–9**: 139–162.

Ife J (1997) *Rethinking Social Work: towards clinical practice*. Melbourne: Longman.

Ife J (2001) *Human Rights and Social Work: Towards Rights-based Practice*. Cambridge: Cambridge University Press.

Iglehart A and Becerra R (1995) *Social Services and the Ethnic Community*. Needham Heights, MA: Allyn and Bacon.

International Federation of Social Workers (2003) Petition to the Australian Prime Minister, John Howard, February 8th, *http://www.ifsw.org/Activities/3.2.4.act.html*

Ion J (1998) *Le travail social au singulier*. Paris: Dunod.

ISUMA: Canadian Journal of Policy Research **2**: 1

Jameson F (2000) Globalization and political strategy. *New Left Review* **4**: 49–69.

Jansson B (2003) *The Reluctant Welfare State* 3rd edn. Pacific Grove, CA: Brooks/Cole.

Jessop B (1994) The transition to post-Fordism and the Schumpeterian workfare state. In: Burrows R and Loader B (eds) *Towards a Post-Fordist Welfare State*. London: Routledge.

Jessop B (2002) *The Future of the Capitalist State*. Cambridge: Polity Press.

Johnson YM (1999) Indirect social work: social work's uncelebrated strength. *Social Work* **44**: 323–334.

Jones A (2000) Social work: an enterprising profession in a competitive environment. In: O'Connor I, Smyth P and Warburton J (eds). *Contemporary Perspectives on Social Work and the Human Services: Challenges and Changes*, pp 150–163. Melbourne: Longman.

Jones C (1983) *State Social Work and the Working Class*. London: Macmillan.

Jones C (1996) Anti-intellectualism and the peculiarities of British Social Work Education. In: Parton N (ed) *Social Theory, Social Change and Social Work*. London: Routledge.

Jones C (1999) Social work: regulation and managerialism. In: Hexworthy M and Halford M (eds) *Professionals and the New Managerialism in the Public Sector*. Buckingham: Open University Press.

Jones C (2001a) Social work and social exclusion. In: Davies M (ed.) *Blackwell Companion to Social Work* 2nd edn. Oxford: Blackwell.

Jones C (2001b) Voices from the front line: state social workers and New Labour. *British Journal of Social Work* **31**: 547–562.

Jones C and Novak T (1993) Social work today. *British Journal of Social Work* **23**: 195–212.

Jones C and Novak T (1999) *Poverty, Welfare and the Disciplinary State*. London: Routledge.

Jones C, Ferguson I, Lavalette M and Penketh L (2003) *Social Work and Social Justice: a Manifesto for a New Engaged Practice*. www.liv.ac.uk/sspsw/manifesto.

Jones K (1994) *The Making of Social Policy in Britain, 1830–1990* 2nd edn. London: Athlone Press.

Jordan B (2001) Tough Love: social work, social exclusion and the third way. *British Journal of Social Work* **31**(4): 527–46.

Jordan B and Jordan C (2000) *Social Work and the Third Way*. London: Sage.

Jupp J (2002) *From White Australia to Woomera: The story of Australia's Immigration*. Cambridge: Cambridge University Press.

Kaplan A (1996) *The Development Practitioners' Handbook*. London: Pluto Press.

Karger HJ (1988) *Social Workers and Labor Unions*. Westport, CT: Greenwood.

Katz M (1989). *The Undeserving Poor: From the War on Poverty to the War on Welfare*. New York: Pantheon.

Keane J (1989) *Democracy and Civil Society* London: Verso.

Keane J (1998) *Civil Society: Old Images, New Vision*. Cambridge: Polity.

Keisling P (1984). Lessons of the Great Society. *The Washington Monthly*. **December**: 50–53.

Kelly A (1992) The new managerialism in the social services. In: . Carter P, Jeffs T and Smith M (eds) *Social Work and Social Welfare Yearbook 3*. Buckingham: Open University Press.

Kenny MA, Fiske L, Ife J (2002) Refugees, asylum-seekers and the law. In: Swain PA (ed). *The Shadow of the Law: the legal context of social work practice*. Sydney: The Federation Press.

Klausen KM (1968) *Kerala Fishermen and the Indo-Norwegian Pilot Project*. Oslo: Universitetsforlaget.

Knickmeyer R (1972) A Marxist approach to social work. *Social Work* **18**: 58–65.

Konopka G (1958) *Eduard Lindemann and Social Work Philosophy*. Minneapolis: University of Minnesota Press.

Korczynski M (2003) Communities of coping: collective emotional labour in service work. *Organization* **10**: 1.

Korten D (1990) *Getting to the 21st Century: Voluntary Action and the Global Agenda*. West Hartford: Kumarian Press.

Kreuger LW (1997) The end of social work. *Journal of Social Work Education*. **33**: 19–27.

Kurien J (1998) *Small-Scale Fisheries in the Context of Globalization*. Thiruvananthapuram: Centre for Development Studies.

Kurzman PA and Solomon JR (1970) Beyond advocacy: a new model for community organization. *Social Work* **16**: 65–73.

Kusmer KL (1973) The functions of organized charity in the progressive era: Chicago as a case study. *Journal of American History* **60**: 657–678.

Labonte R. (1997) *Health Promotion and Empowerment: Practice Frameworks. Issues In Health Promotion Series*. No. 3. Toronto: Centre for Health Promotion, University of Toronto.

Lane M (1997) Community work, social work: green and postmodern? *British Journal of Social Work* **27**: 319–341

Langan M and Lee P (1989) Whatever happened to radical social work? In: Langan M and Lee P (eds) *Radical Social Work Today*, pp 1–18. London: Unwin Hyman.

Larson MS (1977) *The Rise of Professionalism: A Sociological Analysis*. London: University of California Press.

Lascoumes P (1977) *Prévention et contrôle social. Les contradictions du travail social*. Paris: Masson.

Lautier B (1995) Les malheureux sont-ils les plus puissants de la pauvreté (Représentation et régulations Étatiques de la pauvreté en Amérique Latine). Communication au colloque de Royaumont intitulé : *Contribution pour le séminaire préparatoire au sommet mondial pour le développement social* (Copenhague, mars 1995), Royaumont, 9–11 janvier 1995, 21p.

Lavalette M and Mooney G (1999) New Labour, new moralism: the welfare politics and ideology of New Labour under Blair. *International Socialism* **2**: 27–47.

Lavalette M and Mooney G (eds) (2001) *Class Struggle and Social Welfare*. London: Routledge.

Lawani BT (1999) *Non-Government Organizations in Development: Case Study of Solapur District*. Jaipur: Rawat Publications.

LeBlanc A (2001) Social Capital. *ISUMA: Canadian Journal of Policy Research*. **2**: 6–9.

Le Breton D (1995) *La sociologie du risque, collection Que sais-je?* Paris: Puf.

Le Grand J (1993) *Quasi-Markets*. Basingstoke: Macmillan.

Lee S (1997) Competitiveness and the welfare state in Britain. In: Mullard M and Lee S (eds) *The Politics of Social Policy in Europe*. Cheltenham: Edward Elgar.

Legault G (1991) Travail social alternatif en Amérique du sud. *Nouvelles pratiques sociales*. **4**: 193–206.

Lemann N (1988–1989, December/January). The unfinished war, parts I & II. *Atlantic Monthly* **December**: 37–56; **January**: 53–68.

Lenin V (1963) *What is to be Done?* s.l.: s.n.

Leonard P (1975) Towards a paradigm for radical practice. In: Bailey R and Brake M (eds) *Radical Social Work*, pp 46–61. London: Edward Arnold.

Leonard P (1984) *Personality and Ideology, Towards a Materialist Understanding of the Individual*. London: Macmillan Press.

Leonard P (1997) *Postmodern Welfare. Reconstructing an Emancipatory Project*. London: Sage.

Lewis H (1966) The functional approach to social work practice: a restatement of assumptions and principles. *Journal of Social Work Process* **15**.

Lewis H (1972) *Values, knowledge and practice: Issues facing the profession in the '70s*, paper presented at the Ruth E. Smalley Colloquium, April 1972. Philadelphia: University of Pennsylvania.

Lewis H (1973) Morality and the politics of practice. *Social Casework* **53**(7): 404–17.

Lewis H (1982) *The Intellectual Base of Social Work Practice*. New York: Haworth.

Lichtenberg P (1976) Radicalism in casework. *Journal of Sociology and Social Welfare* **4**: 258–276.

Lichtenberg P (1990) Undoing the clinch of oppression. *American University Studies*, Series VIII, Psychology vol. 21, P. Lang.

Lindenboim J (compilador) (2002) *Metamorfosis del empleo en Argentina*. Buenos Aires: Cuadernos del CEPED N° 7. FCE/UBA.

Linhorst DM (2002) Federalism and social justice: implications for social work. *Social Work* **47**: 201–000.

Loney M (1986) *The Politics of Greed: The New Right and the Welfare State*. London: Pluto.

Longres J (1977) *Radical social casework*. Paper presented at the Annual Program Meeting of the Council on Social Work Education, Phoenix, Arizona.

Longres J (1986) Marxian theory and social work practice. *Catalyst: A Socialist Journal of the Social Services* **5**: 14–34.

Longres J (1996) Radical social work: is there a future? In: Raffoul P and McNeece CA (eds) *Future Issues for Social Work Practice*, pp 229–239. Needham Heights, MA: Allyn and Bacon.

Longres J (1997) The impact and implications of multiculturalism. In: Reisch M and Gambrill E (eds) *Social Work in the 21st Century*, pp 39–47 Thousand Oaks, CA: Pine Forge Press.

Lovejoy, O. (1912). Remarks, *Proceedings*. *National Conference of Charities and Corrections*. New York: New York School of Social Work.

Lowe JI and Reisch M (1998) Bringing the community into the classroom: applying the experiences of social work education to service-learning courses in sociology. *Teaching Sociology* **26**: 292–298.

Lozano C (1999) Instituto de Estudios Sobre Estado y Participación: *Inconsistencias estadísticas e injusticia presupuestaria. Análisis del Proyecto de Ley de Presupuesto Nacional para 1999*, Buenos Aires.

Lozano C (2002) La catástrofe social en la Argentina. Documento del Instituto de Estudio y Formación de la CTA, Buenos Aires, junio de 2002.

Lum D (1999) *Social Work Practice with People of Color: A Process Stage Approach*, 3rd edn. Pacific Grove, CA: Brooks/Cole.

Lundy C (2003) *Social Work and Social Justice: A Structural Approach to Practice*, Peterborough, Ontario: Broadview Press.

Lymberly M (2000) The retreat from professionalism: from social worker to care manager. In: Malin N (ed.) *Professionalism, Boundaries and the Workplace*, pp 123–128. London: Routledge.

McAdam D (1994) Culture and social movements. In: Larana E, Johnston H and Gusfield JR (eds) *New Social Movements: From Ideology to Identity*. Philadelphia: Temple University Press.

McAdam D, Tarrow S and Tilly C (2001) *Dynamics of Contention*. Cambridge UK: Cambridge University Press.

McCarthy JD and Zald MN (1977) Resource mobilization and social movements: a partial theory. *American Journal of Sociology* **82**: 1212–1241.

McDonald C, Harris J and Wintersteen R (2003) Contingent on context? Social work and the state in Australia, Britain and the USA. *British Journal of Social Work* **33**: 191–208.

McGrath S, Moffatt K, George U and Lee B (1999a) Practicing citizenship, a study of social planning organizations. *Community Development Journal* **34**: 308–317.

McGrath S, Moffatt K, George U and Lee B (1999b) Community capacity: the emperor's new clothes. *Canadian Review of Social Policy* **44**: 9–24.

McLaren P and Leonard P (eds) (1993) *Paulo Freire: A Critical Encounter*. London: Routledge.

McMurtry J (1997) Free market fallacies: what we need is a rule-based international economy. *CCPA Monitor* **4**: 12–14.

Macpherson CB (1962) *The Political Theory of Possessive Individualism: Hobbes to Locke*. Toronto: Oxford University Press.

Madelin B (2001) Les 'femmes-relais', les 'sans-papiers' du travail social? *Ville-Ecole-Intégration* **124**: 81–91.

Mansanti D (2001) Pauvreté et risque: les déclinaisons de l'urgence sociale. *Revue Française des Affaires Sociales* **1**: 111–132.

Markus A (1995) Legislating White Australia, 1900–1970. In: Kirby D (ed.) *Sex, Power and Justice: Historical Perspectives on Law in Australia*. Oxford: Oxford University Press.

Marseille J (1976) L'industrie coloniale française et l'impérialisme colonial. *Revue d'histoire Economique et sociale* **2–3**: 386–412.

Marshall TH (1950) *Citizenship and Social Class*. Cambridge UK: Cambridge University Press.

Marshall TH (1981) *The Right to Welfare and Other Essays*. London: Heinemann.

Marston G (2003) *Temporary Protection Permanent Uncertainty: The Experience of Refugees Living on Temporary Protection Visas*. Melbourne: Centre for Applied Social Research, RMIT University.

Max-Neef M (1997) On human economics. Presentation at Convergence, The World Congresses of Action Research, Action Learning and Process Management, and Participatory Action Research, Cartagena, Colombia.

May T and Buck M (2000) Social work, professionalism and the rationality of organisational change. In: Malin N (ed.) *Professionalism, Boundaries and the Workplace*, pp 139–157. London: Routledge.

Meinert R (1991) A brief history of the IUCISD: from informal interest group to international organisation. *Social Development Issues* **13**: 1–13.

Melucci A (1994) A strange kind of newness: what's 'new' in new social movements? In: Larana E, Johnston H and Gusfield JR (eds) *New Social Movements: From Ideology to Identity.* Philadelphia: Temple University Press.

Meyer P (1977) *L'enfant et la raison d'Etat.* Paris: Seuil.

Meyer MW and Zucker LG (1989) *Permanently Failing Organizations.* Beverley Hills, CA: Sage.

Midgely J (1995) *Social Development: The Developmental Perspective in Social Welfare.* London: Sage.

Midgely J (1996) Involving social work in economic development. *International Social Work* **39**: 5–12

Midgley J (1997) *Social Welfare in a Global Context.* Thousand Oaks, CA: Pine Forge Press.

Midgley J (2000) Globalization, capitalism and social welfare: a social development perspective. *Canadian Social Work* (Special Issue) **2**:

Midgley J (2001) Issues in international social work: resolving critical debates in the profession. *Journal of Social Work* **1**: 21–35.

Midgley J (2002) Themes in social development: implications for the industrial countries. In: Visvesvaran PK (ed.) *Social Work Today: Present Realities and Future Prospects.* Chennai: Madras School of Social Work.

Midgley J and Jones C (1994) Social work and the radical right: the impact of developments in Britain and the United States. *International Social Work* **37**: 115–126.

Miles R and Phizacklea A (1984) *White Man's Country: Racism in British Politics.* Durango (Colo.): Hollowbrook Publishers.

Ministère de l'économie et des Finances et du Plan (2000) Etude sur l'initiative 20–20 comme option stratégique de développement programme élargi de lutte contre la pauvreté (PELCP).

Ministère de l'économie et des Finances (2002). *Plan d'action pour la mise en œuvre de l'initiative 20 /20.* Sénégal.

Mishra R (1993) Social policy in the postmodern world. In: Jones C (ed.) *New Perspectives on the Welfare State in Europe.* London: Routledge.

Mishra R (1999) *Globalization and the Welfare State.* Cheltenham: Edward Elgar.

Mohan B (1992) *Global Development: Post-Material Values and Social Praxis.* New York: Praeger.

Mohan B (1995) 'Reinventing the Mission.' New Global Development. *Journal of International and Comparative Social Welfare* **XI**: 74–78

Monbiot G (2003) *The Age of Consent.* Basingstoke: Macmillan.

Moreau M (1978) A structural approach to social work practice. *Canadian Journal of Social Work Education* **5**: 78–94.

Moreau M and Frosst S (1989) *Empowerment II: Snapshots Through a Structural Approach to Social Work.* Ottawa: Carleton University School of Social Work.

Moreau M and Frosst S (1993) *Empowerment II: Snapshots of the Structural Approach in Action; Objectives and Practices.* Ottawa: Carleton University Press.

Morell C (1987) Cause is function: toward a feminist model of integration for social work. *Social Service Review* **61**: 144–155.

Moyer B (with McAllister J, Finley M and Soifer S) (2001) *Doing democracy: The MAP Model for Organizing Social Movements.* Gabriola Island, BC: New Society Publishers.

Mullaly B (1997) *Structural Social Work: Ideology, Theory and Practice,* 2nd edn. Toronto: Oxford University Press.

Mullaly B (2002) *Challenging Oppression: A Critical Social Work Approach*. Don Mills, Ontario: Oxford University Press.

Mullaly RP and Keating EF (1991) Similarities, differences and dialectics of radical social work. *Journal of Progressive Human Services* **2**: 49–78.

Murmis M and Feldman S (1992) La heterogeneidad de las pobrezas. In: Minujin A (ed.) *Cuesta abajo. Los nuevos pobres: efectos de la crisis en la sociedad argentina*. Buenos Aires: Unicef/Losada.

Murray C (1984) *Losing Ground: American Social Policy, 1950–1980*. New York: Basic Books.

Nagy G and Falk D (2000) Dilemmas in international and cross-cultural social work education. *International Social Work* **43**: 49.

Neale J (2002) *You are G8, We are 6 Billion*. London: Vision Paperbacks.

Needleman M and Needleman C (1974) *Guerrillas in the Bureaucracy: The Community Planning Experiment in the U.S*. New York: Wiley.

Nes JA and Iadicola P (1989) Towards a definition of feminist social work: a comparison of liberal, radical, and socialist models. *Social Work* **35**: 12–21.

Newdom F (1996) Progressive and professional: a contradiction in terms? *BCR Reports* **8**: 1.

Newdom F (1997) Guilty, your honor, but not guilty enough. *BCR Reports* **9**: 1.

Newman J (2000) Beyond the new public management? Modernizing public services. In: Clarke J, Gewirtz S and McLaughlin E (eds) *New Managerialism, New Welfare?* London: Sage.

Noble C and Briskman L (1996) Social work ethics: the challenge to moral consensus. *Social Work Review* **V111**: 2–8.

Norberg-Hodge H (1997) Learning from Ladakh. In: Rahnema M and Bawtree V (eds). *The Post-Development Reader*. London: Zed Books.

O'Connor J (1973) *The Fiscal Crisis of the State*, New York: St. Martin's Press.

Offe C (1983) Some contradictions of the modern welfare state *Critical Social Policy* **6**: 7–16.

Offe C (1984) *Contradictions of the Welfare State*. London: Hutchinson.

Oommen TK (2002) Social work and human rights: for a feasible linkage. In Visvesvaran PK (ed.) *Social Work Today: Present Realities and Future Prospects*. Chennai: Madras School of Social Work.

Osborne D and Gaebler T (1992) *Reinventing Government*. Reading, MA: Addison-Wesley.

Parfitt T (2002) *The End of Development: Modernity, Post-modernity and Development*. London: Pluto Press.

Patterson T (2001) From safety net to exclusion: ending social security in the UK for persons from abroad. In: Cohen S, Humphries B and Mynott E (eds) *From Immigration Controls to Welfare Controls*. London: Routledge.

Pearson G (1975) *The Deviant Imagination: Psychiatry, Social Work and Social Change*. Basingstoke: Macmillan.

Pease B and Fook J (1999) *Transforming Social Work Practice: postmodern clinical perspectives*. Sydney: Allen & Unwin.

Peile M and Byrne C (2001) *Micro Finance Project Report*. Foresters ANA Friendly Society, December

Peretti-Watel P (2000) *Sociologie du risque*. Paris: Armand Colin.

Peretti-Watel P (2001) *La société du risque*. Paris: La Découverte, collection Repères.

Perlas N (2000) *Shaping Globalization: Civil Society, Cultural Power and Threefolding*. Quezon City, Philippines: Center for Alternative Development Initiatives. (*www.cadi.ph*)

Petras J (1999) NGOs: in the service of imperialism. *Journal of Contemporary Asia* **29**: 429–478

Pettifor A (1998) The economic bondage of debt—and the birth of a new movement. *New Left Review* **230**.

Pieterse JN (2001) *Development Theory: Deconstructions/Reconstructions*. London: Sage.

Pithouse A (1998) *Social Work: The Organisation of an Invisible Trade*, revised edn. Aldershot: Ashgate.

Piven FF and Cloward R (1975) In: Bailey R and Brake M (eds) *Radical Social Work*. London: Edward Arnold.

Piven FF and Cloward R (1995) *Regulating the Poor: The Functions of Public Welfare*, revised edn. New York: Vintage Books.

Pollitt C (1990) *Managerialism and the Public Services*. Oxford: Basil Blackwell.

Powell F (2001) *The Politics of Social Work*. Sage: London.

Pretty J (1995) *Regenerating Agriculture: Policies and Practice for Sustainability and Self-Reliance*. London: Earthscan.

Pretty J (1998) *The Living Land: Agriculture, Food and Community Regeneration in Rural Europe*. London: Earthscan.

Prigoff A (1987) *Progressive strategies: worker–client relationships*. Paper presented at the 1st Annual Meeting of the Bertha Capen Reynolds Society, July 1987, Northampton, MA.

Pusey M (1992) *Economic Rationalism in Canberra, A Nation-Building State Changes its Mind*. Cambridge, UK: Cambridge University Press.

Putnam RD (2001a) *Bowling Alone: The Collapse and Revival of American Community*. New York: Touchstone.

Putnam RD (2001b) Social capital: measurement and consequences. *ISUMA: Canadian Journal of Policy Research* **2**: 41–51.

Quadagno J (1994) *The Color of Welfare: How Racism Undermined the War on Poverty*. New York: Oxford University Press.

Ragg NM (1977) *People not Cases, A Philosophical Approach to Social Work*. London: Routledge.

Rahnema M (1997) Towards post-development: searching for signposts, a new language and new paradigms. In: Rahnema M and Bawtree V (eds) *The Post-Development Reader*, pp 377–403. London: Zed Books.

Ramon S (1999) Collective empowerment: conceptual and practice issues. In: Shera W and Wells LM (eds) *Empowerment Practice in Social Work: Developing Richer Conceptual Foundations*. Toronto: Canadian Scholars' Press.

Rankin K (2001) Governing development: neoliberalism, microcredit, and rational economic woman. *Economy and Society* **30**: 18–37.

Rashid A (2000) *Taliban: The Story of the Afghan Warlords*. London: Pan Macmillan.

Ravon B (2001) Nouveaux emplois de l'intervention sociale urbaine. *Ville-Ecole-Intégration* **124**: 68–80.

Rawls J (1971) *A Theory of Justice*. Cambridge, MA: Harvard University Press.

Rees J (2003) Cairo calling: the Cairo Declaration. *International Socialism* **2**: 23–29.

Rees S (1995) The fraud and the fiction. In: Rees S and Rodley G (eds) *The Human Costs of Managerialism. Advocating the Recovery of Humanity*. Leichhardt: Pluto Press.

Refugee Council of Australia *http://www.refugeecouncil.org.au/html/links/links.html*

Rein M (1970) Social work: in search of a radical profession. *Social Work* **15**: 13–28.

Reisch M (1998) The socio-political context and social work method, 1890–1950. *Social Service Review* **72**: 161–181.

Reisch M and Andrews J (2001) *The Road Not Taken: A History of Radical Social Work in the United States*. New York: Brunner-Routledge.

Reisch M, Wenocur S and Sherman W (1981) Empowerment, conscientization and animation as core social work skills. *Social Development Issues* **5**: 108–120.

Reynolds BC (1934) Between client and community. *Smith College Studies in Social Work* **5**(1).

Reynolds BC (1938) Rethinking social casework. *Social Work Today* **5**: 5–8.

Reynolds BC (1963) *An Uncharted Journey*. New York: The Citadel Press.

Richmond ME (1896) Criticism and reform in charity. *Charities Review* **5(4)**.

Rist G (2002) *The History of Development: From Western Origins to Global Faith* (translated by Patrick Camiller). London: Zed Books.

Rivera F and Erlich J (eds) (1998) *Community Organizing in a Diverse Society*, 3rd edn. Boston: Allyn and Bacon.

Robert P (2002) *L'insécurité en France*. Paris: La Découverte.

Robertson R (1992) *Globalisation: Social Theory and Global Culture*. London: Sage.

Robinson V (1937) *Is unionization compatible with social work?* Paper presented at a forum conducted under the auspices of the National Coordinating Committee of Social Service Employees, June 1937, Philadelphia. Evelyn Butler Archive, Box 29, University of Pennsylvania.

Rogaly B, Fisher T and Mayo E (1999) *Poverty, Social Exclusion and Microfinance in Britain*. Oxford: Oxfam.

Rose N (1999) *Powers of Freedom: Reframing Political Thought*. Cambridge, UK: Cambridge University Press.

Rose N (2000) Community citizenship and the Third Way. *American Behavioral Scientist* **43(9)**: 1395–1411.

Rosenthal BS (1993) Graduate social work students' beliefs about poverty and attitudes toward the poor. *Journal of Teaching in Social Work* **7**: 107–121.

Rowntree (2003) Progress on Poverty, 1997 to 2003/4 *Findings October*, Joseph Rowntree Foundation.

Ruggerio V (2000) *New Social Movements and the 'Centri Sociali' in Milan*. The Editorial Board of *The Sociological Review*, Oxford: Blackwell Press.

Sader E (2002) Beyond Civil Society. *New Left Review (second series)* **17 Sept–Oct**. *http://www.newleftreview.net/NLR25105.shtml*

Sahlins M (1997) The original affluent society. In: Rahnema M and Bawtree V (eds) *The Post-Development Reader*. London: Zed Books.

Saleeby D (ed.) (1992) *The Strengths Perspective in Social Work Practice*. New York: Longman.

Sanders IT (1964) Professional roles in planned change In: Morris M (ed.) *Centrally Planned Change*, pp 102–116. New York: National Association of Social Workers.

Sands RG and Nuccio K (1992) Postmodern feminist theory and social work. *Social Work* **37**: 489–494.

Sarr F (1998) *L'entrepreneuriat féminin au Sénégal: la transformation des rapports de pouvoirs*. Paris: L'Harmattan.

Sarr F (2001) *Analyse de la situation des enfants au Sénégal*. Rapport d'étude Save the Children, Suède.

Schmitz GJ (1994) Democratization and demystification: deconstructing 'governance' as development paradigm. In: Moore DB and Schmitz GJ (eds) *Debating Development Discours*, pp 54–90. Basingstoke: Macmillan.

Schragge E and Ninacs WA (1998) The social economy in Quebec. *Community Stories*. Ottawa: Caledon Institute of Social Policy.

Schrecker E (1998) *Many are the Crimes: McCarthyism in America*. Boston: Little Brown.

Schuller T (2001) The complementary roles of human and social capital. *ISUMA: Canadian Journal of Policy Research* **2**: 18–24.

Schumacher EF (1973) *Small is Beautiful: A Study of Economics as if People Mattered*. New York: Harper Collins.

Sewa EA (1983). Protection et assistance dans un contexte de développement social: sécurité sociale, assistance sociale, réhabilitation. *Cafrades* **2**: 111–156.

Shaw M (2003) Deported Iranian missing: amnesty. *The Age*, 3 September 2003.

Shera W (ed.) (2002) *Emerging Perspectives on Anti-oppressive Practice.* Toronto: Canadian Scholar's Press.

Shera W and Wells LM (eds.) (1999) *Empowerment practice in social work: developing richer conceptual foundations.* Toronto: Canadian Scholars Press.

Shillington R (2004) Who broke social policy? Presentation in February 2004 at the Carleton University School of Social Work, Ottawa.

Shoemaker L (1998). Early conflicts in social work education. *Social Service Review* **72**: 182–191.

Silverstein M (1975) *Social work and social change.* Paper presented at the annual meeting of the Otto Rank Association 19th April 1975, Philadelphia: Evelyn Butler Archive, University of Pennsylvania.

Simon BL (1990) Rethinking empowerment. *Journal of Progressive Human Services* **1**: 27–39.

Simon BL (1994) *The Empowerment Tradition in Social Work Practice.* New York: Columbia University Press.

Simpkin M (1979) *Trapped Within Welfare, Surviving Social Work.* London: Macmillan.

Sklar KK (1993) The historical foundations of women's power in the creation of the American welfare state, 1830–1930. In: Koven S and Michel S (eds) *Mothers of a New World: Maternalist Politics and the Origins of Welfare States*, pp 43–93. New York: Routledge.

Sklar KK (1995) *Florence Kelley and the Nation's Work.* New Haven, CT: Yale University Press.

Smith J, Pagnucco R and Chatfield C (1997) Social movements and world politics: a theoretical framework. In: Smith J, Chatfield C and Pagnucco R (eds) *Transnational Social Movements and Global Politics: Solidarity Beyond the State*, Syracuse, NY: Syracuse University Press.

Smith R (1996) The end of politics and the civil sector: the challenge to social work in the third millennium. In: Ishmael J (ed.) *International Social Welfare in a Changing World*, pp 255–268. Calgary, AL: Detselig.

Social Services Inspectorate (1991a) *Care Management and Assessment: Practitioners' Guide.* London: Department of Health.

Social Services Inspectorate (1991b) *Care Management and Assessment: Managers' Guide.* London: Department of Health.

Soja E (1996) *Thirdspace: Journeys to Los Angeles and Other Real-and-Imagined Places.* Cambridge, MA: Blackwell.

Sourang M (1996) "Implication économique et intégration sociale des femmes du programme caisse d'epargne et de credit du CPRSEI Hadji Omar Thies, Senegal". Unpublished PhD thesis, Ecole Service Social, Université Laval, Senegal.

Spano R (1982) *The Rank and File Movement in Social Work.* Lanham, MD: University Press of America.

Specht H and Courtney M (1994) *Unfaithful Angels: How Social Work Abandoned Its Mission.* New York: Free Press.

Spicker P (1995) *Social Policy: Themes and Approaches.* London: Prentice Hall.

Spronk S (2002) Social capital and the new institutionalists: the liberal-individualist origins of the concept. Annual Conference of Canadian Association for the Study of International Development, Toronto, Ontario.

Stiglitz J (2002) *Globalization and its Discontents.* London: Penguin Books.

Stratton J and Ang I (1994) Multicultural imagined communities: cultural difference and national identity in Australia and the USA. In: O'Regan T (ed.) Critical multiculturalism—a special issue of continuum. *The Australian Journal of Media & Culture* **8**(2).

Strom-Gottfried K (1997) The implications of managed care for social work education. *Journal of Social Work Education* **33**: 7–18.

Supiot A (1999) Travail, droit et lien social. Conférence Publique. novembre 1999 Genève *http://www.ilo.org/public/french/bureau/inst/papers/publecs/supiot.*

Taft J (1939) *Function as the basis of development in social work processes*, paper presented at the annual meeting of the American Association of Psychiatric Social Workers, National Conference of Social Work, June 1939. Philadelphia: Evelyn Butler Archive, University of Pennsylvania.

Tarrow S (1991) *Struggle, Politics and Reform: Collective Action, Social Movements and Cycles of Protest.* Ithaca: Centre for International Studies, Cornell University.

Taylor-Gooby P and Lawson R (1993) Introduction. In: Taylor-Gooby P and Lawson R (eds) *Markets and Mangers: New Issues in the Delivery of Welfare.* Buckingham: Open University Press.

Thompson N (2002) Social movements, social justice and social work. *British Journal of Social Work* **32**: 711–722.

Throssell H (1975) Social work overview. In: Throssell H (ed.) *Social Work: Radical Essays*, pp 3–23. St. Lucia, QLD: University of Queensland Press.

Titmuss R (1958) *Essays on the Welfare State.* London: Allen and Unwin.

Touraine A (1969) *La société postindustrielle.* Paris: Denöel.

Touraine A (1973) *Production de la société.* Paris: Seuil.

Touraine A (1992) *Critique de la modernité.* Paris: Fayard.

Touraine A (2001) *Beyond Neoliberalism* Cambridge: Polity

Truth Overboard, Lies, Damned Lies and Politics (Children' Overboard Affair) *http://www.truthoverboard.com/default.html*

Ungpakorn JG (2003) Challenges to the Thai NGO movement from the dawn of a new opposition to global capital. *http://www.istendency.net/pdf/NGO.pdf*

United Nations Development Program (2002) *Human Development Report 2002.* Available: http://hdr.undp.org/reports/global/2002.

United Nations Development Program (2003) *Millennium Development Goals: A Compact Among Nations to End Human Poverty.* Available: *http://hdr.undp.org/reports/global/2003/*

Van den Bergh N (ed.) (1995). *Feminist Practice in the 21st Century.* Washington, DC: National Association of Social Workers.

Van den Bergh N and Cooper LB (eds) (1986). *Feminist Visions for Social Work.* Silver Spring, MD: National Association of Social Workers.

Van Soest D (1995) Multiculturalism and social work education: the non-debate about competing perspectives. *Journal of Social Work Education* **31**: 55–66.

Van Soest D (1996) Impact of social work education on student attitudes and behavior concerning oppression. *Journal of Social Work Education* **32**: 191–202.

Van Ufford and Philip Quarles (1993) Knowledge and ignorance in the practices of development policy. In: Hobart M (ed.) *An Anthropological Critique of Development: The Growth of Ignorance.* New York: Routledge.

Verdès-Leroux J (1978) *Le travail social.* Paris: Minuit.

Vilbrod A (1995) *Devenir éducateur, une affaire de famille.* Paris: L'Harmattan.

Viner K (2000) Hand-to-Brand Combat. *Guardian* 23 September 2000.

Vuarin R (1999) *Un système africain de protection sociale au temps de la mondialisation.* Paris: L'Harmattan.

Wagner D (1989) Radical movements in the social services: a theoretical framework. *Social Service Review* **63**: 264–284.

Wagner D (1990) *The Quest for a Radical Profession: Social Service Careers and Political Ideology.* New York: University Press of America.

Waine B (2000) Managing performance through pay. In: Clarke J, Gewirtz S and McLaughlin E (eds) *New Managerialism, New Welfare?* London: Sage.

Wald L (1915) *The House on Henry Street.* New York: Henry Holt.

Walker A (1989) Community care. In: McCarthy M (ed.) *The New Politics of Welfare. An Agenda for the 1990s?* Basingstoke: Macmillan.

Waters M (1995) *Globalization.* London: Routledge.

Webb A and Wistow G (1987) *Social Work, Social Care and Social Planning: The Personal Social Services Since Seebohm.* Harlow: Longman.

Webb SA (2001) Some considerations on the validity of evidence-based practice in social work. *British Journal of Social Work.* **31**: 57–79.

Weber M (1967) *L'éthique protestante et l'esprit du capitalisme.* Paris: Plon.

Weick A and Vandiver S (eds) (1982) *Women, Power and Change.* Silver Spring, MD: National Association of Social Workers.

Wenocur S and Reisch M (1989) *From Charity to Enterprise: The Development of American Social Work in a Market Economy.* Urbana, IL: University of Illinois Press.

White V and Harris J (1999) Social Europe, social citizenship and social work. *European Journal of Social Work* **2**: 3–14.

Wieviorka M (1999) *Violence en France.* Paris: Seuil.

Wieviorka M (2001) Faut-il en finir avec la notion d'intégration? *Les Cahiers de la Sécurité Intérieure* **45**: 9–20.

Wieviorka M (2002) Le conflit contre la violence. *Cosmopolitiques* **2**: 14–24.

Wilson A and Beresford P (2000) Anti-oppressive practice: emancipation or appropriation? *British Journal of Social Work* **30**: 553–573.

Wilson MG and Whitmore E (2000) *Seeds of Fire: Social Development in an Age of Globalism.* Winnipeg and Ottawa: Fernwood; New York: Apex.

Withorn A (1976) Helping ourselves: the limits and potential of self-help. *Radical America* 25–39.

Withorn A (1984) *Serving the People: Social Services and Social Change.* New York: Columbia University Press.

Withorn A (1996) 'Why do they hate me so much?' A history of welfare and its abandonment in the U.S. *American Journal of Orthopsychiatry* **66**: 496–509.

Woloch N (1984) *Women and the American Experience.* New York: Alfred Knopf.

Woolcock M (2000) *Using Social Capital: Getting the Social Relations Right in the Theory and Practice of Economic Development,* Princeton, NJ: Princeton University Press.

Woolcock M (2001) The place of social capital in understanding social and economic outcomes. *ISUMA: Canadian Journal of Policy Research* **2**: 11–17.

Workman, T (2003) *Social Torment: Globalization in Atlantic Canada.* Halifax: Fernwood Publishing.

Yeates N (2002) Globalization and social policy. *Global Social Policy* **2**: 1–000

Yeatman A (1994) *Postmodern Revisioning of the Political.* London: Routledge.

Young I (2000) *Inclusion and Democracy.* Oxford: OUP.

Index